MIDDLE ENGLISH HAGIOGRAPHY AND ROMANCE IN FIFTEENTH-CENTURY ENGLAND

MIDDLE ENGLISH HAGIOGRAPHY AND ROMANCE IN FIFTEENTH-CENTURY ENGLAND
From Competition to Critique

Elizabeth Leigh Smith

Mediaeval Studies
Volume 15

The Edwin Mellen Press
Lewiston•Queenston•Lampeter

Library of Congress Cataloging-in-Publication Data

Smith, Elizabeth Leigh.
   Middle English hagiography and romance in fifteenth-century England : from
competition to critique / Elizabeth Leigh Smith.
      p. cm. -- (Mediaeval studies ; v. 15)
   Includes bibliographical references and index.
   ISBN-0-7734-6951-6
      1. English literature--Middle English, 1100-1500--History and criticism. 2. Christianity
and literature--England--History--To 1500. 3. Christian saints--Legends--History and
criticism. 4. Romances, English--History and criticism. 5. Christian hagiography. I.
Title. II. Series.

   PR275.R4 S65 2002
   820.9'3823--dc21
                                                                        2002070195

This is volume 15 in the continuing series
Mediaeval Studies
Volume 15 ISBN 0-7734-6951-6
MS Series ISBN 0-88946-264-X

A CIP catalog record for this book is available from the British Library.

          The Edwin Mellen Press   The Edwin Mellen Press
                 Box 450   Box 67
          Lewiston, New York   Queenston, Ontario
          USA 14092-0450   CANADA L0S 1L0

                          The Edwin Mellen Press, Ltd.
                          Lampeter, Ceredigion, Wales
                          UNITED KINGDOM SA48 8LT

                    Printed in the United States of America

This book is gratefully dedicated to my husband, Michael, whose patience and support have made it possible.

TABLE OF CONTENTS

Preface

Until very recently, for historians and critics of English literature, the fifteenth century remained a largely unexplored black hole, a temporal chasm between the glorious flowering of literary talent that occurred in the latter half of the fourteenth century and, skipping ahead almost one hundred years, the literal Renaissance of poetry, drama, and epic that occurred in the sixteenth century. During the late fourteenth-century reign of Richard II, a cluster of first tier writers contributed to the rich and varied literary *oeuvre* that characterizes the High Middle Ages in England. This group includes: John Gower, author of a vast body of literary pieces in Latin, French, and English including the *Confessio Amantis*; the *Gawain*-poet, author of unquestionable alliterative masterpieces including the Arthurian romance *Sir Gawain and the Green Knight* and the dream vision *Pearl*; William Langland, author of three extant revisions of the lengthy, alliterative allegorical dream vision, *Piers Plowman*; and of course, the jewel in the crown of the Ricardian age, Geoffrey Chaucer, whose early dream visions, *Troilus and Criseyde*, and *The Canterbury Tales* earned him the title of "Father of English Poetry." Chaucer's death in 1400, leaving a legacy that would have been a hard act to follow at any time, seemed to bring a funereal curtain down on this half-century-long literary Golden Age. The sixteenth century saw another such literary flowering, as represented by poets and playwrights who are now virtually household names: Thomas Wyatt, Phillip Sidney, Edmund Spenser, Christopher Marlowe, and the literary jewel in Elizabethan England's crown, William Shakespeare. But what happened in the one hundred year period between these extraordinary bursts of literary productivity?

If popular anthologies of early British literature are any indication--and these collections do seem to take a "greatest hits" approach to the development of literature over time—the fifteenth century would seem to have been a fallow period of literary regrouping at best. Sir Thomas Malory's *Works*, often titled the *Morte D'Arthur*, a translation of the thirteenth-century French Vulgate Cycle of Arthurian romances, exemplifies the literature produced in what anthologies would have us believe was an otherwise unexemplary fifteenth century. Furthermore, sandwiched between the work of such esteemed and beloved writers as Chaucer and Shakespeare, Malory's contribution took on an artificially inflated representational importance that discouraged further investigation of other genres and writers from what is arguably the final century of the Middle Ages. The parts of Malory's bulky collection of knightly adventures that were anthologized, and therefore were recognizable, tended to be about Arthur's attainment of kingship through taking the sword from the stone, the adulterous romance between his best knight Lancelot and his wife Guinivere, or his mortal combat against his illegitimate son, Mordred. So, whatever was known of fifteenth-century texts was skewed in the direction of these courtly and chivalric themes, leaving out the considerable body of spiritual and didactic matter contained in even Malory's *Works*, not to mention other literary productions of the century in which he wrote. But if the fifteenth century represents what John Huizinga called the "Autumn" of the Middle Ages, was it not also the transitional century that as well represents the first anticipation of the Early Modern age? The black hole of the fifteenth century was ripe for both literal and figurative "enlightenment."

Fortunately, in the past decade or so, that black hole has been gradually illuminated through a concerted effort by the TEAMS consortium to make available for teaching other primary texts by fifteenth century authors (besides Malory). These include Thomas Usk, John Lydgate, Thomas Hoccleve, and Robert Henryson. Moreover, exciting work continues to be done in the reconstruction of the textual and performative history of late medieval religious and secular drama, thus providing a richer provenance for the development of playwrights like Marlowe and Shakespeare in the following century. The theoretical discourse of New Historicism, which originated in Renaissance Studies and whose project generally investigated the complex interplay between the political, economic, social, and literary histories of the newly-dubbed Early Modern period, had an additional halo effect on the promotion of Fifteenth-Century Studies, which investigated the chronological period immediately preceding its own temporal focus. Thus, the former tendency to ignore the interim between the Ricardian and Elizabethan ages has been supplanted by a growing recuperation of a sense of the variety and, yes, the *richness* of the literature produced in England in the fifteenth century. *Middle English Hagiography and Romance in Fifteenth-Century England: Competition to Critique* contributes importantly to this recuperation.

Elizabeth Leigh Smith focuses on two popular medieval literary genres that would appear at first glance to have little relation to each other—romances and narratives of the Saints Lives, usually designated generically as "hagiography." Hagiographic narratives can be subdivided further into two separate *foci* of the saint's biography—the *vitae*, narratives of the early life of the saints; and the *passiones*, accounts of the trial, martyrdom, and ultimate death of the saints. The romance was a literary mode well known and widely practiced throughout the long medieval period. Medieval romances were quite elastic in their scope, ranging from the better-known chivalric romances about King Arthur, wherein knights practiced "earthly chivalry," to the lesser-known "romanticized folktales" that had much in common with hagiographic narratives whose saintly heroes, dubbed *milites Christi* or *soldiers* of Christ, were no less chivalric, but practiced "celestial chivalry." Smith reveals in Chapters 4 and 5 how a complex interrelationship between these genres culminated in what she terms a "quarrel" or "debate" between the two modes, as evinced in several important, but rarely discussed fifteenth-century literary texts. As quarrels usually do, this conflict between these dominant genres resulted in the mutual appropriation of characteristics from one mode to the other. This cross-appropriation resulted in the production of some striking literary hybrids by the major authors under consideration in her study: the less known John Capgrave and Osbern Bokenham, and the ubiquitously-anthologized Thomas Malory, as well as other anonymous hagiographers that she considers.

While there is a basic core of Arthurian narrative motifs from which Malory and his thirteenth-century French predecessors could choose in constructing their romances, the Middle Ages venerated an almost limitless plethora of international and local saints, some of whom (even St. Katherine herself, ironically) are no longer considered canonical. Considering the breadth of hagiographic material at her disposal, Smith wisely focuses on doing a comparative analysis of several hagiographers' lives of a particular saint. Chapter 4 thus traces the hagiographic treatment of Saint Katherine of Alexandria, one of the most popular female saints in England, from the thirteenth century *South English Legendary* through several fifteenth-century narratives that cover both the *vita* and *passio* of St. Katherine. Of special interest to Smith are *The Life of St. Katherine*, by Norfolk Austin friar John Capgrave, and the *passio* of St. Katherine that is included in a collection titled *Legendys of Hooly Wummen*, by a protégé of Capgrave, Osbern Bokenhem, also an Austin friar who knew Capgrave at Cambridge. Using the techniques of New Historicism, Smith views both Capgrave's and Bokenham's versions of this particular saint's life against the political tumult of the Wars of the Roses, to show that from opposite political

v

sides of the question, both hagiographers of Katherine's life used aspects of her biography to fulfill their respective political agendas on opposing sides of the War of the Roses. Thus, Capgrave's elaborate defense of Katherine's fitness to rule serves as a defense of the same right of Henry VI. On the other hand, as Smith deftly demonstrates, Bokenham, appropriates Katherine as an articulate speaker for his own pet political cause, the Yorkist claim to the throne. This politicization of hagiography is an aspect of the genre that has received virtually no treatment before Smith's study, rendering her discussion of the differences between these two handlings of the Katherine legend groundbreaking, to say the least. Moreover, Smith also demonstrates how both writers employed the techniques of romance in constructing their lives of this popular saint to serve their respective political designs. This is one example of how hagiography and romance were mutually appropriated to produce biographies of a saint that venture well beyond the expected boundaries of the Saint's Life genre.

Although this book does use the more widely-treated Malory as one of the authors who exemplifies the complex relationship between the genres of hagiography and romance, Smith limits her discussion of the *Works* to Malory's translation of the anonymous thirteenth-century French *La Queste del Saint Graal*, which is more hagiographic than romantic and which, Smith argues, "pictures ideal knighthood as a combination of holiness and chivalry." As she reveals in Chapter 5, Malory considerably altered this text when he translated it into his own *The Tale of the Sankgreal*, which is probably his least discussed and most misunderstood work. Bridging this critical gap, Smith makes a solid contribution to Malory studies by situating his translation within the context of other hagiographic narratives. Through this juxtaposition, she demonstrates how thoroughly Malory rejected the hagiographic model he inherited from his French source as he rewrote the Grail Quest as a chivalric romance, or as she puts it, "By desanctifying Galahad, Malory turns the story of the Grail Quest from quasi-hagiography to romance." He did so, she argues, in order to promote and even champion for his immediate fifteenth-century English audience a revival of earthly chivalry even as this military ideal was inevitably already on the wane.

The title *Middle English Hagiography and Romance in Fifteenth-Century England* conveys only a fraction of the various kinds of information and insights offered by this book. Of course, the critic and student can find clear definitions and characteristics of the genres of hagiography and romance as well as biographical background about the main authors under consideration: Capgrave, Bokenham, and Malory. However, to historically ground her contribution to the critical conversation about the genres of romance and hagiography, in Chapters 1-3, Smith also provides a wealth of information about a variety of other non-literary topics, including the development and decline of the ideals of chivalry and the orders of knighthood in the centuries before the book's focus as well as the role of the Church in medieval politics, especially in the fifteenth century. This contextualization of hagiography and romance narratives within late medieval secular and ecclesiastical politics sets this study apart from many other purely literary analyses. For its depth and originality, *Hagiography and Romance in Fifteenth-Century England* will eventually be considered a beacon in the enterprise whose goal is the total illumination of that former black hole, fifteenth-century English literature.

Lorraine Kochanske Stock

University of Houston

Introduction

In the literature of thirteenth- through fifteenth-century England, the genres of hagiography and romance developed like children of the same family. Their resemblance is undeniable, their relationship important, but troubled. The earliest hagiography, composed in late antiquity and the early Middle Ages, consists mostly of stories about martyrs of the early Church. Because the canonical status of a saint depended upon his making the ultimate sacrifice for the faith, as well as the miracles he performed before and (especially) after his death, the most important part of a saint's life was considered to be his martyrdom, or passion. In the later Middle Ages, when holy men and women who were not necessarily martyrs became eligible for sainthood, hagiographers began to include other events, such as the saint's conversion, divine visions, or mystic marriage. Eventually, such stories about saints' earlier lives, called *vitae*, became more attractive to both readers and writers than the passions. Saints' lives, in both forms, were exceedingly popular throughout the Middle Ages, at least as popular as the romances about knights and their adventures with which modern audiences are more familiar.[1]

---

[1] For evidence of this genre's popularity in the fifteenth century, see Alfred Robert Kraemer, *Malory's Grail Seekers and Fifteenth-Century English Hagiography* (New York: Peter Lang, 1999) 15-29.

As Susan Crane argues in *Insular Romance*, saints' lives and romances represented fundamentally incompatible value systems which competed for the attention of a broad, secular audience. In 1285, the writer of the *South-English Legendary* assures his audience that anyone who enjoys the stock features of romance, brave knights and kings fighting heroic battles, etc., has come to the right place. He even recasts some of the characters in his saints' lives as knights and kings, whereas his sources may refer only to soldiers and emperors. Clearly, for hagiographers who competed with romance writers for the same audience, the common image of the saint as a "soldier of Christ" called to "God's chivalry" was useful because it justified describing a martyred bishop as if he were a knight facing death on the battlefield.

Romance writers appropriated the techniques of hagiography for the same reason. With increasing frequency, the knight's biggest foe turns out to be his own moral weakness, as in *Sir Gawain and the Green Knight*, which no one would mistake for a saint's life. When Gawain returns to Arthur's court, his comrades consider his "adventure" a success[2] because they see it in traditional romantic terms, with the Green Knight as villain—a position often occupied by a giant, a sorcerer, or a witch, i.e. an "other." Surely, a Green Knight carrying his detached head is advertising his otherness, and by coming back to court with his own head safely attached, Gawain would seem to have won. Nevertheless, Gawain knows he has failed because his real enemies are the cowardice and covetousness he confesses to Bercilak. Like a hero of sacred literature, Gawain recognizes the need to fight his own weakness and judges himself by the outcome.

Such similarity may astonish modern readers, who expect chivalric literature to be worlds apart from religious literature. In a sense it is, but the nature of the disagreement is much more complex than the modern conflict between "the sacred" and "the secular." Those two realms were not nearly so

---

[2] *Sir Gawain and the Green Knight*, ed. William Vantuono (New York: Garland Publishing, 1991) 2513-18.

rigidly separate in the Middle Ages as they are today. Even such worldly figures as Geoffrey Chaucer and Thomas Malory would be unlikely to imagine an area of life in which religion was utterly irrelevant. Arthur Ferguson points out that Malory, like other men of his time, "would have found any attempt to define a 'secular mind' or a 'secular civilization' quite outside his intellectual experience."[3] Their ideas of chivalry and right conduct in love, war, government, and a host of other issues were rooted in religious ideals and often expressly connected with them. The Church, for its part, recognized that the monastic ideal of poverty and celibacy was attainable only by a small minority and "often equivocated in order to rationalize the life of the world."[4] Thus, hagiography and romance shared a set of assumptions, including the idea that the "City of God might preoccupy the religious enthusiast to the virtual exclusion of all else. The City of Man could never be considered in and for itself."[5]

In the thirteenth century, some two hundred years before the period on which the present study will focus, competition between hagiographers and romance writers for the same audience created not only the "sacred romances," but also some oddly romantic saints' lives. Competition led writers of both genres to borrow techniques from one another, resulting in a superficial resemblance between them and creating (for us) the illusion of more agreement than in fact there was. The quarrel between hagiographers and romance writers was not about the importance of holiness, but about what really constituted a holy life and whether such a life could ever include worldly, as well as heavenly, reward. The basic difference between the two genres lies in their opposite answers to this question. Romance writers contended that holiness was not only compatible with ideal knighthood (and the glory that it brought), but essential to

---

[3] Arthur B. Ferguson, *The Indian Summer of English Chivalry* (Durham, NC: Duke University Press, 1960) 52.

[4] Ferguson 53.

[5] Ferguson 53.

it. On the other hand, those who wrote saints' lives, usually clerics, presented earthly happiness as incompatible with a holy life.

In the fifteenth century, when the English feudal system began to break down and the Roman Church began to lose its influence, romance and hagiography moved perceptibly closer. The authors of both genres derived their values from medieval England's two dominant institutions, the feudal system and the Church. Thus, the rise of the national state at the expense of both these institutions created similar problems for hagiographers and romance writers. Both saw the ethical codes that, for them, gave meaning to life, gradually losing their influence, but they perceived the decay of old value systems without any way of knowing what would replace them. Consequently, truly unclassifiable works, such as Thomas Malory's account of the Grail Quest, began to emerge. Saints' lives began either to serve worldly political purposes or to attack the chivalric ethic more sharply than in the past. The purpose of this study is to demonstrate and explain this shift in the relationship between hagiography and romance of the fifteenth century.

As cases in point, I will be using several fifteenth-century lives of St. Katherine of Alexandria and Sir Thomas Malory's version of the Grail Quest. I have chosen St. Katherine because scholars consider her "the most important saint in late medieval England,"[6] both in terms of the number of people who venerated her and the intensity of their devotion. As a result of her popularity, many Middle English versions of St. Katherine's life are extant, and the sheer number of them offers an unusually good opportunity to study the development of a single story over several centuries. Katherine Lewis points out, in her invaluable study of St. Katherine's cult, that the development of a saint's legend reveals much about the society that produced it.[7] If this is so, the number and variety of examples surely

---

[6] Katherine J. Lewis, *The Cult of St. Katherine of Alexandria in Late Medieval England* (Suffolk: Boydell Press, 2000) 2.

[7] Lewis 5.

make St. Katherine's legend a rich source of data on medieval England. I select Malory both as the most important English romance writer of the fifteenth century and as the last Middle English interpreter of the Arthurian cycle. Like many saints' lives, the story of King Arthur has been recreated frequently enough to reflect the concerns of a changing society. In particular, Malory's adaptation of the Grail Quest story shows that romance, when important enough to its author, can be as revealing as any saint's life of what a society values.

Although saints' lives have not traditionally attracted as much scholarly attention as romances, interest in them has grown rapidly in the last few years. Especially helpful in explaining the unusual popularity of St. Katherine (and the role of literature in sustaining it) is Katherine Lewis' *The Cult of St. Katherine of Alexandria in Late Medieval England*. Saara Nevanlinna and Irma Taavitsainen provide a straightforward, useful overview of the Katherine legend's development in their edition of *Katherine of Alexandria: The Late Middle English Prose Legend in Southwell Minster*. Sheila Delany provides valuable insights into the political uses of fifteenth-century hagiographaphy in *Impolitic Bodies: Poetry, Saints, and Society in Fifteenth-Century England*. Karen Winstead's *Virgin Martyrs* provides a detailed comparison of two fifteenth-century lives of St. Katherine, as well as some useful discussion of the rhetorical situation in which medieval hagiographers worked.

My understanding of the relationship between hagiography and romance owes much to Susan Crane's *Insular Romance*, in which the author explains how the romance genre developed in England, as distinct from the rest of Europe. Also, Derek Pearsall provides a useful discussion on hagiographers' use of romance techniques in "John Capgrave's *Life of St. Katherine of Alexandria* and Popular Romance Style." In this article, Pearsall points out the passage from the *South-English Legendary* in which its author explicitly offers his work as an alternative to the popular romances. Finally, in *Malory's Grail Seekers and Fifteenth-Century Hagiography*, Alfred Kraemer focuses specifically on the use of hagiographical techniques in Malory's Grail Quest. Although my conclusions are different from Kraemer's, his analysis has been very helpful to the present study.

Regarding the function of hagiography in medieval life, Thomas Noble and Thomas Head offer a concise overview in their introduction to *Soldiers of Christ*, a collection of translated saints' lives. E.J. Dobson discusses the function of the St. Katherine legend specifically in *Origins of* Ancrene Wisse, where he addresses the purpose and probable authorship of the earliest English version of the legend. On the social function of later versions, Lewis, Delany, and Winstead again offer good information. In *A New Song: Celibate Women in the First Three Christian Centuries*, Jo Anne McNamara explores the "soldier of Christ" metaphor and its implications for women in the early Church, up to the time when St. Katherine was said to have lived. She explains how martyrdom offered women the opportunity to appear in literature, specifically hagiography, as military heroes. This provides an important opportunity for hagiographers to utilize romance convention. Furthermore, as I shall argue, the martial metaphors associated with martyrdom explain how the writer of the *South-English Legendary* is able to offer Katherine an alternative to the traditional romance hero.

My understanding of the romance genre in its Middle English form has been assisted by W.R.J. Barron's *English Medieval Romance* and John Finlayson's "Definitions of Middle English Romances," which appeared in the *Chaucer Review*. Also helpful on the question of genre is Susan Crane's work mentioned above. Regarding Thomas Malory, his own source for the legend of the grail quest, the Old French *La Queste del Saint Graal*, is essential. Some see Malory's *The Tale of the Sankgreal* as a straight translation of this "vulgate" version, but a close comparison of the two reveals that Malory's tale is much more a romance and less a saint's life than its original, and therefore more problematic. Helpful secondary work includes *Malory's Grail Quest* by Sandra

Ness Ihle, "The Truest and Holiest Tale: Malory's Transformation of *La Queste del Saint Graal*" by Dhira Mahoney, and "Malory's Lancelot and the Quest of the Grail," by Stephen Atkinson. Of course, Eugene Vinaver's notes to his edition of Malory's *Works* continue to be a good starting point.

My research for this project has necessarily had a historical, as well as a literary, component. The following works on medieval Europe have been important for my understanding of religion, politics, warfare and other cultural issues. On the role of the crusades in the creation of knightly ideals, Arno Borst's *Medieval Worlds* and Frederick Russell's *The Just War in the Middle Ages* offer helpful discussions. Marc Bloch's *Feudal Society* provides a useful overview of the feudal system and the role of the knight in society from the early Middle Ages forward. In *The Indian Summer of English Chivalry*, Arthur Ferguson explains Malory's agenda in terms of the state of English chivalry in the fifteenth century. The reason for this change is nowhere more clear than in Charles Oman's *The Art of War in the Middle Ages*, in which the author explains the development of warfare tactics that, in the fifteenth century, greatly reduced the importance of the mailed knight. Malcolm Vale explains the ramifications of this new kind of warfare for medieval society in *War and Chivalry*. The effect of the Black Death on English feudalism receives mention in many places, two important ones being Frederick Cartwright's *Disease and History* and William H. McNeill's *Plagues and Peoples*. My understanding of the medieval Church has been greatly improved by A. Hamilton Thompson's *The English Clergy*, W.A. Pantin's *The English Church in the Fourteenth Century*, and J.C. Dickinson's *The Later Middle Ages*. C.H. Lawrence chronicles the transformation of religious life in Western Europe in *The Friars*. David Knowles explains the same phenomenon in a specifically English context in *The Religious Orders in England*. Finally, Johan Huizinga's *The Autumn of the Middle Ages* still provides invaluable analysis on the state of chivalry and feudalism in the fourteenth and fifteenth centuries.

As the above sources show, much work has been done on hagiography,

8

romance, and the historical issues that affected them. A few scholars address the borrowing between the two genres as well as other aspects of their relationship. However, those who discuss the connection between sacred and secular literature tend to present it in terms of a monolithic notion of "The Middle Ages," as if it worked exactly the same way in the fifteenth century as it did in the twelfth.[8] Yet, all the historical evidence shows that the positions of knights and clerics in society were far different in the fifteenth century than several centuries earlier.

These differences seem to be due to several factors. First, the Church lost prestige in England while the pope was residing in Avignon. The already anti-clerical and increasingly patriotic English saw no reason to place a French pope above their king, and the schism of 1378 did nothing to increase English reverence for the papacy. Second, the declining feudal system in England, which accompanied the rise of the national state, rendered the knight's role in civic life far less important. At the same time, the heavy plate armor that developed in the late Middle Ages made combat more arduous and expensive for knights, whose income from land did not increase accordingly. Meanwhile, innovations in military strategy rendered him less effective in battle than, for example, a yeoman with a longbow. As the trouble and expense of fulfilling his traditional role increased, knights understandably began to seek new sources of income and new reasons to avoid their military service. Thus, when fifteenth-century hagiographers argued against the values promoted in popular romances, the system those romances glorified was vulnerable, and the contradictions within chivalry appeared much more clearly than in the earlier Middle Ages. The ongoing quarrel between hagiography and romance was bound to reflect this change, and my own research has revealed, ironically, that hagiography and romance begin to resemble one another more closely, at least superficially, as their disagreements become sharper. They now seem to imitate one another in

---

[8] An exception is Alfred Kraemer, who roots his discussion of hagiographical elements in Malory's Grail Quest specifically in the fifteenth century.

order to critique as well as to compete, and both show a defensiveness of their own world-view that never seemed necessary before. My task is not only to establish that this change occurred, but also to explain why it occurred, in terms of the changing positions of the feudal system and the Church.

Chapter One:
The Quarrel

By the fifteenth century, English hagiography and romance were products of several different traditions incorporated into a specific national context. Both genres underwent changes of their own, sometimes as a result of competition between them, but more often as a result of linguistic, political, and religious forces outside literature which found expression in what were, after all, two of the most popular genres of the time. By the thirteenth century, the Church in England was at the height of its power and no longer needed to use all its resources for strengthening its political position. At that point, it began redirecting its energies toward comprehensive reforms which made organized religion a larger part of ordinary people's lives than ever before.[9] For example, enforced confession and detailed penitential manuals gave the Church "unprecedented control over the daily behavior of parishioners."[10] With the founding of the friars, as we shall see, clerics focused their efforts more than ever on preaching and education of the

---

[9] W.A. Pantin, *The English Church in the Fourteenth Century* (Toronto: University of Toronto Press, 1980) 2-3.

[10] Susan Crane, *Insular Romance: Politics, Faith, and Culture in Anglo-Norman and Middle English Literature* (Berkeley: University of California Press, 1986) 93.

12

laity and less-tutored clergy. Susan Crane interprets the so-called "homiletic" or "exemplary" romances as the "lay resistance to the constraints that [the Church's new] supervision imposed."[11] In support of this interpretation, Crane points out an important distinction between romances and saints' lives. Romances, even "pious" or "exemplary" ones, validate worldly achievement and reward the hero's valor or holiness not only in the next life, but in this one.

On the other hand, hagiography rewards its heroes only in the next world. Since the genre originated in late antiquity with stories of martyrdom, called *passiones* (literally, *passions*), it naturally features heroes who scorn any prize short of Heaven. For example, St. Perpetua, whose story will appear in more detail later, was a wealthy Roman matron. Upon her conversion to Christianity, she broke all ties with her influential family and sought an opportunity to bear witness to her faith. *Martyr* literally means *witness*, and most saints of late antiquity and the early Middle Ages were martyrs. They accept torture and death not with fear or even resignation, but with joy, since it brings the only reward they value. Upon their deaths, miracles are said to occur, and these miracles constitute the martyr's claim to sainthood. In the central Middle Ages, when the Church had become so powerful that few Christians could expect to pay the ultimate price for their faith, a new kind of saints' life, the *vita*, became popular. These *vitae* (literally, *lives*) tell the story of the saint's life before the martyrdom. A martyred saint, such as Katherine of Alexandria, might then be the subject of two different legends, circulating separately, one about her early life, conversion, good works, etc., and the other about her martyrdom and the miracles that followed. On the other hand, a later saint, such as Francis of Assisi, would have no *passio*, since he was not a martyr. His *vita* would therefore contain all the information about his life—and the miracles following his death—that affect his canonical status. The emergence of *vitae* presented numerous creative options, but they did not substantively alter the standard for sainthood. Even if a saint was not called upon

---

[11] Crane 101.

to die for his beliefs, he still had to show the same disregard for earthly wellbeing that made Katherine or Perpetua embrace martyrdom. Again, St. Francis is a good example, as are his contemporary, St. Dominic, and his *protégé*, St. Clare.[12]

While exemplary Middle English romances may promote a Christian ideal, they ratify secular concerns in a way that saints' lives rarely do. For example, *Guy of Warwick* has been called a "hagiographical"[13] romance because of the hero's service to God and rejection of worldly honors. Crane notes a superficial parallel between *Guy of Warwick* and the legend of St. Alexis because both heroes leave their prominent families soon after their weddings to serve God in poverty and anonymity.[14] However, as Crane also notes, their means of serving God differ greatly. Alexis becomes a beggar, while Guy serves God in combat, often fighting for secular causes, e.g. to avenge his friends or "to make Inglond fre."[15] Unlike any hagiographer (at least, before the fifteenth century), the author of *Guy* considers such causes consistent with the hero's commitment to serving God. Moreover, he allows Guy to rejoin his family. Shortly before his death, Guy reveals his identity to his wife and begs her pardon for leaving her.[16] Alexis, like Perpetua, rejects all earthly ties and sees nothing for which to apologize.

For this reason, Crane rightly judges the exemplary romances of the thirteenth and fourteenth centuries not as a product of church reform, but as a protest against it. They argue not only for the legitimacy of secular concerns, but

---

[12] See summary of Francis's and Clare's *vitae*, below.

[13] Constance Birst West, *Courtoisie in Anglo-Norman Literature* (Oxford: Oxford University Press, 1938) 61. Dieter Mehl sees *Guy* as an ideal example of the English tendency to meld hagiography with romance. He even goes so far as to claim that such combining of technique sometimes made it difficult to tell what was hagiography and what was romance. See Dieter Mehl, *The Middle English Romances of the Thirteenth and Fourteenth Centuries* (New York: Barnes and Noble, 1969) 19.

[14] Crane 110-111.

[15] *Guy of Warwick: The First or 14th—Century Version*, ed. Julius Zupitza (London: EETS E.S. 59, 1891) 248.

[16] *Guy* 293.

14

also for the consistency of such causes with a holy life. Guy, the author implies, has a right to avenge his friends and seek the good of his country; such projects are consistent with his dedication to God's service. Thus, "hagiographic romances" are still romances. While they borrow ideas from saints' lives, their values remain chivalric rather than saintly. Certainly, the Church's condemnation of "pious" romances along with "courtly" ones argues against the idea of a separate genre.[17] Furthermore, readers of the time clearly recognized the challenge that exemplary romances presented to the Church's increasing power and intrusiveness. Like the saints' legends, they depict a hero who is a model of piety, but their heroes are rewarded with riches, love, or renown as well as salvation. The authors present "worldly and spiritual endeavor" as being not only compatible with, but as "a necessary part of the life of the true knight."[18] In turn, religious writers argue that the only way to salvation is through renunciation of earthly success. Once again, as Ferguson explains, the City of God is enough for those who devote their lives to it, but the City of Man cannot stand on its own.[19] For the Church's presentation of this argument, hagiography was an important tool, as were the homiletic romances to the "lay resistance."

To understand why, one needs to realize the importance of hagiography in medieval society. The overt purpose of saints' lives had always been to provide Christians with examples of virtuous conduct, and they helped make sermons more appealing because people loved to hear them.[20] Contemporary readers have difficulty appreciating how popular saints' lives were in the Middle Ages, probably due to "[m]odern prejudices against the coexistence of entertainment

---

[17] Crane 94.

[18] Ferguson 52.

[19] Ferguson 53.

[20] On the use of St. Katherine's legend in sermons, see Lewis 15-20.

and didacticism."[21] Yet, they have everything we recognize as necessary for pleasing crowds. The heroes and heroines are noble, the villains satisfyingly villainous, and the plots full of violence and dramatic conflict. In other words, they are appealing for many of the same reasons romances are appealing, and saints' lives were much clearer in their application to the lives of their hearers. People throughout the Middle Ages celebrated with enthusiasm the feast days of saints.

The saints were not only charismatic, engaging heroes, but also influential figures who could intercede with God on behalf of the living. It has become conventional to speak of the Heavenly Kingdom in which Christ is king and the saints are the nobility.[22] As with any court, if an ordinary person desires a favor from the king, the patronage of a noble is invaluable. Accordingly, Christians would ask the help of whatever saint had influence over the area in which they needed help. For example, the (now uncanonical) St. Christopher was the patron saint of travelers; St. Jude was the patron saint of hopeless causes. Of course, different professions also had their particular saints,[23] and individuals might feel an attachment to saints with whom they shared a name or profession. The faithful would visit the shrines of these saints and offer their prayers. The saints, in return, would use their influence for the benefit of those who venerated them. Thus, saints were more influential than most living role models, and a preacher or religious writer could reasonably use a story about a popular saint to influence behavior. Even when the Church became sufficiently powerful that martyrdom was not a likely danger unless one purposely sought it, stories about martyred

---

[21] W.R.J. Barron, *English Medieval Romance* (Essex: Longman House, 1987) 57.

[22] Thomas Noble and Thomas Head, ed. and intro, *Soldiers of Christ: Saints and Saints' Lives From Late Antiquity and the Early Middle Ages* (University Park: Pennsylvania State University Press, 1995) 14.

[23] St. Clare is the patron saint of needleworkers; St. Arnold is the patron saint of brewers; St. Katherine, oddly, is the patron saint of wheelwrights, on account of the Katherine Wheel designed to torture her.

16

saints were still useful to promote whatever virtues the saint exemplified.

A. Middle English Hagiography

1. The Anglo-Saxon Perspective

Anglo-Saxon Christianity was Germanic in tone, combining the Christian teachings of Roman missionaries and Celtic monks with the older Anglo-Saxon heroic ideals that produced *Beowulf* and *The Battle of Maldon*.[24] When Anglo-Saxon writers applied the ideals of their own warrior elite to Christian subjects, the result was a "Germanicized" Christianity that was uniquely English. Its sensibilities are apparent in the Anglo-Saxon poem *Dream of the Rood*, which features a warrior-hero, eager for the coming battle. The Holy Cross, who is the speaker in the poem, recalls the following:

> Geseah ic þa Frean mancynnes
>
> Efstan elne micle, þæt he me wolde on gestigan.
>
> þær ic þa ne dorste ofer Dryhtnes word
>
> Bugan oððe berstan, þa ic bifian geseah
>
> eorðan sceatas. Ealle ic mihte
>
> feondas gefyllan, hwaeðre ic fæste stod.
>
> Ongyrede hine þa geong hæleð – þæt waes God Aelmigtig! –
>
> Strang and stiðmod.[25]

The poet refers to Christ as a *dryhten*, for which there exists no real modern English equivalent. A *dryhten*, the leader of a *dryht* or Anglo-Saxon comitatus, shared with his followers bonds of kinship and loyalty. Here, the Holy Cross acts in the role of a loyal retainer, whose leader and protector is Christ. The word *hæleð* can mean either "warrior" or "hero," since the Anglo-Saxon concept of

---

[24] Noble and Head 33.

[25] *The Dream of the Rood*, ed. Bruce Mitchell and Fred Robinson, *A Guide to Old English*, 5th ed. (Blackwell: Oxford, 1992) 33-40. Saw I the Lord of Mankind/hasten with much courage in his wish to mount upon me./I bore him that dared not over the word of the Lord/Bend or burst, then I saw shake/the earth's/surface. I might all/of the enemies have felled, however I stood fast./Against that young hero – that was God Almighty!/Strong and resolute. (My translation)

heroism has mostly to do with conduct in battle. When this Germanic ideal mixes with the Christian teachings of the missionaries, the result is a specifically English version of Christ who little resembles the meek, suffering figure of other narratives.

English saints, after the example of Christ, are eager warriors for God against evil. As Noble and Head point out, they include "hermits who wrestled demons in fetid bogs," such as St. Guthlac, and "kings who were martyred by pagan rivals," such as Edmund.[26] Guthlac leaves his monastery for a desolate fen, in order to live as a hermit. Every night, the evil spirits who inhabit the place torment him spiritually, by placing fears and doubts in his mind, as well as physically, by literally beating him with iron whips. Unable to make him abandon his resolution, they eventually leave him in peace, and he becomes an authority figure for others who wish to live holy lives. Edmund earns his victory in the same passive/aggressive way. The Viking invaders cannot make him fight, and after torturing him with arrows (which do not kill him), they cut off his head and hide it from his followers. Yet, even this does not kill him. When the invaders leave, the faithful search for his head, and it calls to them. They eventually find it between the paws of a wolf, who was keeping it safe until the right people should find it. Like Guthlac, Edmund defeats his enemies by refusing to abandon his beliefs, even under horrific torture. These saints are warriors for God and might have rightly said, with the older, less aristocratic St. Martin of Tours, "I am Christ's soldier. I am not allowed to fight."[27]

English saints, like those of the Roman and Frankish tradition, generally come from the nobility,[28] but deny themselves the material comforts their position

---

[26] Noble and Head 33.

[27] Noble and Head 8.

[28] Noble and Head 34.

would otherwise afford them.[29]   Their nobility not only makes them people of consequence whose "blessings and curses carried weight among their contemporaries,"[30] but it also makes their renunciation meaningful.   Sons and daughters of the rich and powerful give up inherited wealth and the chance for power, entering into a life of voluntary poverty.   Others remain at a royal court or a wealthy house to use their influence in God's service, but they take steps to avoid material comfort, such as wearing a hair shirt beneath their fashionable clothes.   Anglo-Saxon England produced many such holy people, as collections such as Bede's *Ecclesiastical History of the English People* or the Old English *Martyrology* show.[31]

Because their battleground is not physical, their ranks can include women, such as Etheldreda and Leoba.   However, the women tend to be painted in less martial terms.   Instead of living in the wilderness, exposed to the attacks of demons, they seclude themselves in convents or devote themselves to good works.   For example, Etheldreda is a queen who gives up her wealth and status to live in a monastery and serve the poor.   Leoba teaches and even has disciples, but she ends her life as the abbess of a convent.

The narratives of non-native saints make women more public, active members of God's chivalry.   These include the late Roman saints' lives, which entered England via Latin texts and were then rendered into Old English by Ælfric and others.[32]   For obvious reasons, many of these are *passiones* or stories of violent martyrdom, although they do include other categories, such as the

---

[29] For Continental examples see Jo Ann McNamara and John E. Halborg with E. Gordon Whatley, trans., *Sainted Women of the Dark Ages* (Durham, NC : Duke University Press, 1992).

[30] Noble and Head 32.

[31] For a comprehensive guide to Old English hagiography, excluding the martyrologies, see E. Gordon Whatley, "An Introduction to the Study of Old English Prose Hagiography: Sources and Resources," *Holy Men and Holy Women: Old English Prose Saints' Lives and Their Contexts* (Albany, NY: State University of New York Press, 1996).

[32] For details, see Whatley 9.

desert fathers. One of the most influential *passiones* is that of St. Cecilia, who "retain[s] her virginity by converting her husband on their wedding night."[33] Both eventually suffer martyrdom, and their example seems to inspire other "chaste marriages."

2. Female Sanctity and Martyrdom

Martyrdom has always carried with it martial imagery, and in the first three Christian centuries, it came to be "recognized as a transcendental victory over the physical conditions of mortality. It was the ultimate act of salvation where, mystically, women became men."[34] The most specific description of this process appears in the journal of St. Perpetua, the Roman matron mentioned above who was thrown to the lions in 203. While her story does not appear in Old English, it merits mention here as the only record to show, from the saint's viewpoint, how martyrdom could enable a woman to transcend her socially defined role. When she embarks upon a course that she knows will end in her execution, Perpetua pointedly gives up both her husband and her baby.[35] Jo Ann McNamara interprets this act as a renunciation of "everything that made her a woman and a matron,"[36] and Perpetua certainly seems to have seen it that way. The night before her execution, Perpetua has a dream in which she is already in the arena, where, "there came to me comely young men, my helpers and aiders. And I was stripped, and I became a man."[37] Stripped of everything that made her a woman, Perpetua is now ready to be a warrior. Perpetua's dreams about the day of her "victory" are not nearly as frightening as one would expect. They are all

[33] McNamara 99.

[34] JoAnn McNamara, *A New Song: Celibate Women in the First Three Christian Centuries.* Women and History 5 (1983) 88.

[35] For a fuller discussion of this saint and her personal account of the events leading to her martyrdom, see Joyce Salisbury, *Perpetua's Passion* (New York: Routledge: 1997) 85-148.

[36] McNamara 105.

[37] McNamara 105.

appealing, even erotic. For example, after the comely young men strip her, they rub her naked body with oil, "as they are wont to do before a contest."[38] Her former slave, Felicity, who dies with her, shares her view of martyrdom as victory and worries that "her martyrdom would be postponed because of her pregnancy."[39]

3. Female Sanctity and Virginity

McNamara puts to rest a popular misconception that the ideal of virginity was somehow imposed on women by men in the early Church. A common theme in legends of female saints is the struggle of the young maiden to keep her virginity, which means defying the authority of parents and even, ironically, religious leaders. Usually, it means remaining unmarried, although some, such as Cecilia, do persuade their husbands to share their commitment to chastity and thus avoid the familial responsibilities that marriage normally entails. Chaucer so emphasizes Cecilia's sweetness and humbleness[40] that a reader could easily fail to notice what a subversive example she is setting. By refusing to consummate her marriage, she fails not only to submit to her husband, but also to become a mother. Like Perpetua, she rejects the responsibilities that her family and community expect her to fulfill, and the freedom she gains thereby allows her to give her whole self to God through martyrdom.

From the early days of the Church, a select group of women wished to follow the example of St. Cecilia and other holy maidens. By choosing to remain virgins, they were, in effect, refusing to fulfill the roles of wife and mother normally expected of women, and many of them met with as much resistance from Christian authorities as the early saints met from unbelieving parents and

---

[38] Salisbury believes that Perpetua is trying to avoid the eroticism of this image, as well as the similarity to pagan combat scenes. See Salisbury 107.

[39] Salisbury 115.

[40] Geoffrey Chaucer, *The Second Nun's Tale*, *The Riverside Chaucer* (Boston: Houghton Mifflin, 1987)129.

husbands. Mothers and fathers, as well as clerics, begged and commanded women under their authority to take husbands. When Christina of Markyate, in twelfth-century England, emulates St. Cecilia by refusing to consummate her marriage, she encounters fierce opposition from both her family and Church authorities.[41] In fact, the trouble and suffering that Christina endures to keep her virginity is much more severe than that of Cecelia.[42] Christina's husband does not readily see the matter her way, and her family, especially her mother, becomes violently abusive, attempting to make her submit to her husband.[43] Thus, women in the central Middle Ages who wished to remain virgins were, like the early saints, in a position of rebellion.

Church leaders, whom one would expect to praise their efforts to imitate the saints, found them dangerous, and for good reason. Without husbands or children, they were able to study, preach, lead, and face martyrdom as well as their male counterparts, especially in the early years, when strict regulations about what functions women could perform had yet to be agreed upon. The Church began to establish organized female religious communities because clerics, such as Clement of Alexandria, saw that the alternative was groups of religious women over whom the Church had little or no control.[44] In Alexandria, many women who were called to a religious life were highly educated and influential in the community. When they chose to remain celibate, and therefore independent, they

---

[41] The hair-raising story of Christina's escape from her husband and hiding under torturous conditions is recorded in *Christina of Markyate: Of S. Theodora, a Virgin, Who Is Also Called Christina*, trans, C.H. Talbot, *Medieval Women's Visionary Literature*, ed. Elizabeth Petroff (Oxford: Oxford University Press, 1986) 144-150.

[42] Karen A. Winstead, *Virgin Martyrs: Legends of Sainthood in Late Medieval England* (Ithaca: Cornell University Press, 1997) 20.

[43] *Christina* 144.

[44] McNamara 90.

represented a serious danger to the authority of the Church.[45] Yet, such women could also be important for the growth of the Church's influence. As McNamara observes, clergymen in the early Church "were aware of the value of educated aristocratic women to their cause."[46] Since many in Alexandria were prominent citizens with wealth and influence, incorporating them seemed to Clement a much better idea than ignoring them.

Katherine of Alexandria, whose story will appear in more detail later, was a typical example of the charismatic aristocrat of the late Roman period who renounces worldly wealth and power. Martyred at the beginning of the fourth century, Katherine was one of the most popular saints of the Middle Ages, both in England and in Continental Europe. She is a queen, the beautiful and learned daughter of King Costus, but following her "Mystic Marriage" with Christ, she embraces martyrdom at the hands of the Roman emperor. The emperor tempts her with promises of wealth and power, in exchange for an end to her public and embarrassingly articulate protests against his sacrifices to pagan gods. Katherine scoffs at the worldly riches and honors the emperor offers and eagerly endures both torture and martyrdom, in anticipation of reaching her real bridegroom the sooner.

Katherine became a popular heroine in English hagiography, possibly because she exemplified Anglo-Saxon ideals as well as the newer ones promoted by the friars of the thirteenth and fourteenth centuries. The English found her story appealing for the same reason they found the martyrdom of their own St. Edmund appealing. Like Perpetua, she approaches her own martyrdom as combat between good and evil. The emperor's execution of Katherine is a clear victory for the apparent victim and a clear defeat for the perpetrator. As Chapter Four of

---

[45] In the early fourth century, Katherine of Alexandria was exactly the kind of independent, educated, "man-like" celibate woman who would have aroused the concern of the local bishop. For a detailed discussion of her, see Chapter 4.

[46] McNamara 89.

the present study will show, the emperor orders Katherine's death only after he fails, with threats, promises, and even torture, to make her relinquish Christ. Oddly enough, as Eugen Einenkel points out, the reader might well find himself pitying the evil emperor, as he battles "an opponent weak in appearance, but in reality too strong for him."[47] Undoubtedly, her story made perfect sense to those who were familiar with an Anglo-Saxon tradition of sanctity.

4. Female Sanctity and the Friars

After the thirteenth-century arrival of the friars in England, another aspect of St. Katherine's story became important. England's native female saints, such as Etheldreda, usually achieved sainthood by giving up wealth and position to retire to monasteries. Katherine, far from retiring to a monastery, engages with the imperfect world, preaching and debating in defense of her religion at every opportunity. Her involvement with the world of human beings made her an ideal role model for the new religious orders that emerged in the early thirteenth century. At that time, the traditional monastic ideal of "personal salvation through withdrawal and salvation of society through prayer was eclipsed" by the founding of the friars, "a new religious role. . .whose core was a combination of evangelical preaching and radical renunciation of material support."[48]

The earliest order of friars, the Franciscans or Friars Minor ("little brothers") attempted to imitate the disciples of Christ as closely as possible, according to the noble and difficult example of St. Francis. Francis, born into the knightly class of late twelfth-century Italy, served in the military for a short time before suddenly relinquishing his wealth and power to live as a hermit in absolute poverty. Claiming to have heard the words of God in a dream, he conceived the idea of an apostolic "life of poverty devoted to evangelising the unconverted in

---

[47] Eugen Einenkel, intro., *Seinte Katerine* (London: EETS O.S. 80, 1884) xx.

[48] Caroline Walker Bynum, *Jesus as Mother: Studies in the Spirituality of the High Middle Ages* (Berkeley: University of California Press, 1982)13.

which the missionaries were supported by alms."[49] Unlike the older monastic orders, the Franciscans could own no property, even collectively. Instead of living in cloisters, isolated from the community, they slept and begged for their sustenance in the cities where they preached. Because they lived within secular communities, they were able to bring the laity into fuller participation in religious practice than the monastic orders had been able to do.

In the thirteenth century, the growth of cities and the number of literate, religiously-minded laymen produced heresy as well as piety. St. Dominic and his associates formed the second major order of friars to combat the heresy of the Cathars, whose leaders set an example of personal austerity that anyone who wished to discredit them would have to match.[50] The Dominicans were, from the beginning, a learned order of preachers and students who could argue intelligently with sophisticated heretics. When the Dominicans, or Friars Preachers, became mendicants, they often worked with the Franciscans, bringing high quality preaching and other services to the towns. [51] Thus, the mendicant preachers made possible the reforms of the thirteenth century, many of which were designed to give the laity better pastoral care.

By the middle of the thirteenth century, the Dominicans and Franciscans were well established in England.[52] Although the two orders shared a devotion to poverty and preaching, rivalry between them eventually suggested another use for saints' lives. For some time, religious communities had been using saints' relics and legends to increase their influence, gain ascendancy over one another, or even begin new religious communities. In the thirteenth century, Franciscans and Dominicans created or recreated legends of the saints in order to gain adherents,

---

[49] C.H. Lawrence, *The Friars: The Impact of the Early Mendicant Movement on Western Society* (London: Longman Group, 1994) 32.

[50] Lawrence 68.

[51] Lawrence 87.

[52] Lawrence 103.

from the lay public and from one another.[53] During the thirteenth and fourteenth centuries, competition between these orders produced a number of new narratives with already popular saints promoting the ideals of each order. Clearly, the kind of religious ideal promoted by the friars would demand a different kind of hero from the monastic ideal.

St. Francis himself has always fascinated hagiographers, with the result that his personality comes down to our own time much more clearly, at least in popular images, than that of Dominic.[54] His sacrifice of family wealth in order to live in absolute poverty and service to the poor attracted numerous followers and emulators. The heroes of Franciscan narratives are the ones who imitate most perfectly the absolute poverty of Francis, and for women, this imitation often involves conflict with authority, even Church authority. St. Clare, St. Francis's *protégé* and founder of the Poor Clares, desires only to live a life as close as possible to that of St. Francis, in "penance, humility, and poverty."[55] She comes into conflict with the Church's power structure after the death of Francis because of her insistence on the "privilege of poverty," i.e. the right of her order not to own property.[56] When the friars try to "compel the sisters to acquire enough property to make them self-supporting,"[57] Clare must argue her case before the authorities, which she does vigorously and successfully. While she would rather be in her enclosure, ministering to the poor, Clare fights for her "privilege" of imitating Francis and eventually wins it.

While the Franciscan ideal emphasized poverty, the Dominican ideal, originating as it did in the struggle against heresy, emphasized preaching and

---

[53] Rudolph M. Bell, *Holy Anorexia* (Chicago: University of Chicago Press, 1985) 127.

[54] Lawrence 66.

[55] Petroff 233.

[56] Petroff 234.

[57] Petroff 235.

argument. The saints of Dominican narratives are therefore much more outspoken and confrontational than those of Franciscan narratives. Both orders eventually excelled in both areas, but the hagiography they produced reflects important differences in their early character. The Dominican heroine, unlike St. Clare, is typically "individualistic, even faintly heretical, outgoing and public."[58] A good illustration is a story about Agnes of Montepulciano, in which the Virgin Mary allows Agnes to hold the baby Jesus. When Mary tells Agnes to give him back, she refuses, and the two "engage in a fierce tug-of-war,"[59] which Mary eventually wins, but not before Agnes snatches a cross from around the child's neck (the cross is still venerated as a relic in Montepulciano). Bell paints an almost humorous picture of "Agnes, the bride of Christ, engaged in a struggle for possession of her husband's body against her mother-in-law."[60] By the time Dominicans needed suitable heroines to promote their vision among religious women, the story of St. Katherine had been in England for a considerable period. As Chapter Four will show, her learning, her skill at public debate, and her confrontational defense of both her religion and her right to remain a virgin made her an ideal Dominican heroine.

B. Middle English Romance

1. Definition and Types

Romance, despite its relatively shorter history, is more difficult to describe in terms of its essential elements and the purposes it served. Much recent scholarship has succumbed to the temptation to oversimplify romance as aristocratic self-justification.[61] While conceding that medieval romance glorifies a

---

[58] Bell 130.

[59] Bell 132.

[60] Bell 132.

[61] For a Marxist interpretation of medieval romance, see Stephen Knight, "The Social Function of Middle English Romances" and Toril Moi, "Desire and Language: Andreas Capellanus and the Controversy of Courtly Love," *Medieval Literature: Criticism, Ideology & History*, ed. David Aers (Brighton: Harvester, 1986) 15-29;125-31. Knight and Moi contend that

code of conduct that only the ruling class could practice, I would note that the need to justify the privileges of the knightly class comes fairly late in the history of romance. More importantly, the category is too diverse for such simple explanations. As Finlayson points out, "anyone reasonably familiar with Middle English fictitious narratives will be aware that the only thing which many of them have in common is the fact that the *personnae* are aristocratic."[62] The genre covers such a wide assortment of literary works that "[c]ritics are increasingly abandoning the concept of a romance genre as unhelpful."[63] Furthermore, the genre we call *romance* "comprises as many types and sub-types as the modern novel."[64] Therefore, when Finlayson sets out to formulate a workable definition of romance that really explains the genre in its own terms, he divides it into three types.

Finlayson's first type, the "romanticized folktale," in which the author superimposes chivalric elements on a fairytale to make it "contemporary and modish,"[65] is interesting because it helps explain what some hagiographers, including the writer of the *South-English Legendary*, were doing with their saints' lives. In defining this category, Finlayson's discusses fairy tales, such as Chaucer's *Wife of Bath's Tale*. He observes that this work is not actually a romance, but an old fairy tale "tricked out in Arthurian clothes."[66]

---

the knightly class, which produced the chivalric romances, imbued knights with numerous virtues to justify their privileged position. By making the ruling class appear morally superior, romance writers made the social order appear natural, necessary, and beneficial to everyone. This interpretation has much to recommend it, but I believe that it ignores the variety and complexity of Middle English romance.

[62] John Finlayson, "Definitions of Middle English Romance," *The Chaucer Review* 15 (1980): 45.

[63] Barron 57.

[64] Barron 57.

[65] Finlayson 177.

[66] Finlayson 178. Because the solution to the problem comes not from the knight's new knowledge, but from magic, Finlayson considers this tale a "deliberate failure" to be a romance.

Although Finlayson seems to have only fairy tales in mind, his definition of "romanticized folktale" applies equally well to hagiography.[67] Saints' lives were surely as important a part of medieval folklore as fairy tales, and probably more so, judging from the large number of them still extant. They also seem subject to "updating" by those who wrote them down and circulated them among their contemporaries. In Chapter Four, I give the example of St. Katherine of Alexandria, showing how the *South-English Legendary* author "romanticizes" her story, turning soldiers into knights and describing the saint under torture as "wounded" but "steadfast." But the case of Katherine is only a single instance of a consistent effort by hagiographers to appeal to readers who enjoy the popular romances. Derek Pearsall points out a section of the *South-English Legendary*'s Prologue, in which the author states:

> Men wilneth much to hure telle . of bataille of kynge
>
> And of knightes that hardy were . that muchedel is lesynge
>
> Wo so witneth much to hure . tales of suche thinge
>
> Hardi batailles he may hure . her that nis no lesing
>
> Of apostles & martirs . that hardy knightes were
>
> That studeuast were in bataille . & ne fleide noght for fere.[68]

Here, the author acknowledges that his contemporaries enjoy hearing about the exploits of fearless knights in battle, although many such tales, i.e. romances, are lies. Anyone who wishes to hear that kind of story, he assures his reader, will find it here. He can provide equally exciting stories about fearless apostles and martyrs, and his stories have the advantage of being true. Apparently, the saints' lives of the *South-English Legendary* have been "romanticized" for the reason that Finlayson believes fairytales were, and I doubt that many critics would wish

---

[67] In an important sense, it applies better. Since no actual fairy tales survive from the Middle Ages, the assumption that many romances originated in fairy tales is highly problematic. The existence of individual saints' lives is much easier to document.

[68] *S. Katerine, Early South-English Legendary*, ed. and intro. Carl Horstmann (London: EETS O.S. 87, 1887) 59-64.

to start calling them romances. At the time of the *South-English Legendary*, which was around 1285, the line between romance and hagiography is still quite clear, despite the stealing of techniques that might result from any rivalry. Coke may imitate Pepsi's marketing strategies, but it remains Coke, or the competition ends. For this reason, I question (as Finlayson does) the viability of the "romanticized folktale" as a category of romance.

On the other hand, Finlayson's "basic" definition of romance describes with some (though not absolute) accuracy the English popular romances of the thirteenth and fourteenth centuries. According to Finalyson, "the basic definition of *romance*. . .is that it is a tale in which a knight achieves great feats of arms, almost solely for his own *los et pris* in a series of adventures which have no social, political, or religious motivation and little or no connection with medieval actuality."[69] Here, Finlayson distinguishes between the popular "romance of adventure" and the aristocratic "courtly romance," referring more to the audience than to the characters, since romance heroes are always aristocratic. Both begin with the same idea: "the knight rides out alone to seek adventure."[70] The popular variety, exemplified by *King Horn* and parodied in Chaucer's *Tale of Sir Thopas*, features a "meaningless (or purely glory-hunting) series of adventures."[71] Predictably, the aristocratic variety, modeled after the works of Chrétien de Troyes, is more complex, and the adventures the knight encounters are arranged in meaningful order to reveal progressively the hero's character. Perhaps the best English example of this subgenre of romance prior to Malory is *Sir Gawain and the Green Knight*, which rejects the glory-hunting valorized in the popular romances and uses Gawain's adventure as a "vehicle for a presentation and

---

[69] Finlayson 55.

[70] Finlayson 55.

[71] Finlayson 56; Finalyson oversimplifies *King Horn* when he refers to the heroes adventures as "meaningless." In fact, they address important issues for early English culture. See Barron's and Crane's interpretations of *King Horn*, below.

examination of the chivalric ethic"[72] in the manner of Chrétien.

Sir Gawain could also be included in Finlayson's third category, the religious or homiletic romance. In this type, the knight's quest turns inward, and his reward is salvation or enlightenment, rather than love or glory. As noted above, Gawain knows he failed in his quest because he understands that the enemies he had to fight were his own cowardice and covetousness. Therefore, he must wear the green band as a "token of vntrawþe" as long as he lives.[73] The rest of Arthur's court "reads" his story as a popular romance and therefore sees it as a success. They laugh and comfort Gawain, agreeing that:

> lordes, and ladis, þat longed to þe Table—
>
> Uche burne of þe Broþerhede a bauderyk schulde haue,
>
> A bende abelef hym aboute of a bryȝt grene,
>
> And þat, for sake of þat segge, in swete to were.
>
> For, þat watȝ acorded þe renoun of be Rounde Table,
>
> And he honoured þat his hade euermore after,
>
> As hit is breued in þe best boke of romaunce.[74]

The homiletic romance often owes much to the saint's life in terms of plot structure and the values it promotes. The knight's adventures may be a series of ordeals in which great suffering tests his faith or teaches him humility or otherwise brings him closer to a state of grace. Homiletic romances, like saints' lives, can have female heroes, such as Chaucer's Griselda of the Clerk's Tale, whose saint-like steadfastness in the face of the mental torture of her husband earns her happiness at the end. However, as already noted, these romances differ from actual saints' lives in that the hero receives his or her reward in this world, as well as the next.

---

[72] Finlayson 56.

[73] Sir Gawain 2509.

[74] Sir Gawain 2515-2521.

In fact, Chaucer may not have intended Griselda's eventual reunion with her family to compensate her adequately for so many years of deprivation. The fact that Walter is not God and is in no position to offer her the Kingdom of Heaven makes Griselda's story questionable as a homiletic romance. Furthermore, the Boccaccio tale on which *The Clerk's Tale* is based ends with a pointed condemnation of the husband's behavior. Finally, Griselda's suffering lacks the meaning that it has for a saint, who usually welcomes the chance to suffer for Christ. If the Clerk means, as he says, that her patience with the trials imposed by a mortal man teaches us all how to "Receyven al in gree that God us sent,"[75] he certainly has not painted a very pretty picture of how God behaves. In many of the saints' lives, as Chaucer seems to have noticed, God behaves a lot like Walter, subjecting the most virtuous people to extreme and often painful tests of faith. For this reason, I see *The Clerks' Tale* as a contribution to the ongoing debate between hagiography and romance. Chaucer, as a civil servant and manifestly secular figure, would almost certainly side with the "lay resistance"[76] to the Church's expanded role in daily life following the founding of the friars. Chaucer's negative opinion of friars (which he shared with many of his contemporaries, including Langland and Gower) is too well established to require much support here. In *The Canterbury Tales*, the *Friar's Tale*, the *Wife of Bath's Tale*, and the image of the pilgrim friar in the *General Prologue* all draw the same picture. Chaucer's friars are uniformly hypocrites who use their position of trust to gratify their vices.

2. Development and History

The English romance of Chaucer's time, the fully developed genre which Finlayson describes, is the product of several traditions, just as the genre of hagiography is. The story, however, is shorter, since there is no such thing as

---

[75] Geoffrey Chaucer, *The Clerk's Tale*, *The Riverside Chaucer* (Boston: Houghton Mifflin, 1987) 1151.

[76] Crane 101.

English romance until about a century after the Norman Conquest.[77] In 1066, the Normans brought their language and literature to England, along with the feudal system, which provides the necessary context for romance. Most of the Anglo-Saxon thanes died either at Hastings or shortly thereafter, and William the Conqueror parcelled out their land to his own followers.[78] At that point, the language of the ruling class in England became Norman, while the commoners continued to speak Old English. In the century that followed, Anglo-Norman developed as the language of the English aristocracy, who, by this time, were born in England, rather than Normandy. Englishmen who wished to advance in society learned Anglo-Norman as quickly as possible, and distinctively English romances were written in Anglo-Norman. The most famous of these is probably the Anglo-Norman version of *King Horn*, which predates the English version by some fifty years.[79]

King Horn differs from French romance in several respects. First, English history at the time of the Viking raids "provides the violent social context of the action."[80] In other words, it deals with the "matter of England," a new subject in formal court literature. Second, *King Horn* resembles the Anglo-Saxon "folk-tale of the exile-and-return type involving the familiar motifs of revenge, recovery of the patrimony, and the winning of a bride."[81] It seems, then, to have its origin in the oral tradition of the Anglo-Saxons. Its emphasis on ritual and kinship bespeaks a specifically English sensibility. Barron points out that the hero goes through the same kind of adventure six times, crossing water on each occasion. Each time, he must free himself (or is freed) from the power of a king, starting

---

[77] Barron 48.

[78] Barron 50.

[79] Barron 65.

[80] Barron 65.

[81] Barron 65.

with his father, whose death Horn never sought, and ending with Fikenild, the last rival for his bride, Rymenild.[82] Horn also shows a Saxon concern that "to marry a princess and become a king is a disloyal act against a reigning monarch."[83] In short, *King Horn* is what Crane would call "insular romance." Its cultural context, the values it promotes, and the ritual challenges the hero faces all come from the Anglo-Saxon tradition.

Formal literature was not written in English until the decline of Anglo-Norman, which occurred in the thirteenth century. With the rise of Francien as the standard language of France, Anglo-Norman became a "provincial dialect liable to excite ridicule in the courts of France."[84] Therefore, the English nobility taught their children Continental French, and the language of everyday business became English, though an English altered by prolonged exposure to French and Anglo-Norman. The earliest English romance was, of course, *King Horn*, written around 1225.[85] The English version is about a quarter the size of its Anglo-Norman original, and the dramatic episodes "follow one another without explicit connection,"[86] relying on the repeated theme to establish structure.

Even more in the English version than in the Anglo-Norman, Horn differs from the heroes of French romance. The hero of traditional courtly romance struggles with the internal contradictions of chivalry, whereas the hero in the "insular romances" of the thirteenth century struggles in Anglo-Saxon fashion with the "oppressive forces of a wicked world."[87] Unlike the heroes of French

---

[82] *King Horn: A Middle English Romance*, ed. Joseph Hall (Oxford: Oxford University Press, 1901) 51-64;1508-10.

[83] Barron 66.

[84] Barron 51.

[85] Barron 65.

[86] Barron 67.

[87] Barron 85.

34

romance, Horn feels "no problematic conflict between his own desires and those of his society."[88] All his challenges are external, and he meets them with no self-doubt or hesitation.

"Courtly" love, which leads to so much of the conflict "between private identity and public expectations"[89] and which is so integral to Continental romances, is not an element of the insular romances. Nor is it as much a primary concern of later English romances. Even Malory, whose hero, Lancelot, is surely the courtliest lover of them all, "seems to have had little feeling for the courtly love tradition."[90] His valorization of adultery, which courtly romance requires, is rather hesitant compared to his French sources. Whereas no one could accuse Malory of inadequate detail on most issues, he presents the love affair between Lancelot and Guinevere laconically: "as the Freynshhe book seyth, the quene and sir Launcelot were togydirs." He then hastens to add, "whether they were abed other at other maner of disportis, me lyste nat thereof make no mencion, for love that tyme was nat as love ys nowadayes."[91] English writers seem, as a rule, to be "less tolerant of adultery than their French counterparts,"[92] and Malory writes as if he would like to acquit his hero of the charge altogether, if this were possible.

Critics offer different reasons why the English romance writers seem less interested in love than were their French contemporaries. Ferguson suggests that the English, almost by nature, would be less inclined to approve wholeheartedly of a literary phenomenon whose essence is love outside marriage.[93] Crane

---

[88] Crane 14.

[89] Crane 13.

[90] Ferguson 48.

[91] Thomas Malory, *The Works of Thomas Malory*, ed. Eugene Vinaver (Oxford: Oxford University Press, 1971) 676.

[92] Ferguson 50.

[93] Ferguson 48.

suggests that the tranquil and de-militarized barony of England was inclined to see "the human drama [as] collective, a communal search for stability."[94] The hero, in his struggle against whatever "pagans, usurpers, monsters, and wrong-headed kings" threaten "properly established order" represents the community, which, since the time of Henry II, was much more subject to the power of the crown and the courts than was the barony in France.[95] A story in which the hero represents society will have little use for the kind of passionate love which serves, in French romance, to dramatize conflict between individual desire and societal expectations. Barron sums up English romance of the thirteenth century as "an amalgam less courtly and exclusive, more eclectic and broadly based than its Continental counterpart and, in the width of its appeal, a significant indicator of the future potential of English narrative literature."[96]

By Chaucer's time, the history of English romance strongly resembles the history of English hagiography. Both were products of several traditions, including Anglo-Saxon folklore, various learned texts in Latin, and French ideals of both holiness and courtliness. The romances and saints' lives which entered England via France also had a strong effect on the development of England's own tradition. In the thirteenth and fourteenth centuries, the new religious ideals of the Dominicans and Franciscans affected them both, with hagiographers and romance writers responding in opposite, though related, ways to the growing role of organized religion in daily life. English saints' lives and romances both have noble heroes, in the sense of personal qualities as well as social status. The hero in both represents the author's idea of perfect conduct, and after several exciting battles with the forces of evil, the hero earns the ultimate prize, whether it be the love of the perfect woman, the restoration of a birthright, or direct entry into the

---

[94] Crane 83.

[95] Crane 14.

[96] Barron 85.

Kingdom of Heaven. They deal with similar questions, both in a uniquely English way. Their differences, which in some ways are less interesting than their similarities, lie in the way they answer those questions. In a sense, then, their disagreement is a family quarrel, not a battle for survival or a struggle for predominance.

In the fifteenth century, as both the Church and the feudal system begin to lose influence with the growing power of the secular state, the ideological quarrel between hagiographers and romance writers becomes sharper. Both see the decline of values they cherish, and in a characteristically medieval way, they interpret change as decay.[97] Not knowing that they are also witnessing the dawn of the Renaissance, both sacred and secular writers contrast their own decadent times with a bygone Age of Gold,[98] when knights were noble and Christians sincere. Understandably, they blame one another for the decline of their own cherished institutions, and their historic quarrel takes on a new dimension. In the next two chapters, I shall explain how and why these institutions lost influence in the later Middle Ages. Then, in Chapters Four and Five, I shall illustrate the effects of their collapse on literature through several fifteenth-century lives of St. Katherine and the grail quest narrative of Thomas Malory.

---

[97] Ferguson 57.

[98] Ferguson 57.

Chapter Two:

Chivalry and Feudalism in Malory's Time

In the late fifteenth century, when Thomas Malory composed his version of the Grail Quest, English chivalry was in greater need of defenders than ever before. As the rise of the national state reduced the knight's civil authority, the success of new military tactics incorporating advanced weaponry diminished his importance in battle. Men of the knightly class saw increased danger and expense in the fulfillment of their traditional roles, but not the prestige that knights had once enjoyed. Being practical men, they declined the formal "honor" of knighthood in droves, turning to less romantic, but more profitable occupations, such as business and banking.[99] Those who refused to take this course found themselves compelled, for reasons they scarcely understood, to offer their skills as men-at-arms for money. However understandable their reasons, they were avoiding their traditional obligations and thereby incurring the contempt of their

---

[99] Even the meaning of "knightly class" changed from the thirteenth century to the fifteenth. For reasons that will become apparent shortly, a rising professional and merchant class gained political power in the later Middle Ages, and rank began increasingly to be based on wealth, rather than birth. By the fourteenth century, "distraint of knighthood" (the requirement that men of a certain rank become dubbed knights) had begun. The category of those eligible for distraint of knighthood was defined, not by aristocratic birth, but by an income of ƒ40 a year. See Christopher Dyer, *Standards of Living in the Later Middle Ages: Social Change in England c. 1200-1520* (Cambridge: Cambridge University Press, 1989) 30.

more idealistic contemporaries.

Moreover, because their services had ceased to be crucial to the public good, they became easy targets for criticism. For example, clerics who had reservations about the genuine holiness of the knightly code saw little or nothing in the behavior of actual knights in their own time to justify either their violent profession (which they were often too lazy or cowardly to practice anyway) or their high status in society, which they no longer bothered to earn. If the Malory mentioned in the court records is the same Malory who wrote the King Arthur tales, he was far from the consistent defender of the Church demanded by the knightly code.[100] In short, by Malory's time, knighthood was easy to attack, but hard to defend, and Malory's own life may have typified what he himself seems to find objectionable. However, the very difficulty of the task made it, for Malory, that much more important to attempt. Therefore, he "translated" an anti-chivalric religious text, the Old French *Queste del Saint Graal*, into an elaborate defense of the High Order of Knighthood. To understand his transformation of the ultimate knightly quest, one must first understand the difference between knighthood as the French *Queste* author would have understood it and knighthood as Malory would have known it.

A. The Knight in Battle: Agincourt and Military Strategy

Much of the difficulty of Malory's project stems from the declining position of the knight in society. Warfare, from which knights had always derived their principal importance, changed dramatically in the fifteenth century, reducing the impact of the mailed knight in battle. Ironically, the knightly Henry V, on whom Malory and his contemporaries looked back with such longing, was "a keen

---

[100] For information on the controversy, see Chapter Five.

professional soldier rather than a knight-errant."[101] In fact, without intending to do so, he contributed significantly to the decline of chivalry through effective use of innovative strategy and advanced weaponry. The success of his campaigns in France, especially against superior numbers, was largely due to Henry's willingness (and the unwillingness of the French) to abandon chivalry[102] when necessary to gain strategic advantage. Henry took Harfleur in a very modern way: by pounding it into submission with artillery. The large number of English casualties was attributable more to disease than to combat.[103] The Battle of Agincourt, on which Malory looked back with nostalgia,[104] illustrates with particular clarity the ascendancy of modern methods of warfare and the declining importance of the mailed knight.[105]

To anyone observing, the battle must have appeared impossible for the English. As Oman relates, the English troops were dying of starvation and disease when heavy rains halted their march to Calais. With much difficulty, Henry managed to get his men across the swollen Somme river and took up a

---

[101] Charles Oman, *The Art of War in the Middle Ages A.D. 378-1515*, 2 vols. (New York: Burt Franklin, 1924) 380. Henry himself seems to have gone to considerable trouble to be seen and remembered as a knightly king. For examples of how he "played to the chivalric gallery," see Ferguson 39-41.

[102] By *chivalry*, I mean the battle of knights on horseback (*chevaliers*), as well as the warrior ethic that causes a knight to throw a sword to his enemy, surrendering an advantage to give his opponent a fair fight. When medieval authors use the term *chivalry*, they are almost always referring to the knight in his military capacity. For a concise description of the chivalric ideal at its height, see Gervase Matthew, "Ideals of Knighthood in Late-Fourteenth-Century England," *Studies in Medieval History Presented to Frederick Maurice Powicke*, ed. R.W. Hunt, et. al. (Westport, CT: Greenwood Press, 1948) 354-362.

[103] John Keegan, *The Face of Battle* (New York: Viking Press, 1976) 80.

[104] Ferguson 44.

[105] Some historians have suggested that chivalric warfare was already outdated by the time of Agincourt. See Keegan 317 and Malcolm Vale, *War and Chivalry: Warfare and Aristocratic Culture in England, France, and Burgundy at the End of the Middle Ages* (Athens: University of Georgia Press, 1981) 100. Certainly, Edward III had used equally modern weapons at Crecy, as had the Black Prince at Poitiers, and both were more than willing to overlook the requirements of chivalry to gain a tactical advantage. For details, see Oman 124-147; 160-178.

40

position on a narrow strip of land with rain-soaked fields between his own army and the French. With floodwaters on one side and an enemy outnumbering them four to one on the other,[106] the English desperately needed something to happen. If Henry could not get the French to attack, he would have to come out and fight them on whatever terms they chose or his soldiers would starve where they stood. For this reason, the French, despite their superior numbers, could simply have continued blocking the road to Calais and waited for the English to come to them. In fact, D'Albret, the constable of France, suggested doing exactly that.[107] Monstrelet says "the wisest of [the French] had their fears, and dreaded the event of an open battle,"[108] but he does not say why.

The problem, oddly enough, was that D'Albret was leading the noblest knights in France. This was a problem for two reasons. First, the French nobility, which was well represented at Agincourt, was not easy to command.[109] Whereas English strategy since the time of Edward III had depended more and more on yeomen with longbows, French tactics relied on noblemen who were far too important to take orders. Oman explains that "D'Albret was not really a responsible commander in charge of an army which would obey; there were so many royal counts and dukes present, that he was really only the president of an unruly council of war."[110] This brings us to the second problem with French chivalry at Agincourt. This "unruly council of war," the flower of French chivalry, would not want to wait for the enemy to attack. Every knight present

---

[106] Four to one is Oman's conservative figure. Monstrelet says six to one. See Enguerrand de Monstrelet, *Chronicles*, trans. Thomas J. Ohnes (London: Henry G. Bohn, 1853) 340.

[107] Oman 381.

[108] Monstrelet 340.

[109] For a comparison of the English and French nobility, see Crane 7-9.

[110] Oman 381.

wanted to be the first to ride into battle.[111] Henry, knowing his opponents, edged his army forward about four hundred yards, until they were just within "extreme bowshot," i.e. about 300 yards.[112] Looking across the fields, the English saw "a shiver pass over the whole front of the enemy's first line"[113]: the lances coming down for the charge. Henry stopped immediately, fixed the stakes again, and waited.

The situation could not have been less suited to a full-scale cavalry charge. The fields, which Henry had carefully placed between himself and the enemy, were so wet that the horses sank up to their fetlocks and the men up to their ankles in mud. Henry had had to bring his men further out into the open than he would have liked, but not nearly so far as the French would have to go under heavy fire from the English archers. To make matters worse, the French answer to increasing concerns about the English longbow had been to make their armor thicker and heavier.[114] Therefore, every step was an ordeal as the charge proceeded at a "funereal pace."[115] English archers shot down most of the French cavalry long before they reached the English line.[116] Arrows struck horses as often as they struck men, and a large number of wounded, maddened horses

---

[111] The French had already suffered a crushing defeat at Nicopolis in 1396 for the same reason. When the Hungarian commander who was to lead their assault on the Turks placed the French troops into the rear guard, the knights among them, resenting the "insult," launched an attack on their own, and were badly beaten. See Johan Huizinga, *The Autumn of the Middle Ages*, trans. Rodney J. Payton and Ulrich Mammitsch (Chicago: University of Chicago Press, 1996)104-5; Norman Housley, *The Later Crusades: From Lyons to Alcazar* (Oxford: Oxford University Press, 1992) 76-79.

[112] Keegan 90.

[113] Oman 383.

[114] Oman tells of older knights "of a stout habit of body" dying of heart failure in their heavy armor before making any contact with the enemy. See Oman 377. For a concise description of armor and its weight in the fifteenth century, see C.J. Ffoulkes, *The Armourer and His Craft From the XIIth to the XVth Century* (London: Longman 1912) 119.

[115] Oman 377.

[116] Monstrelet 342.

created chaos in the French lines.[117]

Those knights that did arrive, most of them on foot, managed to push the English back somewhat. Although better rested than their opponents by this time, Henry's knights were nevertheless weak from hunger and marching. At this point, the English king took the unusual step of sending his archers into the fray, armed with swords, mallets, and axes.[118] Unencumbered by heavy armor, they readily knocked their opponents to the ground. Clearly, heavy armor had become a liability, especially once the wearer was exhausted.[119] Moreover, a knight that falls down in such armor is helpless—he can only wait like a turtle on its back to be killed at his enemy's leisure.

The Battle of Agincourt showed the decline of English chivalry[120] for several reasons. First of all, Henry V, despite his continual (and successful) efforts to appear knightly, was certainly as willing to dispense with chivalric virtue as with chivalric warriors when conditions demanded. Henry's conduct at Agincourt, as indicated earlier, was less that of a knight-errant than that of a skillful general. For example, "in a tight moment at Agincourt,"[121] he instructed his soldiers to execute their captives—hardly a knightly act. Monstrelet says this order occasioned "an instantaneous and general massacre of the French prisoners,"[122] although other accounts suggest that Henry met with something less

---

[117] Monstrelet 342; See also Vale 100.

[118] Monstrelet 342.

[119] Oman 384.

[120] The same observation could certainly be made of Crecy or Poitiers, both of which show the ability of English archery, under the right circumstances, to defeat heavy cavalry. I have chosen Agincourt to describe in detail because of its importance to Malory's ideas about the lost Golden Age, when England celebrated the victories of its last knightly king.

[121] Ferguson 40.

[122] Monstrelet 342.

than immediate obedience.[123] Furthermore, Henry consistently took the strategic advantage, even when it meant choosing the less knightly course.[124] He fought a defensive battle not only at Agincourt, but every chance he got during his long campaign in France. Since the primary advantage the English had was their archery, the wisest thing for them to do was set up stakes to protect their bowmen from a cavalry charge and goad the enemy into attacking.

After the success of this strategy for his predecessors at Crecy and Poitier, Henry had good reason to try it at Agincourt. At Crecy in 1346, as Jonathan Sumption vividly shows, the French were unable to understand why their Genoese crossbowmen were being slaughtered without firing a shot.[125] Obviously, because of the longer range of their weapons, the English archers were able to hit the Genoese troops before they got into crossbow range. Nevertheless, many in the French cavalry were quick to brand them traitors and cowards,[126] not recognizing a technological advantage for what it was. Ten years later, at Poitiers, the French knights again charged into a line of longbows, giving their crossbowmen even less chance to compete with the English archers.[127] The result was another slaughter scene, perhaps even worse than the one at Crecy. Predictably, the knights were knocked off their horses by English arrows before they could get close.

---

[123] Many soldiers refused "whether from compassion or for financial reasons," since noble prisoners meant ransoms. Henry had to send some of his personal retinue to carry out the killings. See Oman 385.

[124] Huizinga mentions an exception to this rule, which occurred the night before Agincourt. Henry had accidentally marched his troops beyond the village where they were supposed to stay for the night. Rather than "retreat" in battle dress, he spent the night where he was and sent his advance troops ahead from there. (See Huizinga 111.) Being a shrewd politician, Henry minded appearing unchivalrous much more than he minded being unchivalrous.

[125] Jonathan Sumption, *The Hundred Years War I: Trial By Battle* (Philadelphia: University of Pennsylvania Press, 1990) 525-530.

[126] Sumption 528.

[127] Oman 169.

44

The refusal of the French knighthood to adjust to the new situation was partly a result of their playing their parts too well. Unlike the English, who were ready to ignore the chivalric ideal in the interest of practicality, the French seem romantically willing to lose. For example, when the French attacked Flanders in 1382, the knights refused to enter by an unexpected route. Using such surprise tactics "would show that we are not proper knights."[128] When they did invade, they all wanted to be in the advance guard, and whoever was placed in charge of the rear guard resisted, despite the fact that someone has to command in the rear.[129]

During a raid on the English coast in 1404, the leader of the French troops planned to attack the English flank, for the good reason that the defenders had dug a deep trench along the beach in front of them. His plan might have succeeded, had a French nobleman not called their adversaries "a troop of peasants." As soon as his knights heard that, they insisted that "it would be shameful to avoid meeting such opponents head-on."[130] Like the knights at Agincourt, they overruled their leader to give up a tactical advantage in the name of chivalry, and the result was much the same.

Given these tendencies, as well as the experiences of his predecessors, Henry need not have understood French chivalric thinking exceptionally well to realize what his adversaries would do. Bound by the knightly code, of which they were the shining examples, they would disdain to fight a defensive battle against inferior numbers. They would certainly not understand how a handful of yeomen could defeat so many armored knights.

Only after Agincourt did the French abandon the romantic cavalry charge and begin to deal intelligently with English archery. They hid behind castle walls

---

[128] Huizinga 112.

[129] The French also made the same mistake at Nicopolis in 1396. See Housely 76.

[130] Huizinga 112.

or reconciled themselves to using surprise tactics.[131]   In short, they became practical. The English became even more so. At Crecy, the number of bows to lances had been fairly even, and even there, the longbows had decided the outcome. At Agincourt, the archers who ensured the victory outnumbered the knights, five to one.[132] The English were quick to learn from this experience, and the number of bows to each lance nearly doubled over the next twenty years.[133]

Malory's nostalgia for this last shining moment of English chivalry is therefore doubly ironic. After all, the High Order of Knighthood is based on the idea of a ruling military class. When another group of soldiers becomes more important in battle, the knight's role in society becomes more difficult to define. As we shall see, "Sir Thomas Malory, Knight," feels more strongly than his predecessors the need to argue for the importance and relevance of chivalry. Yet, Henry V himself, England's last knightly king, contributed as much as any individual could to the creation of an England where such arguments were necessary. Of course, Henry had no thoughts of altering the social order, any more than Edward III or the Black Prince had; he merely needed to win a battle. Nevertheless, the success of his tactics against seemingly impossible odds continued a process that could not be reversed. Although cavalry continued to have a place in fifteenth-century warfare,[134] it now required fewer mailed knights.

Moreover, as the knight's equipment became heavier and more expensive,[135] the danger and difficulty of battle increased. While his status in the community diminished, his administrative responsibilities did not, and the king's

---

[131] Oman 386-393.

[132] Actual figures vary from one chronicle to the next. Oman cites several, which estimate the number of lances at eight hundred or nine hundred and the number of bows anywhere from five thousand to ten thousand. Monstrelet says thirteen thousand.

[133] Oman 379.

[134] Vale 128.

[135] Ferguson 109.

46

demands for money and service often outstripped his income from land. Finally, a large proportion of the English nobility in the fifteenth century derived its status from "its property ownership, not...its descent."[136] Due to the resulting entry of wealthy merchants into the "nobility," the knightly class gradually came to be dominated by men who had neither interest nor training in traditional chivalry. By Malory's time, the status of a knight had ceased to depend on his actual role in warfare, which was hopelessly at odds with the role depicted in romances or, for that matter, that lingered in the popular imagination.

Ferguson contrasts this situation with the one that existed in the late thirteenth century, when

> [a]ll the administrative responsibilities that devolved upon the knight could be considered in one way or another connected with his protective function and with his monopoly of the means of enforcing justice. From his land might derive his legal status, but from his sword sprang his authority.[137]

The ruling class was a military class, and the knight's prestige stemmed from his role as soldier and protector.[138] When the importance of this role diminished, the task of defending knighthood fell to those who, like Malory, felt a personal commitment to the High Order of Knighthood as a good in itself.

B. The Knight in Society: Economic Changes

---

[136] S.H. Rigby, *English Society in the Later Middle Ages: Class, Status and Gender* (London: Macmillan, 1995) 204.

[137] Ferguson 109.

[138] For this reason, the romances of the thirteenth century need not have been as concerned with justifying the privileges of the knightly class as Stephen Knight and others claim. Those who are responsible for providing defense and administering justice do not have a desperate need to justify their existence. Certainly, the ruling classes of other times and places have provided less service and felt no such need for justification. Since the knight's status as warrior-hero made his duties an honor and perhaps a pleasure, it seems to me more probable that the romances acted as propaganda not for the peasants, but for the knights themselves.

As the knight began to lose his traditional importance as a warrior, he retained his popular prestige because of romances and chivalric displays, what Huizinga calls the "beautiful play of courtly life."[139] Certainly, Malory, as we shall see, did what he could to keep the ideal alive. However, as the illusion replaced the reality, the lifestyle and courtly displays expected of the knight became more elaborate and expensive. As long as the knight relied on land for his income, his means could not increase to match his expenses. Even Malory, who obviously saw traditional knighthood as worth preserving, probably could not meet his expenses by serving an overlord in the time-honored fashion. The reluctance of noblemen to accept the formal honor of knighthood, with all the financial and military obligations it implied, therefore makes perfect sense. Forced by necessity into such unchivalrous occupations as business and banking[140] (or in some casees, highway robbery), they had less time for and less to gain from the glory of battle.

Thus, Henry's campaign against the French, of which Agincourt was the defining moment, contributed greatly to the England Malory knew, where noblemen declined the honor of knighthood and became bankers, landlords, or even politicians in the modern sense. Warfare still required cavalry, but these were as likely as not to be mercenaries.[141] When English knights came home from the French wars and experienced the heavy demands that the crown placed on a diminishing number of them, they often found themselves forced to "Sell their services to the highest bidder."[142] Knights who needed employment but disliked the idea of going into business, at least found a lucrative market for their skills in

---

[139] Huizinga 120.

[140] Ferguson 115.

[141] Even across the channel, the full-scale cavalry charge ceased to be employed exclusively regardless of conditions. More often, heavy cavalry was used for its offensive "shock" effect, in combination with arrows or pikes. See Vale 125.

[142] Ferguson 115.

a country preparing for civil war. If knights in the service of their king were not perfectly chivalrous, they could hardly be expected to be so in the service of an employer.

Furthermore, knights no longer enjoyed the authority or respect in civilian life that their ancestors had. In late medieval England, the knight's administrative duties were performed, more and more frequently, by professionals like Chaucer's Franklin.[143] As the number of dubbed knights shrank, law and public service became professionalized. The knight might become a lawyer or politician and sit in the House of Commons, but he was no longer, by definition, an administrator of justice. In earlier times, this responsibility had fallen to the knight because he was the only person with the might to carry it out. (As Ferguson says, "from his sword sprang his authority."[144]) By the middle of the fifteenth century, this was no longer true, and Malory's need to glorify knighthood is therefore understandable.

While advances in military strategy explain the knight's declining position, even in civilian life, it does not explain the professionalizing of services such as law, politics, and banking. Few of the new professions that knights found attractive would have existed if the English economy had not undergone a palpable shift. The replacement of the feudal system by a cash economy happened slowly, but two forces hurried it along. One was the Black Death, which affected the English economy much more than it affected harder-hit countries on the Continent. The other was the centralizing of political power, which, as much as anything else, would bring England into the Renaissance.

Before the arrival of the plague, English feudalism was already in danger of collapse. One reason was the wider circulation of money. Since feudalism is a

---

[143] Ferguson points out that, even in Chaucer's time, the Franklin could "be contrasted effectively to the Knight himself, who...typified the older and purer tradition of military knight-errantry." The professional administrator became much more the rule in the fifteenth century. See Ferguson 113.

[144] Ferguson 109.

system of reciprocal obligations, it depends upon money's being very scarce.[145] As soon as money becomes readily available, a certain number of people will hire out the services they owe to their overlords. For example, a knight who would rather not go to war will hire soldiers instead of going himself. An ambitious peasant could become a tradesman or even a small landlord, paying someone else to till his land. In the thirteenth century, a combination of good luck and good management had brought England a large surplus of bread corns, such as wheat, barley, and oats. Landowners, especially the Church, exported this surplus and acquired not only foreign goods, but also a great deal of money.[146] The ability to commute service for cash trickled down to the free peasantry, who also began to buy and sell land. Even unfree peasants could lease land, demand money for the work they did, or even—more and more often—purchase their freedom.

This last possibility placed additional strain on the system because landowners did not necessarily want those who worked their land to become free. Especially in highly cultivated areas near the Continental markets, the wealthiest peasants encountered the most obstacles to buying their freedom. The poorest peasants, in areas with the least farm land, had an easier time.[147] The objection of wealthier peasants to this state of affairs is as natural as the insistence of landowners that it continue. Even without the Black Death, English feudalism would probably not have continued indefinitely in the face of such discontent and the growing influence of Lady Meed. In any case, by the time the plague did reach England, in the mid-fourteenth century, the feudal system had already weakened as it had not on the Continent.

In England, even more than Continental Europe, the "economic impact of the Black Death was enormous."[148] While it brought the war between England

---

[145] Frederick Cartwright, *Disease and History* (New York: Signet, 1972) 38.

[146] Cartwright 39.

[147] Cartwright 39.

[148] William McNeill, *Plagues and Peoples* (Garden City, NY: Anchor Press, 1976) 162.

50

and France to a hasty (though, of course, temporary) truce in 1349, it also ended England's vigorous trading with the Continent.[149] Peasants were the hardest hit, due to close living conditions and lack of sanitation, and the resulting labor shortage placed those who survived in a stronger bargaining position with their overlords.[150] The urgent need of landowners to reap the harvest in autumn of 1349 exacerbated this situation, and even small landowners, who might be peasants themselves, had to pay much higher prices. Field laborers enjoyed a higher standard of living, not only because they could negotiate for a higher wage, but also because a diminishing market had driven down the price of meat, grains, and other foods. For the first time, day laborers could travel to wherever the wages were highest, i.e. where labor was needed most, and landowners had to hire them or risk letting the harvest rot in the fields. This is the situation Langland decries in *Piers Plowman*, where peasants are no longer satisfied with anything less than fresh meat, wheaten bread, and good brown ale.[151]

Langland need not have worried. Landowners moved quickly to bring prices under control, asserting their feudal prerogatives whenever possible and refusing to allow peasants to commute service for cash.[152] England also passed the Statute of Laborers in 1350, limiting the wage a laborer could demand or a landowner offer. Peasants, who were now used to better conditions, did not accept these measures passively. A major reason the 1381 Rising occurred when it did was "the abundance and prosperity in which the common people then lived."[153] As is usually the case, people rebelled to keep from losing a privilege,

[149] Cartwright 46.

[150] Henry E. Sigerist, *Civilization and Disease* (Chicago: University of Chicago Press, 1943) 16.

[151] Cartwright 47.

[152] Cartwright 49.

[153] Jean Froissart, *Chronicles*, ed. and trans. Geoffrey Brereton (London: Penguin, 1968) 211.

not to gain a new one. "If they worked for their masters," says Froissart disapprovingly, "they wanted to have wages for it."[154] Thus, the new regulations on the price of labor and the revoking of accustomed privileges led many to believe that "they were held too much in subjection."[155]

Similar revolts occurred on the Continent wherever legal measures were employed to keep wages down. Froissart perhaps finds the English revolt so disturbing because similar uprisings were occurring in France for the same reasons. However, the so-called English Peasants' Revolt had more serious long-term effects. Although it failed in the short run, landlords realized that they could not bring back English feudalism as it was before the plague. The times when the wealthiest peasants in the most arable areas could be kept from buying their freedom were never going to return. As landlords and peasants made negotiated the best agreements they could, laborers became tenant-farmers, and the feudal system in England "lost much of its meaning within two generations."[156]

Thus, by Malory's time, the feudal system in England, from which the knight derived most of his importance, had ceased to function. Therefore, if Malory was more interested in justifying chivalry than in correcting its flaws, as Chapter Five discusses, he had practical reason. To a man who derives all his ideals from the knightly code, an imperfect, earthly chivalry, sincerely practiced, would be infinitely better than no attempt at chivalry at all. However, if peasants could not be forced to continue fulfilling their feudal obligations, much less so could knights. Those who came home from the French wars to find their families and communities destroyed by the plague no longer had a definite position to go back to. Since a knight was also a landholder, he would find the labor shortage driving up his expenses, just at a time when the accoutrements of knighthood

---

[154] Froissart 212.

[155] Froissart 211.

[156] Cartwright 49.

were also becoming more expensive. Thus, the need for more income might drive him either into selling his services as man-at-arms or entering one of the less-than-knightly professions discussed earlier in this chapter.

Moreover, there was a shortage of knights as well as laborers. England had always had a much smaller proportion of nobles than France had.[157] Now, because of the plague as well as the war, there were too few knights in England to perform the administrative duties traditionally expected of them. Hence, professional administrators, paid in coin, were needed to take up the slack. In the military, squires made up for the lack of knights, fighting on an essentially equal basis with them.[158] As a result of these role changes, military service had been professionalized in England, by the time of Agincourt, as it had not in France. The history of that battle certainly shows that knights in the older tradition do not necessarily have the advantage over professionals. While professional soldiers may be less loyal, less willing to die for their cause than knight-errants, they are also more disciplined and easier to command.

However, a professional soldier, no matter how personally ethical, is not a knight. A knight has feudal obligations to govern and defend, from which he derives his status. When a system of payment for services replaces a system of obligations, knights can no more be expected to live up to the knightly code than peasants can be expected to continue working for no wages. Malory perceived that knights no longer commanded the respect that they once did and that their failure to live up to expectations was, in large measure, a result of this fact. Therefore, his version of the Grail Quest, as Chapter Five will show, glorifies knighthood and presents the knightly search for "worship" as laudable and worth preserving because it inspires virtue.

When the French wars ended in the 1450s, the returning English knights

---

[157] Froissart says there were too many laborers, but to say that is to say much the same thing. See Froissart 211.

[158] Ferguson 115.

found their own country bristling for armed conflict. It cannot be a coincidence that the Wars of the Roses began in earnest only two years after the expulsion of the English from France. As long as the men-at-arms were across the channel, hostilities between York and Lancaster could go only so far. As soon as they returned, knights without established affiliations were "often at pains to sell [their] services to the highest bidder,"[159] as, for example, Malory joined the Earl of Warwick. The knight, whose exalted position depended upon the feudal system, had become a professional, as had the laborer.

C. The Knight and the Church: The Relationship and Its History

The final cause of chivalry's decline in the fifteenth century was the weakening of its religious underpinnings. By that time, as the knightly class's preoccupation with business shows, chivalry had nearly ceased to be a Christian vocation. Yet, the ideal of knighthood is as much an inherently Christian ideal as it is an inherently feudal one. Although much has been made of Malory's "secularization" of the Grail Quest,[160] Malory understood, probably better than we do, that ideal knighthood cannot be thoroughly secularized without turning into something very different. To imagine what it would turn into, one has only to look at the warrior profession before the Church imposed a Christian ideal on it.

"Knighthood" began, ironically, with the "hot-headed warriors" of ninth-century France who could not have had less of what we would call chivalry.[161] After the collapse of Charlemagne's empire and the social order it provided, these warriors "came to represent the only authorities, violent, arbitrary and demanding,

---

[159] Ferguson 115.

[160] See discussion in Chapter Five.

[161] Arno Borst, *Medieval Worlds: Barbarians, Heretics, and Artists in the Middle Ages*, trans. Eric Hansen (Chicago: University of Chicago Pres, 1991) 148.

that men knew."[162]   The only fighters strong enough to defend a village against foreign invaders, they lacked not only strong religious feelings, but also the seemingly secular virtues that we associate with knighthood.[163]   The fellowship that Malory prizes so highly[164] was conspicuously absent.   They fought one another constantly—for vengeance or to display their strength—and acquired whatever wealth they needed through violence.[165]   While they defended their lands from outside attack, they had no scruples against attacking anyone they thought to be weaker, robbing travelers, torturing prisoners, beating and raping women.[166] Much of their violence was directed against the Church, and so it happened that clerics joined with peasants and merchants to bring the nobles under control.[167]

The Church, with the help of its own warriors, began the medieval "peace movement"[168] in the late tenth century.   The first major step was the Peace of God, which prohibited violence against certain classes of people, such as unarmed clerics and, later, merchants.[169]   It also forbade anyone to plunder churches or steal peasants' livestock.[170]   From these prohibitions, one can glean a fairly clear idea of what type of not-so-chivalrous activity was common among the knights of this time.   In the first of many peace councils, called in 990, the bishop asked those

---

[162] Jonathan Riley-Smith, *The Crusades: A Short History* (New Haven: Yale University Press, 1987) 14.

[163] Borst 147.

[164] See Chapter Five.

[165] Marc Bloch, *Feudal Society*, trans. L.A. Manyon (Chicago: University of Chicago Press, 1961) 411.

[166] Borst 147.

[167] Frederick H. Russell, *The Just War in the Middle Ages* (Cambridge: Cambridge University Press, 1975) 34.

[168] Russell 34.

[169] Bloch 414.

[170] Bloch 414.

present to vow to keep the peace and not steal from churches or the poor. Modest as this proposal seems, the nobles refused until the bishop produced warriors of his own, forcing them to take the oath and provide hostages to guarantee their compliance.[171] This first "peace pact" was therefore concluded, as one chronicle says, "with the help of God."[172]

The next question, once the bishops organized the peace councils, was how to enforce the agreements. The old system, whereby the local lord would be responsible for apprehending brigands, had shown itself unequal to the task. However, as the success of the first peace council shows, the Church had already evaluated the problem realistically and concluded that those who favored peace could not always be strict pacifists.[173] Bishops and abbots had their own retinues of knights,[174] and other knights saw that an end to the natural state of all against all would be in their long-term interest. As Bloch explains, the warlords realized better than anyone else "the disasters which they brought in their train."[175] Naturally, those who favored this new social contract had also to enforce it. Knightly fellowship began when "the sworn associations, whose sole object had originally been to bind men together by a comprehensive pledge of good behavior, tended to be transformed into executive organs."[176] Nobles organized militias and appointed judges, enforcing the traditional right of any community to defend itself against lawbreakers. Thus, knights became responsible for the righting of wrongs because only they could effectively "protect society" against

---

[171] Bloch 415.

[172] De Vic and Vaissete, qtd. in Bloch 415.

[173] Russell 34.

[174] Riley-Smith 14.

[175] Bloch 412.

[176] Bloch 415.

56

the unregenerate robber barons among them.[177] In this way, the Church and the "sworn associations" of warriors (which it helped create) joined forces to end the reign of violence and disorder.[178] Thus, the Church played a vital role in the creation of chivalry as we know it. Not surprisingly, then, when the warrior profession in the late Middle Ages lost its close connection with the Church, some, like Malory, again became robbers.

Still another way the Church tried to reduce the frequency of violence was the Truce of God, which "limited violence to certain time periods."[179] Really, it was an extension of an older law forbidding war on Easter. Eventually, it extended to ordinary Sundays and then to the three days preceding Sunday. Its purpose was to reduce private war and feuding among the nobles, and "no law would have been more salutary—if it had not for the most part remained a dead letter because it asked too much."[180] Three days a week was apparently not yet enough for the knights to pursue their feuds.

The Church found in the Crusades a more effective means of stopping noblemen from fighting one another.[181] In 1078, Pope Gregory VII sowed the seeds by declaring that knights could not pursue secular warfare without sin, but that they could fight for justice when instructed by their bishops.[182] He even

---

[177] Ferguson 112.

[178] John of Salisbury, the English cleric, saw a definite purpose for knighthood. He writes in *Policraticus* in 1159, "What purpose does ordained knighthood serve? To protect the church, to battle against disloyalty, to honour the office of the priesthood, to put an end to injustice towards the poor, to bring peace to the land, to let his own blood be spilled for his brothers, and, if necessary, to give up his own life." Qtd. in Borst 148.

[179] Russell 34.

[180] Bloch 414.

[181] Writers also found in the crusading movement the real-life inspiration for the Grail Quest. See discussion of the Old French *Queste* and the Knights Templar, below.

[182] Russell 34.

required bishops to provide the papacy with troops.[183] This policy shows that the Church had a definite use for knights: to wage a *"bellum Christi* against heretics and other enemies of God and the Roman Church."[184] The decisive moment came in 1095, when Pope Urban II delivered his famous speech at the Council of Clermont, admonishing knights to "desist from their wicked combats against Christians and to fight the righteous war against the infidel."[185] A knightly class, somewhat tamed by the Peace of God, responded enthusiastically, partly because of a "growing piety" among them, and partly because the project appealed to them.[186] The crusades, the ultimate marriage of knighthood and Christianity, yielded some of the highest ideals that the warrior profession was ever to know. By no accident, at the height of the crusading movement, the author of the Old French *Queste del Saint Graal* pictures ideal knighthood as a combination of holiness and chivalry.

The Church, especially Pope Urban II, used good rhetorical strategy to promote the first crusade. Much of the violence perpetrated by the knights of the ninth and tenth centuries was for plunder and personal revenge. To those who went to war against the infidel, the pope promised, in addition to salvation, "the temporal rewards of peace, prosperity and plunder."[187] Furthermore, preachers explained the crusades in terms of the blood-feud and personal vendetta. Christians, their brothers, were being oppressed, and God, their father, had been injured and banished from his rightful estates by the heathen. They were bound to avenge these wrongs, even more so than if their blood relatives had been so

---

[183] Russell 35.

[184] Russell 35.

[185] Russell 36.

[186] Riley-Smith 15.

[187] Russell 36.

wronged.[188] Finally, the crusades offered laymen a chance for salvation. Prior to the first crusade, laymen could seek their salvation only indirectly by donating to the monastic orders, where *miles Christi* fought evil through prayer and penance.[189] A new kind of *Militia Christi*, defined as "knightly bellicosity now obedient to papal purposes and initiative" began in 1078 when pope Gregory VII preached the first crusade.[190] People who fought in defense of Christ and the Church could now have their sins forgiven and achieve a spiritual status almost equal to that of monks.[191] Thus, the Church harnessed the violent impulses that were keeping society in chaos and redirected them to its own purposes.

Only after this surprising alliance between the warrior class and the Church does one begin to see knights with qualities such as fellowship, piety, mercy, justice, and pity that Malory prized so highly and that we still associate with "chivalry." By the eleventh century, the traditional blessing of the sword had developed into a religious ritual in which the cleric himself armed the newly "ordained" knight.[192] When the knight received his consecrated sword, he usually took an oath to fulfill a set of obligations. While these varied from one region to another, they all included the familiar expectations of knightly conduct: "[T]he sword thus consecrated. . .had been given to the knight first of all that he might place it at the service of good causes. . .With this sword, the dubbed knight will defend Holy Church, particularly against the infidel. He will protect the widow, the orphan, and the poor. He will pursue the malefactor."[193] Furthermore, in

---

[188] Riley-Smith 16.

[189] J.M. Upton-Ward, introduction, *The Rule of the Templars: The French Text of the Rule of the Order of the Knights Templar*, trans. J.M. Upton-Ward (Woodbridge: Boydell Press, 1992) 2.

[190] Russell 35.

[191] Riley-Smith 9.

[192] Bloch 315.

[193] Bloch 318.

battle, he will not slay a defenseless foe; in public life, he will not take part in false judgments or treason; in everyday life, he will not give evil counsel to a lady and will give help to the needy whenever possible.[194] As Chapter Five of the present discussion will demonstrate, Malory's King Arthur requires the Knights of the Round Table to swear exactly the same kind of oath. Thus, no matter how "secular" the chivalric ideal seems, especially in the hands of Malory and other chivalric writers, it never existed separately from its religious component and would never have come to be without the intervention of the Church.

No reasonable observer would claim that knights on the crusades (or anywhere else for that matter) behaved chivalrously at all times. Gervase Matthew describes chivalry as a "standard of values, at time consciously followed, at times consciously sinned against, but always presupposed."[195] Crusaders sought the promised plunder with enthusiasm, and the victims were not always the heathens they were sent to fight. For example, the fourth crusade began with a shortage of funds, which the crusaders solved by attacking a Christian town.[196] The military religious orders were also accused of conducting themselves with something less than the selfless piety expected of them.[197] This problem would eventually do irreparable damage to the Christ-like knightly ideal, as the next chapter of this discussion will establish. Nevertheless, cooperation between the Church and the warrior class created chivalry, the code of conduct that finally turned an ungovernable pack of "hot-headed warriors" into knights, as we understand the term. Thus, while the requirement that a good knight show loyalty to his king (as shown by Malory) developed very late, the connection between chivalry and religion existed from the beginning. Accordingly, the most compelling causes for knights in the High Middle Ages were not the political

---

[194] Bloch 318.

[195] Matthew 354.

[196] Riley-Smith 125.

[197] Riley-Smith 210-215.

aspirations of a monarch, but the crusades.[198]

D. A New Knighthood: The Rise and Fall of the Templars

As noted above, the ideal of "heavenly chivalry" that the thirteenth-century author of *La Queste del Saint Graal* valued so highly came from the crusades. Its exemplars, on whom the Old French version of Galahad is based, were supposedly the knights of the military religious orders: the Templars, the Hospitallers, and the Teutonic Knights. The Knights of the Temple, founded in 1119 or 1120 to protect pilgrims on the dangerous journey to the Holy Land,[199] was the most influential in France and England. These knights were a new "combination of monk and soldier": warriors who lived under a Rule based on the Rule of the Cistercians and took vows of poverty, chastity, and obedience.[200]

Of course the term "soldier of Christ" had long existed, but it traditionally referred to a monk or saint who did not use a sword to fight evil. Martyrdom, with the military imagery that usually accompanied it in saints' lives, was the most a soldier of Christ could do for his God. Of course, as indicated above, the Church had allowed and even encouraged laymen to bear arms in its defense, and not only because it was impossible to keep warriors from fighting. Skillful fighters were necessary for the Church to enforce the Peace of God as well as to begin the crusades. However, monks were still strictly forbidden to bear arms, and the "Church's recognition of a religious community dedicated to fighting as well as prayer was a revolutionary step."[201] St. Bernard of Clairvaux, a Cistercian monk who supported the Templars, remarks with pride that the order contains

---

[198] Borst 148.

[199] Riley-Smith 58.

[200] Upton-Ward 2-3.

[201] Riley-Smith 58.

many former criminals who now fight only for their Savior, incarnating "the ideal qualities of both monks and warriors."[202] The Templars brought monastic discipline to the battlefield and became the natural allies and protectors of the crusading armies.[203] Thus, Bernard compellingly articulated the "connection between the peace movement and the crusade," explaining that the violent criminals of Europe became the Holy Land's "faithful defenders."[204]

In this way, the first ideal of knighthood, what Borst calls the "Christ-like knight"[205] was born in the early twelfth century. Throughout the Middle Ages, the "ascetic element" continued to be an essential part of the knightly ideal, at least when "professed in its purest form."[206] This is the ideal valorized in the Old French *Queste*, and as Huizinga points out, the "ideal of the noble propertyless warrior," embodied in the "knight-errant as well as the Templar," still exists.[207] We moderns have difficulty, certainly more than Malory had, recognizing its religious underpinnings. Yet, the qualities which make the heroic warrior so appealing remain "the higher elements of religious consciousness[:] compassion, justice, and fidelity."[208] In our own cinema, the old West gunfighter, the heroic vigilante, and the *ronin* all appeal to their audiences for the same reasons. Without wealth or earthly ties, they fight for pure principle.

Of course, over time, values such as love of women and fellowship with brothers-in-arms, in which Malory was much more interested than the French *Queste* author, altered the knightly ideal and created conflicts within it. For

---

[202] Russell 37.

[203] Upton-Ward 6.

[204] Russell 37.

[205] Borst 148.

[206] Huizinga 82.

[207] Huizinga 82.

[208] Huizinga 82.

62

example, a knight such as Lancelot must choose between devotion to his God and love for his lady or between love for his lady and loyalty to his overlord.[209] Nevertheless, the religious ideal came first and remained essential to idealized knighthood. As Huizinga explains, "The first knightly orders, the three great orders of the Holy Land. . .arose as the purest embodiment of the medieval spirit from a combination of the monastic and knightly ideals at a time when the fight against Islam had become a wondrous reality."[210] Love or fellowship alone, important as they were, could never have brought the warrior class under control. Only the Church, first through the Peace of God, then through the crusades, could have brought the civilizing effects of piety to men whose greatest joy was in fighting and thereby provide fertile ground for the other virtues to grow. Thus, to understand Malory's idea of chivalry, one needs also to understand what happened to this "Christ-like knight" between the thirteenth century (when *La Queste del Saint Graal* was written) and the fifteenth, when our knight-prisoner wrote his own Grail Quest.

For the first decade or so of its existence, the Order of the Temple was very poor and few in number. In 1129, the founder of the Order, Hughes de Payns, appealed to the Council of Troyes for formal recognition.[211] At that time, it received a Rule of its own, partly written by Bernard de Clairvaux, "the greatest preacher of his day,"[212] whose eloquence and reputation overcame the opposition at the Council and won full acceptance for the Templars.[213]

In the next few years, the Templars began to prosper under the leadership

---

[209] This is the apparent conflict that Malory's Lancelot must resolve. Malory's resolution is a "triple scale of values" which holds that fidelity to one's beloved is a good thing, but that serving God is a higher good, before which other goods must give way. See Ferguson 54.

[210] Huizinga 92.

[211] Riley-Smith 89.

[212] Riley-Smith 94.

[213] Upton-Ward 4.

of Hughes de Payns, who spent two years in Europe, successfully recruiting members and wealthy supporters. When Hughes' successor, Robert de Craon, acquired open support from Pope Innocent II, the Order "emerged as a full-fledged military order with a hierarchical structure."[214] Bernard de Clairvaux, who "created the image of the warrior monk,"[215] continued to lend his prestige to the Templars' cause, assisting their expansion tremendously.[216] Increasing piety among laymen also worked to their material advantage, and the Templars' holdings in the West increased steadily throughout the twelfth century. They acquired estates, which included serfs, animals, mills, wine-presses, etc. They also acquired a large amount of liquid capital and began to finance lay crusaders, including Louis VII, whose successor, Philip II, repaid the Temple handsomely.[217] In this way, the Templars "added banking to their other functions,"[218] and the officials, bailiffs, craftsmen, servants and benefactors of the Temple soon came to greatly outnumber the actual knights.[219] Thus, by the end of the twelfth century, the Order had "developed in to an international corporation, administering estates and handling large sums of money belonging to the crowned heads and leading lords of Christendom."[220]

The rise of the Order of the Temple contained the seeds of its fall. The Temple's wealth and prestige reached its highest level in the mid-thirteenth

---

[214] Upton-Ward 5.

[215] Russell 296.

[216] Malcolm Barber, *The Trial of the Templars* (Cambridge: Cambridge University Press, 1978) 7.

[217] Barber 9.

[218] Upton-Ward 7.

[219] Barber 9.

[220] Barber 9.

64

century,[221] when only the military religious orders had the resources to defend the Latin settlements in the East.[222]   Not coincidentally, this was also the time when an anonymous French monk composed *La Queste del Saint Graal*, promoting the same "celestial chivalry" that Bernard of Clairvaux had so compellingly described. To its writer, the successful Grail knights represented an ideal that was not only attainable, but vitally important to the future of Christendom. The importance of knighthood to the Church had never been clearer, and the Templars seemed to embody its highest application.

Other orders naturally grew to resent the Temple's wealth and privileged position, as well as its papal protection and immunity from secular authorities.[223] Even the papacy, so supportive of the Templars since Bernard's time, became decidedly less so. Barber cites various examples of both lay and clerical writers ascribing the worst possible motive to every decision the Templars make. While not assuming that these detractors are correct, Barber notes that they show how much resentment the Templars incurred at the height of their power. As early as 1207, Pope Innocent III "condemned the Templars for their pride and their abuse of their privileged position."[224]   During a dispute in 1265, Pope Clement IV sternly reminded the Grand Master of the Temple that "if the Church removed for a short while the hand of its protection from you in the face of the prelates and the secular princes, you could not in any way subsist against the assaults of these prelates or the force of the princes."[225] The turning point came in 1291, when Acre fell to the Muslims, and the Order therefore "lost its base and its *raison*

---

[221] Riley-Smith 60.

[222] Upton-Ward 9; Barber 10.

[223] Barber 11-12.

[224] Barber 13.

[225] qtd. in Barber 13.

d'etre.[226] Huizinga explains the result:

> As long as the Templars and Hospitalers flourished and were still active in the Holy Land itself the knightly way of life had served a real political function and the knightly orders really were practical organizations serving functions of great significance. . .[but by the beginning of the fourteenth century] their economic success. . .had eaten away their political usefulness.[227]

Now that the French king no longer needed their services, he became more resentful of the Templars' wealth and immunity from royal authority. Really, the 1265 warning from Clement IV suggests that princes resented the Templars long before the fall of Acre. However, afterwards, such princes were much more willing to act on their resentment. On 13 October 1307, early in the morning, every Templar in France who could be caught was arrested on charges of heresy.

Even today, scholars disagree as to whether they were guilty or not.[228] The charges against them were certainly "bizarre in the extreme."[229] Barber includes the complete Articles of Accusation in *The Trial of the Templars*, Appendix A. These include the following charges:

> Item, that they made those whom they received spit on a cross, or on a representation or sculpture of the cross and an image of Christ, although sometimes those who were being received spat next [to it].
>
> Item, that they sometimes ordered that this cross be trampled underfoot. . .

---

[226] Upton-Ward 9.

[227] Huizinga 92.

[228] For an in-depth examination of both sides, see G. Legman and Henry Charles Lea, et. al., *The Guilt of the Templars* (New York: Basic Books, Inc., 1966). G. Legman makes the case against the Templars, and Henry Charles Lea makes the case for them.

[229] Riley-Smith 210.

Item, that sometimes they urinated and trampled, and caused others to urinate, on this cross, and several times they did this on Good Friday. . .

Item, that they adored a certain cat, [which] sometimes appeared to them in their assembly.

Item, that in the reception of the brothers of the said Order or at about that time, sometimes the receptor and sometimes the received were kissed on the mouth, on the navel, or on the bare stomach, and on the buttocks or the base of the spine.

- Item, [that they were kissed] sometimes on the navel. – Item, [that they were kissed] sometimes on the base of the spine. – Item, [that they were kissed] sometimes on the penis. . .

Item, that they told the brothers whom they received that they could have carnal relations together.

Item, that it was licit for them to do this.

Item, that they ought to do and submit to this mutually. . .

Item, that in each province they had idols, namely heads, of which some had three faces, and some one, and others had a human skull.

Item, that they adored these idols or that idol, and especially in their great chapters and assemblies. . .

Item, that they venerated [them] as God. . .

The Articles go on in that vein for many pages. Riley-Smith observes that "very few have believed that the Templars were guilty of the crimes of which they were accused."[230] Although G. Legman makes an intricate argument that they were guilty, the final consensus of most scholars is that their guilt or innocence was irrelevant: Philip's reasons for wanting to be rid of them had nothing to do with heresy, homosexuality, idol worship or the adoration of cats. Riley-Smith sums up the situation laconically: "They were rich and King Philip IV's government

---

[230] Riley-Smith 210.

was short of cash."[231]

Whether or not they were guilty, by 1307, this reason would probably have been sufficient. Henry Lea, who contends that the riches of the Temple are generally exaggerated, nevertheless believes that "the wealth of the Order was more than sufficient to excite the cupidity of royal freebooters, and its power and privileges quite enough to arouse distrust in the mind of a less suspicious despot than Philippe le Bel."[232] Not only their immunity from royal power, but also their close connection with the pope represented a serious challenge to Philip's authority.[233] In short, Philip had the chance to remove an annoyance and, at the same time, increase his treasury considerably. All 138 Templars arrested in France were questioned closely, and many were tortured.[234] Not surprisingly, all but four confessed, and many were burnt to death, including Jacques de Molay, the Grand Master, and Geoffroi de Charnay, the preceptor in Normandy.

In England, the response was much milder, but the king, Edward II, could not ignore such serious charges against the Order in France. Upon hearing news of the Templars' arrest in October 1307, Edward expressed astonishment and assured Philip that he and his council would examine the matter closely. The charges, in Edward's view, were so shocking as to be scarcely believable, and he refused to lift a finger against them until they should be legitimately convicted.[235] The Templars "held a respected, trusted and privileged position in the domains

---

[231] Riley-Smith 210.

[232] Lea 151.

[233] To call the conflict between Philip IV and Clement V a "power struggle" would be an understatement. Clement's predecessor, Boniface VIII, had died of "shock" only four years earlier, after being kidnapped by one of Philip's ministers. Some consider Philip's denial of ecclesiastical justice for the Templars to be a deliberate attack on Church authority. See Riley-Smith 211 and Lea 151.

[234] Lea 186-97.

[235] Lea 197.

ruled by the Norman and Angevin kings,"[236] and Edward would not believe evil of them without clear proof, despite the financial rewards that he could have gained by having them arrested.[237] He wrote letters to the kings of Portugal, Castile, Aragon and Naples, and finally to the pope, begging them not to accept the slanders of envious men without more compelling evidence.[238]

Accordingly, the trial of the Templars proceeded in England with much less harshness than in France. Edward ordered the Templars arrested in January 1308, in obedience to a papal bull, but the sophisticated legal system in England did not allow torture. This prohibition apparently caused great frustration to the papal inquisitors, who were unable to extract the needed confessions without it.[239] Eventually, Edward had to allow the inquisitors to use whatever methods their duties required "in accordance with ecclesiastical law," but the accused Templars retracted their confessions as soon as the torture ended, and it failed to produce convictions.[240] The only useful information the inquisitors could discover was that some Templars erroneously believed their preceptors could absolve them from sin. This may not even have been the official Templar position: most of the brothers were poorly educated and may have "failed to grasp the difference between sacramental absolution by priests and absolution by the Master for breaking the Order's rules and regulations."[241]

Eventually, the Templars in England were dispersed into various monasteries and assigned penance until the Holy See could make a decision about

---

[236] Barber 194.

[237] Barber 193.

[238] Barber 194.

[239] Lea 198-9.

[240] Lea 200.

[241] Barber 208.

their future. Nothing further was done about them,[242] but the Order was clearly in disgrace, and the image of the Christ-like knight retreated into theory. As so often happens, reality had given "the cruel lie to the ideal," and it "sank more and more back into the realm of imagination, where it was able to preserve features of noble asceticism that were rarely evident in the midst of social realities."[243]

E. The Result: Malory's England

By the fifteenth century, the idea of heavenly chivalry, as compelling as it was when Bernard of Clairvaux described it, was no longer meaningful. Its shining exemplars, the Knights of the Temple, were gone. Malory, as we shall see, utterly rejects the distinction that the Old French *Queste* author draws between "celestial chivalry" and "earthly chivalry." Although his view of ideal knighthood has religious underpinnings, he has no use for a knight whose holiness renders him useless for keeping order in an earthly kingdom.[244] A country in the midst of civil war, such as Malory's England, does not need its natural leaders to go on a solitary quest for religious perfection. It needs them, at least in Malory's view, to fulfill their traditional obligations to put down renegades and reestablish order.

Furthermore, the idea that serving the Church was more important than serving the state, which seemed so obvious in the thirteenth century, was not nearly so obvious in the fifteenth. Malory's England, with its well-developed court system and army of professional administrators, was rapidly moving towards a Renaissance idea of the state, in which the knightly code, shorn of its religious and militaristic implications, would be reborn in the Renaissance

---

[242] Lea 200.

[243] Huizinga 82.

[244] See discussion of Galahad in Chapter five.

gentleman, whose virtue lay in service to the crown.

At the time of the Old French *Queste*, knighthood had needed no defense. It had several obvious purposes, which clerics and laymen alike could understand and support: to maintain the social order, to protect the weak, and to defend the Holy Church. By Malory's time, knighthood was no longer necessary for any of these functions. The knight's legal and administrative duties could be performed just as well by professionals like Chaucer's Franklin. These were needed anyway because there were not nearly enough knights left in England to do all their traditional tasks. In battle, from which the knight's chief importance had always come, squires were performing the same functions on an almost equal basis, and lightly clad yeomen were more important than either of them. The decline of English feudalism and the fall of the military religious orders thus left the knightly ideal an empty shell which lacked a real social function.

Thus, not only had knighthood ceased to serve a holy purpose, but the purpose it did serve was becoming difficult to explain. Sir Thomas Malory, if he was the same Thomas Malory in prison for disloyalty to the crown, had little to gain from justifying the vocation that he himself practiced so imperfectly. Yet, Malory seems to have had much personal investment in the knightly ideal, and he was certainly the most capable Englishman to undertake its defense when such a defense was most difficult. Thus, the courtly knight continued to live in literature and in the popular imagination beyond his natural life-span. Hagiographers, most of whom were clerics, no longer viewed knighthood as necessary for the defense of the Church and condemned the knightly ideal
for its glorification of violence. However, romance writers, including Malory, continued to see in chivalry the only code of civilized behavior available to ordinary people who could not become monks or saints.

Chapter Three:

The English Church in the Fifteenth Century

Thomas Malory and his contemporaries correctly viewed their time as an age of decaying institutions. The last chapter showed the effects of a declining feudal system on knighthood and, inevitably, on chivalric literature. This chapter concerns the other medieval institution that lost power to a growing English state. I refer, of course, to the Church, whose authority reached its height in the thirteenth century and then began a slow decline in the fourteenth.[245] The weakened Church of the fifteenth century, like the weakened feudal system, affected both of the major literary genres. Hagiographers, many of whom were clerics, became defensive as romance writers became anti-clerical. Other changes, not so obvious, in the English Church caused clerical writers to show an involvement in politics that their predecessors would have scorned. To make sense of the secular concerns of fifteenth-century hagiographers, one needs to examine relations between the Church and the increasingly powerful state of the late Middle Ages. A. Hamilton Thompson has noted that one cannot discuss the English Church in the fifteenth century without also considering in some detail events that preceded it. Ecclesiastical institutions at the end of the Middle Ages

---

[245] Crane 101.

72

"wore a settled form which had been achieved at an earlier date."[246]

For this reason, I shall have to return for a moment to the early fourteenth century. The refusal of Philip the Fair to allow the Templars the traditional right to trial in an ecclesiastical court, as explained in the last chapter, was correctly interpreted as a message of defiance directed at Clement V. His predecessor, Boniface VIII, had met disaster "by his attempt to domineer over kings"[247] at a time when kings had ceased to need the support of the papacy. The unfortunate Templars, who admittedly had abused the pontiff's willingness to protect them, were caught in the middle of a power struggle whose outcome shows which way the wind was blowing. Most historians of this period consider the fall of the Templars "a good example of what the developing state machinery could do at a time when the crown controlled the inquisition and the papacy was on the defensive."[248]

In England, where the state machinery had developed early and "something very closely akin to a national feeling"[249] caused Englishmen routinely to side with their king against the pope, Edward I and his successors often enjoyed the advantage in their dealings with Rome. Moreover, English anti-clericalism, fed by abuses in an overly powerful Church and the efforts of reformers such as John Wycliffe (1320-84), increased throughout the fourteenth and fifteenth centuries. The anti-clericalism of Chaucer and Langland was standard fare in popular literature, and the situation became decidedly worse in the fifteenth century, when graft, pluralism, and secular politics were so common in the Church as to make it an easy target for satire. Ultimately, fifteenth-century

---

[246] A. Hamilton Thompson, *The English Clergy and Their Organization in the Later Middle Ages* (Oxford: Clarendon Press, 1947) 1.

[247] Thompson 11.

[248] Riley-Smith 210.

[249] J.C. Dickinson, *An Ecclesiastical History of England: The Later Middle Ages From the Norman Conquest to the Eve of the Reformation* (London: A&C Black, 1979) 251.

clerics found themselves in the same position as fifteenth-century knights: with their prestige appallingly low, they needed to defend and justify themselves to the lay public as never before.

A. Anglo-Papal Relations

The first force molding the English Church in the late Middle Ages was the relationship between crown and papacy. In the fourteenth century, the age of papal absolutism, Anglo-papal relations seem to consist of an elaborate chess game in which the ordinary clergy "were caught between a relentless church and a relentless state."[250] Both wanted control over patronage, and both needed the ability to tax the clergy. Disputes over benefices were common, and neither side could afford to give in, since both were claiming expanded influence over the power structure of the English Church. At stake in this chess game was whether bishops and other high-ranking clergy would owe their sinecures to the crown or the papacy, and individual disputes could last as long as fifty years.[251] Furthermore, the Pope, residing at Avignon since 1309, was cut off from his major source of income and needed new taxes to support his large retinue. These, however, he was willing to share with the king to gain his compliance.[252] The clergy, squeezed from both sides, protested loudly, and the English kings duly used these complaints to gain leverage in their bargaining with the pope.[253]

During "England's asinine engagement in the Hundred Years War,"[254] Englishmen in general heartily resented the interference of a French pope in their

---

[250] James Westfall Thompson and Edgar Nathaniel Johnson, *An Introduction to Medieval Europe* (New York: Norton, 1937) 970.

[251] Pantin 80-81.

[252] Thompson and Johnson 969.

[253] Dickinson 247.

[254] Dickinson 252.

74

affairs, but Edward II and Edward III (in his youth) were weaker monarchs than Edward I, and the papacy generally had the upper hand. When Edward III succeeded to the throne, he was very young and easily dominated by his mother, Isabella, and her lover, Mortimer. W.A. Pantin accurately describes a letter from the eighteen-year-old Edward to Pope John XXII as "like a letter for help smuggled out of prison."[255] There, Edward tells his "Most Holy Father" that, in the future, letters which contain the secret code "Pater Sancte" in the king's own hand contain his real wishes.[256] Eighty-four-year-old John XXII was as strong as Edward was weak, and John shows paternal concern for Edward's difficulties. For this reason, the Avignonese popes generally "did what they would with English benefices."[257]

On the other hand, Edward did not remain weak. During "the most vigorous period of Edward III's reign," in the mid-fourteenth century, England was at war with France, and Pope Clement VI was "thoroughly French in his sympathies."[258] At this point, Edward became decidedly less conciliatory and Anglo-papal relations began to resemble the negotiations between equals that had characterized the reign of Edward I. In the late fourteenth century, the balance of power shifted in favor of the crown, where it remained until Henry VIII's final break with Rome.

This shift, which created the English Church of the fifteenth century, was the result of three factors. The first was the strong machinery of government that already existed in England. By the fifteenth century, as explained in the last chapter, England no longer had a functioning feudal system. When the knightly class ceased to be large enough or wealthy enough to do all the work of

---

[255] Pantin 77.

[256] Pantin reproduces the letter on pages 77-78. It is also available in facsimile in C. Johnson and H. Jenkinson, *English Courthand* (Oxford: Oxford University Press 1915) plate xxii.

[257] Thompson 11.

[258] Pantin 81.

government, the state grew enormously. Since the time of Henry II, Englishmen could rely on a sophisticated court system to resolve their disputes and determine punishments in criminal matters. Like everyone else, the clergy depended upon the king's justice, and Edward I found that denying the clergy protection of the law persuaded the pope to cease his threats of interdict. By the time of Henry V, the jurisdiction of ecclesiastical courts was severely limited in cases of advowson and benefit of clergy.[259] Furthermore, England had a well-developed tax system and a large number of professional administrators to run the larger, more powerful government. In short, the English king needed no help from the outside, and English citizens, including clerics, resented the intrusion of foreigners, especially of foreigners who held court in France. For this reason, as Chapter Four will show, fifteenth-century hagiographers show an interest in national issues that would have surprised their predecessors, who saw themselves as churchmen first.

The anti-papal protests in England were largely due to the second factor that affected Anglo-papal relations in the fifteenth century: a feeling which historians of the period are tempted to call "patriotism." The hesitation one hears in Dickinson's "something very closely akin to a national feeling"[260] is understandable, since the rise of the national state, as much as anything else, marks the close of the Middle Ages and the beginning of Renaissance Europe. Nevertheless, England existed as a political unit under the authority of a recognized king long before the same could be said of France, Italy, or Germany. This does not mean there was no disagreement as to who should rule, as the Wars of the Roses clearly show. Nevertheless, a strong, capable king, such as Henry IV, could achieve peace in his kingdom, especially given the relative tranquility of the English barony. Moreover, a charismatic king, such as Henry V, could stir his subjects into such nationalistic fervor against a foreign enemy that they

[259] E.F. Jacob, *The Fifteenth Century: 1399-1485, The Oxford History of England,* ed. Sir George Clark (Oxford: Clarendon Press, 1961) 265.

[260] Dickinson 251.

entirely forgot for a long while their differences about the succession.[261]

Because of this early sense of patriotism was defined by loyalty to the king, "the military loyalty of the knight had been transferred from the feudal lord to the king."[262] Ironically, when Malory tries to recall a Golden Age of chivalry, he equates chivalric virtue with loyalty to a king, which is much more characteristic of his own day than of the real heyday of English chivalry. Thus, in the early fifteenth century, those who would have been most able to create division in the realm had the strongest sense of patriotism. Trouble came, as it did after the expulsion of the English from France, when there was a real question about who the rightful king was, i.e. to whom a true knight owed his loyalty. Malory, whose defense of the knightly code is often vehement,[263] nevertheless probably died in prison for following the Earl of Warwick against Edward IV. John Capgrave, St. Katherine's greatest biographer (of whom we shall see much more later) shows equally intense, though vacillating, concern about which claimant to the throne will best secure the happiness of England.

Therefore, even a pope who did not reside in France would have found the English king a powerful adversary. His traditional weapons of interdict and excommunication worked only if they made it impossible for the king to govern. From the late fourteenth century forward, the English parliament showed marked "hostility to the provisory authority of the pope."[264] Legislation designed to limit the pope's influence over English affairs strengthened the king's bargaining position.[265] For example, the Statute of Provisors, enacted in 1351, forbade

---

[261] These differences, stemming from the usurpation of Henry IV, resurfaced during the reign of the weaker Henry VI, resulting in the Wars of the Roses.

[262] Ferguson 128.

[263] See discussion of Malory in Chapter 5.

[264] Thompson 15-16.

[265] K.B. McFarlane, *John Wycliffe and the Beginnings of English Nonconformity* (New York: Macmillan, 1953) 53-54.

appeals to the Roman Curia on temporal matters such as patronage; the Statute of Praemunire, enacted in 1353, declared it a crime to place a foreign power above the king.[266] With a nation whose patriotism so often manifested itself in such anti-papal demonstrations, even a strong pope would have to proceed cautiously, and the popes of this late period were not as strong as their predecessors.

On the contrary, a weakened papacy was the third factor that brought about the shift in Anglo-papal relations. The schism of 1378 destroyed most of the gains that the Avignon popes had made, and the authority of the papacy never recovered from the nearly forty years in which there were two popes. An English monarch did not have to be as clever as Henry IV or Henry V to realize that he could play the two of them against each other, threatening to support the pope at Avignon if the pope at Rome did not do as he wished. Naturally, the English inclined toward the Roman popes who, anxious to keep their support, complied with most of the king's requests.[267] Thus, the days of protracted struggles between monarchy and papacy about whose nominee should receive the papal provision were over. Generally speaking, the king nominated, and the pope approved. Then, the local chapter would be told "whom they were to elect."[268] In other words, the crown and the papacy came to the understanding that the pope would provide the royal nominee, and the king would not dispute the pope's right to provide whomever he wished.[269]

Occasionally, the pope would test this agreement, and disputes over whose nominee should receive the bishopric clearly show how far the advantage had shifted to the crown. Only the pope could make a provision, but the king controlled the "temporalities," i.e. the funds, and he could simply withhold them

---

[266] Pantin 85.

[267] Jacob 268.

[268] Jacob 268.

[269] Thompson 16.

from a papal provisor with whose selection he did not agree. After the schism, English kings were much freer to use this weapon, as Henry IV did in 1400 against Boniface IX's nominee. In that case, the see of Bath and Wells had fallen vacant, and Boniface provided Richard Clifford, dean of York and archdeacon of Canterbury. Henry, who had nominated Henry Bowet, refused the temporalities to Clifford. Without a struggle, Clifford got the see of Worcester, and Bowet got Bath and Wells, as Henry wished.[270]

The weakness of the papacy in this case becomes obvious if one compares it to a similar conflict which arose in 1205 between Innocent III and King John. In summer of that year, the archbishopric of Canterbury fell vacant, and the local chapter quarreled with the bishops of the southern provinces over whether the bishops had a right to participate in the elections. The bishops appealed to Rome, and the monks elected their subprior, who immediately left for Rome himself. When John arrived, he was furious that the chapter had held the election without consulting him—in fact, had speeded up the process to avoid doing so. He insisted that the chapter elect his candidate, John de Grey, then bishop of Norwich, and the result was a "tangle" to be unraveled by "the eminent lawyer, Pope Innocent III."[271] The unfortunate John was overmatched. Innocent III, entirely unaffected and unimpressed by royal pressure, suggested Stephen Langton, a highly respected theologian in the Roman Curia. The chapter agreed, and Langton received the appointment. However, John furiously objected to an Archbishop of Canterbury's being selected without consultation with the crown and seized all the chapter's considerable revenues.[272] The pope placed him under interdict, then excommunicated him, and considered declaring him deposed

---

[270] Thompson 18.

[271] Dickinson 219.

[272] Dickinson notes that John had a reasonable complaint. The Archbishop of Canterbury played a major role in secular government and controlled a great deal of wealth and patronage. English tradition required that the crown be fairly consulted before this office could be filled: 219-220.

before John became terrified at the idea of the king of France invading England with the pope's approval, something Philip Augustus would have dearly loved to do. So John accepted Langton as Archbishop of Canterbury, promised to return the revenues he had seized, and surrendered his kingdom to the pope, receiving it back from him as a papal fief. This "colorful concession" theoretically made the king of England "a vassal of the papacy,"[273] although later popes had little success in asserting their feudal rights.

It would be hard to imagine a more complete defeat for the English crown. Despite the king's control of the temporalities, the pope held all the highest cards. Interdict would deny to everyone in the kingdom the services of priests, including sermons and all the sacraments except baptism and confession for the dying. Excommunication would make the king a "spiritual leper,"[274] with whom all Christians would have to avoid contact. The strongest king could not have continued to rule under these circumstances and would have had to conciliate the pope, as John's much stronger father, Henry II, had to do after his conflict with Becket. However, these powerful weapons were not available to later popes. In a world with two popes, threats of interdiction and excommunication would have been meaningless, since the king could simply turn to the other pope, who would cheerfully accept his support. Therefore, when the king presented his nominee, "amid the difficulties of the Great Schism, the popes were compliant."[275] Although the schism ended in 1417, the papacy never regained its prestige. Thus, the combination of a strengthened state and a weakened papacy made English kings essentially independent of the pope. After 1378, the papacy simply needed the crown more than the crown needed the papacy, and this fact had important implications for the English clergy, from whose ranks the fifteenth-century hagiographers mostly came.

---

[273] Dickinson 222.

[274] Dickinson 220.

[275] Thompson 15.

B. Patronage and Provisions

English clerics in the fifteenth century, like their contemporaries outside the Church, had begun consciously to think of themselves as English and to participate in English politics. When papal provision became more or less a rubber-stamping of the king's nominees, English clerics owed everything they had, directly or indirectly, to the favor of the king or, perhaps, one of the great magnates who became influential during the minority of Henry VI. The clergy thus became involved in secular politics because their fortunes depended upon it. In order to understand why, one has to realize how beneficed clergy came by their appointments.

When a medieval see became vacant, a replacement could come from any of five places: the religious orders (later including friars), the universities, the civil service, the Roman Curia, or the high aristocracy. A king could also, with the pope's approval, "translate" a bishop from one see to another. In the twelfth and thirteenth centuries, the Church was surprisingly meritocratic, compared with other institutions in society, and "social origins were not of decisive importance."[276] Many bishops came from the religious orders, and the most important sees often went to very able monks and, in the later thirteenth century, friars.[277] Many others came from the universities, not only in the form of graduates, but also of serious academics who had made their reputations in the universities. An important part of thirteenth-century Church reform was the education of the clergy and the promotion of scholar bishops.[278]

However, in the fourteenth century, the number of scholars and religious

---

[276] Dickinson 254.

[277] Pantin 18.

[278] Pantin 18.

among high-ranking clergy fell dramatically. At that time, a growing number of civil servants needed to be rewarded with benefices, and these began to figure prominently among the bishops in the middle of the fourteenth century. Many continued to hold high offices in government in addition to a bishopric and perhaps other offices as well.[279] On the other hand, the only official of the Roman Curia ever actually nominated by the pope and appointed to an English bishopric was Rigaud de Asserio, canon of Orleans and papal tax collector, who received his office by papal provision in 1320. Asserio's appointment "represents the high-water mark of papal pressure on English church patronage, under the strongest pope and the weakest king of the century."[280] Thus, while the formal necessity of papal provision made the appointment of aliens to high positions in the English Church possible, the actual practice was almost nonexistent.

A few high aristocrats always appeared among the English bishops, but their numbers were negligible until the late fourteenth century. At that time, a major change began to take place in the make-up of the English Church at the highest levels. More and more often, bishops were aristocrats, such as Bishop Beaufort of Lincoln, the twenty-three-year-old son of John of Gaunt and Katherine Swynford, who had little or no interest in spiritual matters.[281] In fact, Beaufort was one of the bishops that some members of Parliament had in mind when they proposed a bill that would have forced bishops "to reside in their dioceses and not at court."[282] This increase in the number of aristocratic bishops accompanied a decrease in the number of civil servant bishops. Pantin paints the

---

[279] Pantin 11; Such pluralism was possible because general opinion, outside as well as inside the Church, regarded a benefice as a sinecure rather than a full-time job. For a discussion of pluralism, see below.

[280] Pantin 21.

[281] Thompson notes that the fifteenth-century English episcopate was still remarkably meritocratic. A man like Beaufort may gain notice because he is the king's cousin, but he receives preferment because he demonstrates unusual ability. However, the ability he demonstrates is now more likely to be political than spiritual. See pp. 41-42.

[282] Dickinson 254.

scenario in broad strokes: "whereas in the reign of Edward III bishoprics had been given as administrative salaries or rewards, in the reign of Richard II we find them given as political rewards or retainers."[283] By the beginning of the fifteenth century, "[n]o appointment of a bishop, at any rate to the more important see, was made without respect to his possible services to the government."[284]

Because of the compliance of the papacy, it became much easier for a king to translate a bishop from one see to another. Translation then became a weapon that the king could use for rewarding his friends and punishing his enemies.[285] Someone who was in special favor with the crown might be given a wealthy, influential see such as London or York, whereas someone who was out of favor might go to a poorer see, such as Ely, or a less influential one, such as St. Andrews. During the schism, St. Andrews was "a kind of ecclesiastical Botany Bay, being in the hands of the anti-pope."[286] Ely was (and still is) a tiny village dwarfed by a monstrous cathedral—it could not possibly yield the tithes that the bishop of a prosperous city could expect. In short, the fifteenth century "marks a steady growth in the influence of the Crown over the choice of spiritual rulers of the Church."[287]

In reference to this period, the "crown" often means the English government, rather than the king personally. The great magnates in parliament were sometimes able to force the king's hand, as did the Merciless Parliament of 1388, when bishops who obtained their appointments through the royal favor were translated to the poorer or otherwise less desirable sees, while baronial supporters got the more lucrative bishoprics. Conversely, when the king

---

[283] Pantin 23.

[284] Thompson 15.

[285] Dickinson 253.

[286] Pantin 24.

[287] Thompson 31.

prevailed, as during Richard II's "second tyranny" in 1397, royalist bishops were again "promoted."[288] During the minority of Henry VI, episcopal appointments became even more "liable to become the prey of manoeuvring [*sic*] by top people."[289] The king's council, which essentially ruled in his name, was composed of high aristocrats, including several bishops and the Archbishop of Canterbury. In 1425, when several sees became vacant at the same time, the council simply "divided the episcopal spoils" among themselves and their favorites.[290]

The role of the papacy in English episcopal politics was becoming complex. By the fifteenth century, the pope was certainly in the habit of approving anyone the king might nominate for a bishopric. However, in the case of Henry VI, the "will of the king" must be interpreted loosely. It sometimes meant "whoever had influence over the king," since the official letter of nomination from the king to the pope might be the result of manipulation or even compulsion by one or more lords in his council. For example, in 1448, the see of London fell vacant, and Henry agreed with Pope Nicholas V that Thomas Kemp would be ideal. Shortly after Nicholas made the provision, he received a letter from Henry recommending Marmaduke Lumley, whose patron was the Earl of Suffolk, the dominant voice in Henry's council. The pope might even disregard the stated wishes of the king in favor of someone more influential. Whatever magnate was in control of Parliament usually got the appointments for his own *protégés*, with or without the king's approval. For example, in 1457, the king recommended John Arundel for the see of Durham, but Calixtus II gave it to Lawrence Booth, who was favored by the nobles and, significantly, the queen.[291]

---

[288] Pantin 24.

[289] Dickinson 253.

[290] Dickinson 253.

[291] Jacob 270.

The appointment of Booth raises the question of why the pontiff would choose to satisfy the nobles rather than the king. The answer, in the estimation of fifteenth-century writers, was rather modern: money. Both Thompson and Jacob quote Thomas Gascoigne, chancellor of the University of Oxford, as follows: "there are three things today that make a bishop in England: the will of the king, the will of the pope or the court of Rome, and the money paid in large quantities to that court."[292] The papacy, weakened as it was by this time, was chronically short of cash and therefore vulnerable to corruption at every level. By the middle of the fifteenth century, graft in the papal administration was such that "most of the offices in the chancery, camera, and penitentiary could be bought."[293] Apparently, then, whoever had the best financial backing had the best chance of securing the provision. Furthermore, the pope had to choose carefully with whom to throw in his lot. For the same reason he could not afford to alienate a strong king in 1400, he could not afford to alienate the lords in power in 1425. He needed their support, while they could do without his.

As a result of these changes, a new kind of bishop was emerging in the English Church. When writers of the time satirized worldly bishops, they knew whereof they spoke, but their critiques are subject to modern misinterpretation. The offending bishops were not churchmen who had become worldly and sinful. Rather, they were worldly noblemen who had received bishoprics for secular, political reasons. Their positions depended entirely upon whether the king or the great lords in parliament had control of the English government, and many of them, being lords themselves, continued their involvement in secular politics unhindered by clerical responsibilities. Therefore, the "association of bishops with politics. . .became more constant in the fifteenth century."[294] A good

---

[292] Thompson 24; Jacob 269; Interpreting what Gascoigne meant by "the will of the king," Jacob suggests the loose interpretation given above, and for the same reason I have adopted it here.

[293] Thompson and Johnson 972.

[294] Thompson 42.

example is Thomas Arundel, who was promoted from Ely to York by the Merciless Parliament in 1388, demoted to St. Andrews with Richard's "second tyranny," and promoted again to Canterbury after the coup of 1399. Arundel tried to visit the University of Oxford in 1411, where John Rote, one of his political opponents, was Dean of Oriol. Pantin reports a conversation that took place, between Rote and a colleague, who supported Arundel. Rote says, "The archbishop had better take care; he tried to visit the University once before [i.e. in 1397], and at once was banished from the realm." The colleague responds, "Sir John, why do not you remember what happened to those [i.e. Richard II and his party] who insulted the archbishop, and how gloriously he himself returned."[295] This deep involvement of clerics in secular politics, unheard of before the fourteenth century,[296] became standard in the fifteenth.

These aristocratic bishops, like the lay magnates, had extensive patronage of their own. They appointed archdeacons, canons, parish priests, and other beneficed clergy, in addition to all positions in their cathedrals.[297] A new bishop would, of course, want to appoint his own *protégés* to any of these positions that might fall vacant. On the other hand, the king or great lord who had recommended the bishop could then pressure him to appoint favorites that the patron wanted to reward, and the bishop would be hard-pressed to refuse. Furthermore, when a bishopric was vacant, the king had a "regalian right" to exercise the bishop's patronage, as well as take over his lands and revenues. Because bishops appointed so many offices that the king could use to reward his servants, the regalian right "was stretched to the utmost."[298]

Thus, we need not wonder why the English clergy were patriotic or why

---

[295] Qtd. Pantin 25. The original source is *Snappe's Formulary*, ed. H.E. Salter (Oxford Historical Society 80: 1923) 200-1.

[296] Pantin 25.

[297] McFarlane 47.

[298] Pantin 31.

even their hagiographic texts seem to have political agendas. Many clerics, especially at the higher levels, were not in religious orders. Bishops were political men whose fortunes depended upon which faction controlled the government. The lower clergy were appointed either by aristocratic bishops or by kings exercising their regalian rights. Thus, they owed everything they had either to the king or to some powerful person, and their politics became polarized when their patrons' did. The Austin Friars, for example, were mostly Yorkist because "the patronage of religious houses was constantly used for the promotion of clerks whose services could be used to advantage by the patrons."[299] Now that papal provision was essentially *pro forma*, the English clergy had become English in their outlook and were divided by the same political forces that divided the rest of the nation.

C. Anti-Clericalism and Reform

These developments in the English Church necessarily colored the popular view of clerics in the fifteenth century. Englishmen, who became increasingly patriotic during the Hundred Years War, had little regard for a French pope and protested loudly against papal interference in English affairs. Of course, the return to Rome did nothing to increase respect for the papacy because it precipitated the schism. Furthermore, Englishmen outside the Church realized that their bishops were far from being men of God. Mature people understood that their leaders could not always live up to their ideals, but now, the Church leadership seemed to have no interest at all in the spiritual needs of the people. Moreover, a system where one class of men made the money while another class did the work was hardly conducive to good pastoral care. Anti-clerical thinkers, who had long been common in England, now found an easy target in the fifteenth-century Church.

---

[299] Thompson 105; See also discussion of Osbern Bokenham in Chapter Four.

The most radical anti-clerical views were those articulated at Oxford near the end of the fourteenth century by the "eminent but irascible don, John Wycliffe."[300] Wycliffe and the Lollards, who carried his ideas into the fifteenth century, condemned the increasing wealth and worldliness of the Church. The reforms that the Lollards sought were many and varied, but nearly all concern the Church as a hierarchical institution. Wycliffe regarded the true Church as the whole community of Christian faithful, whose only head was Christ, and he scoffed at the idea that monks somehow practiced a higher grade of Christianity than others. Nor was he willing to grant to priesthood a special authority over Christian believers. He considered all ranks in the Church to be against Scriptural law, including the idea that the pope was the head of the Church.[301] He disapproved of all the sacraments (except marriage) and ridiculed the doctrine of transubstantiation. All of these ideas he based upon a literal reading of the Bible, which he believed every Christian should be able to do for himself, without the official interpretations of clerics. Accordingly, he promoted the translation of the Bible into English. In short, he was "as thorough-going a radical as the conservative Protestant leaders of the sixteenth century."[302]

Building on William of Ockam's ideas about the roles of Church and state, Wycliffe argued that the law of Christ, as set forth in the Scriptures, forbids the Church from owning any property. Therefore, he reasoned, the state should confiscate all Church property and "secular lordships, that clerks have full falsely against God's law and spend so wickedly, shulden be given by the King and witty lords to poor gentlemen that wulden justly govern the people."[303] At first, the king and witty lords found his views congenial. His patron, John of Gaunt, and others

---

[300] Dickinson 315.

[301] The pope, predictably, condemned his writings, and only the firm support he had in London shielded his person from the vengeance of Rome. See McFarlane 79-88.

[302] Hamilton and Thompson 978-9.

[303] Qtd. in Thompson and Johnson 980.

like him considered the idea of seizing Church property eminently sensible, although they were not able to put it into practice until the sixteenth century. Moreover, his tirades against the pope fell on sympathetic ears just before and during the schism.[304]

Nevertheless, his anti-hierarchical writings were ultimately too subversive for fifteenth-century English society to tolerate. The wealthy, powerful clerics of whom he complains were so much so that Oxford could not protect him indefinitely from their wrath. After the 1381 Rising, for which the Lollards were unjustly blamed,[305] Oxford condemned his views, and Lollardy was driven underground. In the process, the English Church leadership might have missed an opportunity to avert the disaster that befell them in the sixteenth century. Because they gave no serious consideration to Wycliffism, but relentlessly suppressed it, "it ultimately emerged in power as unconsidered protest movements are apt to do."[306]

Although good information on an outlawed movement is hard to come by, evidence of Lollardy appears at odd intervals throughout the fifteenth century and into the sixteenth, long after it was supposedly suppressed. In September 1413, Sir John Oldcastle, a knight of Herefordshire, was accused of Lollardy and locked in the Tower of London. His friends helped him escape, and he spent the next two months planning a rebellion. The king, Henry V, discovered the plot through his spies and had the group arrested on January 8, 1414. They numbered about sixty and were hanged in London on January 13.[307] After this "violent and political phase," Lollardy continued as an English puritan movement "of the latent

---

[304] Dickinson 323.

[305] Dickinson 321.

[306] Dickinson 255.

[307] For details, see McFarlane 160-185.

and obstinate kind."[308]   In 1428, several Norfolk priests were convicted of Lollardy, and the movement was apparently active in the North of England in the early sixteenth century.[309]   In *The Later Lollards*, John Thomson traces the influence of Lollardry on heretics from Oldcastle to the eve of the Reformation.[310]

Anyone who examines what was happening to the English Church at the end of the Middle Ages will see the source of the Lollards' complaints. The clerics with "secular lordships" are obviously the aristocratic bishops who hold high offices in the government and therefore spend more time at court than in their dioceses. Thompson observes that "nothing, of course, is easier than to condemn a course of conduct so inconsistent with a strict view of the pastoral office, and the political bishop who was at the beck and call of the government of his day was fair game for the satirist."[311] Such conduct was also fair game for the humorless Wycliffe. He pilloried as "Caesarean clergy" those who "owed their advancement in the church to their sovereign's patronage,"[312] the implication being that they engaged in Caesar's work rather than God's. Several historians, including McFarlane and Dickinson, have pointed out that many of these "Caesarian prelates" were sincere men who used their income for the benefit of the public, including, ironically, poor students at Oxford. Nevertheless, Wycliffe had pointed to a real problem in the late medieval Church. The common view of a benefice as a perquisite rather than a full-time job led to abuses that neither the

---

[308] Jacob 282.

[309] Jacob 282.

[310] John Thomson, *The Later Lollards: 1414-1520* (Oxford: Oxford University Press, 1965); The title of this book is somewhat misleading. Thomson has done an exhaustive study of heresy in fifteenth-century England and identified all heresies consistent with Wycliffite doctrine as Lollardy. For example, a person who denies the sacrament of confession is automatically called a Lollard. Nevertheless, Thomson provides compelling evidence that Lollardy existed, uninterrupted, as an organized, underground movement in every section of England throughout the fifteenth century.

[311] Thompson 44.

[312] McFarlane 70.

Roman Curia nor the English parliament made any serious effort to check.

Pluralism, the holding of more than one benefice by a single cleric, was a common target for anti-clerical criticism.[313] Admittedly, most pluralists were not exceedingly wealthy. Few held more than two benefices, and still fewer held more than one with the "cure of souls," such as a parish church.[314] A "typical pluralist" might hold one parish church and a prebend in a collegiate church or cathedral.[315] Still, the possibility existed for the other extreme, and late medieval England had plenty of examples. The most successful pluralist was probably William of Wykeham, former Lord Chancellor of England and Keeper of the Privy Seal, who was bishop of Winchester from 1367 to 1404. He held the archdeaconry of Lincoln and a dozen other positions yielding a total of £873 per year and, for obvious reasons, was a particular target of Wycliffe's rhetoric.[316]

As manifestly corrupt as the practice seems, pluralists naturally defended it. Dickinson reports that:

> A fourteenth-century pluralist, commissary to the bishop of Hereford and holder of a rectory, five prebends and a portion, urged complacently that an industrious and educated person (a category in which he certainly included himself) could look after two or even ten churches better than some others look after a single one, so that it is better for a parish to have a good incumbent at a distance than a bad or indifferent one on the spot—a judgment which, of course, ignores that advantage of having a good one on

---

[313] Dickinson 267.

[314] Pantin 37; To hold more than one benefice with cure of souls, one needed a papal dispensation, and these were either rarely sought or rarely granted. Perhaps one cleric in a diocese might have one. Pantin uses statistics from the *Registrum Simonis de Sudbiria*, ed. R.C. Fowler and C. Jenkins (Canterbury and York Society, 1938) xxxvii-xLiii and *Registrum Simonis de Langham*, ed. A.C. Wood (Canterbury and York Society, 1947-8) 1-109.

[315] Pantin 37.

[316] McFarlane 48.

the spot.[317]

No matter how capable such a man is, he cannot be everywhere at once. Thus, the care his parishioners are getting depends upon his deputy,[318] who might do the job well enough. Still, even pluralists seem hard-pressed to explain the advantage of this system for anyone besides the holder himself.

Another abuse that followed naturally from pluralism was absenteeism. A bishop who continued to hold secular offices, as so many did, would probably not reside in the community where he held the appointment. The attempt to force men like Beaufort to reside in their dioceses failed, and the tendency of bishops to live in London increased dramatically throughout the fifteenth century.[319] The anti-clerical Gascoigne accuses one very political bishop, John Kempe, of spending no more than two or three weeks at a time, perhaps ten or twelve years apart, in his diocese. While noting that Gascoigne is not the most objective source, Thompson finds evidence in Kempe's own records that the claim is not greatly exaggerated.[320]

The absenteeism of the minor clergy also increased in the fifteenth century, as they followed the example of their superiors. While canons and parish priests did not have high offices of state keeping them in London, they were as able as their superiors to collects benefices. Needless to say, a cleric with prebends in two or more churches could hardly be expected to work in both. Furthermore, the canons in the fifteenth century discovered a means of "disguised absenteeism," by which they could appoint "vicars choral" to sing services in their places when they had to be absent.[321] The canons' appointments were so

---

[317] Dickinson 268.

[318] Thompson 46.

[319] Thompson 43.

[320] Thompson 43.

[321] Dickinson 269.

92

lucrative that they became "major prizes for royal nominees who increasingly came to regard them largely as mere financial assets, whose revenues they pocketed but whose functions they did not fulfil in person."[322] As a result, the major cathedrals in fifteenth-century England were almost double-staffed. Dickinson gives the example of Lincoln Cathedral, which, at the end of the fifteenth century, had fifty-eight canons on the payroll, but rarely more than five in residence.[323]

Historians still debate whether the conduct of these "Caesarian prelates" was really as reprehensible as it looked to Wycliffe and other anti-clerical writers.[324] However, regardless of the extent of the abuses, a system in which "one set of men did the work and another set of men received the rewards"[325] did not produce the quality of pastoral care that the reformers of the thirteenth century had sought. It did perpetuate two distinct classes of English clerics: "the higher clergy, the *sublimes* and *litterati*, men of birth and lettered clerks, and the crowd of inferior clergy, vicars, curates, and chantry chaplains, whose education was rudimentary and who lived on small stipends."[326] The higher ranks included both aristocrats like Beaufort and Bourchier and university graduates of fairly humble origin. In the late Middle Ages, educated clerics were much in demand, and bishops often granted their *protégés* leave to study at universities. Moreover, noblemen such as William of Wykeham often sponsored university students. A graduate could then gain preferment through service to the crown or some aristocrat and thereby acquire a government position or a benefice "and might

---

[322] Dickinson 269.

[323] Dickinson 270.

[324] Even Wycliffe's biographer doubts that his censure of Wykeham was reasonable or productive. See McFarlane 70.

[325] Pantin 43.

[326] Thompson 72.

even become a pluralist."[327]

However, Dickinson notes that "many graduate holders of preferment were not primarily engaged in pastoral work, such responsibilities being in varying degree passed on to hired clergy."[328] This category obviously included bishops, who, in the fifteenth century, received their appointments almost exclusively for political reasons. Since their fortunes depended upon government politics rather than job performance, they had every reason not to make diocesan issues their primary concern. As a result, when they had to deal directly with some diocesan problem, they often treated it "lightly or negligently."[329] In short, the most qualified people, from bishops to parish priests, were the least likely to work directly with parishioners; every reward in the system encouraged them to do otherwise.

Not surprisingly, discussions of English clerics in the late Middle Ages speak less of widespread abuses than of mediocrity. Pantin observes that clerics like "William of Wykeham and Thomas Arundel were worthy enough men in their own way and cannot be called scandalous; but neither were they the type of zealous and learned bishop envisaged by Innocent III."[330] Dickinson's remark that "the diocesans were not necessarily devoid of solid virtues"[331] is hardly an unqualified endorsement. Then, he points out the "not surprising" fact that "of all the English archbishops and bishops who lived in the two centuries before the Reformation, not a single one has captured any great interest from posterity."[332] Thompson, who takes particular care to explain their position, finally avers that "[t]aken as a whole the English bishops of the fifteenth century were not a strong

---

[327] Thompson 276.

[328] Thompson 276.

[329] Thompson 44.

[330] Pantin 43.

[331] Dickinson 254.

body of men: the period of the loss of France and the Wars of the Roses produced many clerical politicians, but no great clerical statesman."[333]

D. Conclusion

In general, the fifteenth century was a time when old institutions ceased to function and old assumptions lost their meaning. Both the Church and the feudal system were rapidly losing power to the national state. Whereas the knight's feudal devotion to his lord could be turned into patriotism, the cleric simply had to carve out a place for himself in a world where the Church depended upon temporal authority. In other words, England was quickly moving toward the Renaissance and the final break with Rome. Already, both the clergy and the laity depended so much on the state's patronage that the idea of something higher than the state had ceased to be viable. English clerics thus became English subjects first and clerics second.

The decision was really made for them by the late fourteenth century, when papal patronage became a non-factor, due to the "Babylonian captivity" and the schism of 1378. By then, most of the high-ranking clergy were already secular aristocrats who regarded Church offices as sinecures. The parish priests and prebendaries whom the bishops appointed often saw their positions the same way. By the fifteenth century, most beneficed clergy in England owed their appointments either to the king or to some aristocratic patron. When their patrons became divided over politics, they naturally became divided, too.

Thus, throughout the fifteenth century, clerics became, if anything, more political and less clerical in their concerns. Aware of anti-clerical feeling that was growing throughout England, the clergy did not take the opportunity to reexamine their duties as churchmen toward the laity. They saw a decline in respect for the

---

[332] Dickinson 255.

[333] Thompson 45.

Church without understanding the reason for it or considering what would replace it. Like romance writers, hagiographers at this time saw all change in terms of decay and may, like them, have wished for a vanished time when they could have pursued their professions independently of politics. Yet, also like romance writers, they felt compelled to defend the institution to which they owed their positions, even when it became nearly impossible to defend.

Chapter Four:

The Case of St. Katherine of Alexandria

I have referred to St. Katherine as one of the most popular saints of the Middle Ages. Judging from the number of lives of St. Katherine still available, she seems to have a provided an interesting subject for hagiographers as well as for the many Christians who venerated her. She also appears frequently in medieval paintings, usually with her spiked wheel, sword, book, and wedding ring. In fact, as Winstead reminds us, she was "often designated as God's favorite saint, second only to the Virgin Mary, and more lives were written of her than of any other virgin martyr." [334] She was the patron saint of virgins, Christian philosophers, and female scholars, among others. Her feast day on November 25 was celebrated in many English towns from the early thirteenth century forward, with the local maidens ritually placing a crown on a statue of Katherine, after the saying that only a virgin had the right to "bonnet St. Katherine."[335] Unfortunately, she enjoys less popularity in our time, and the Catholic Church suppressed St.

---

[334] Karen Winstead, *Chaste Passions: Medieval English Virgin Martyr Legends.* (Ithaca: Cornell University Press, 2000) 115.

[335] Saara Nevanlinna and Irma Taavitsainen, introduction, *St. Katherine of Alexandria: The Late Middle English Prose Legend in Southwell Minster MS 7* (Cambridge: D.S. Brewer, 1993) 7-61. See also Lewis 155-160.

Katherine's feast in 1969, on the grounds that she may never have existed.

Nevertheless, the many available Middle English lives of St. Katherine allow us to see the development of her legend over the course of several hundred years.[336] As it developed from the thirteenth century to the fifteenth, her story changed according to the rhetorical goals of the various authors, the situation of the audience, and the surrounding political and social realities. Katherine's life proved better suited for the methods of romance than we might expect from a story about a virgin martyr of the early fourth century. In each new retelling, the author (who is usually anonymous) uses the techniques of romance for his own purposes to an ever-increasing degree, even while explicitly condemning the values of romance. By the middle of the fifteenth century, a subtle but startling transition has occurred. Thirteenth-century religious writers employed romance techniques to make hagiography more appealing to a broad audience. Fifteenth-century authors often used the conventions of romance to critique the very romances they imitated. Moreover, they began to use hagiography for a variety of purposes, some of which were surprisingly secular. Issues such as what makes a good ruler and what should be the relationship of the individual to the state are traditional subjects of courtly romance, which the St. Katherine narratives begin pointedly to address by the middle of the fifteenth century. In addition, one rarely-studied life of St. Katherine from c.1420 reads more like the popular romances of the fourteenth century than like any tradition of saints' lives. In this work, while copying the romance style, the author criticizes the ethics and assumptions underlying romance. He seems to be drawing the audience into his work so that he can admonish them for being so easily drawn. Thus, the Middle English St. Katherine legends, as they develop from the thirteenth century to the fifteenth, reveal the changing relationship and growing conflict between romance and hagiography, as well as the increasing influence of secular values.

---

[336] Lewis argues that Katherine was "the most important saint in late medieval England" (2), indicating the extensive treatment she receives from John Capgrave, as well as the fourteen Middle English lives of St. Katherine that survive.

St. Katherine of Alexandria lived, if she lived at all, at the end of the third century, and was martyred at the beginning of the fourth. There is no unequivocal historical evidence that she did exist, although some scholars, such as Eugen Einenkel, have suggested that she may be a Christianized version of the ancient philosopher Hypatia. The earliest known account of her was written in the tenth century by the eminent Greek hagiographer Simon Metaphrastes.[337] This version provides the basic framework of Katherine's *passio*, which we find near the end of the tenth century in *Menologium Basilianum*, a collection of legends compiled near the end of the tenth century, during the reign of the Emperor Basil II.[338] The legend reached Normandy in 1020, when Simeon of Treves, a monk of Rouen (in Normandy) brought a relic (supposedly a knucklebone) of St. Katherine back from Alexandria. This relic seems to provide the reason for the founding of the Abbey of Rouen.[339] In the 1040s, Ainard (a monk at Rouen) wrote a long *passio* of St. Katherine in Latin, perhaps to publicize the relic.[340] The legend may have entered England in 1044, when Robert, the Abbot of Rouen monastery, became Bishop of London. Robert became Archbishop of Canterbury in 1051, and by the beginning of the twelfth century, St. Katherine was well known in the south of England.[341] The various Middle English versions of the Katherine legend share a

---

[337] The later Greek and Latin versions, upon which the Middle English versions are founded, share this original source. See Lewis 47.

[338] Lewis 47. Lewis's source for the dating of this version is Jennifer Relvyn Bray, *The Legend of St. Katherine in Later Middle English Literature*, Ph.D. thesis, (Birkbeck College, University of London, 1984) 6. Nevanlinna and Taavitsainen date it from the reign of Basil I (d.886), as do D'Ardenne and Dobson, in their introduction to *Seinte Katerine*, ed S.R.T.O. d'Ardenne and E.J. Dobson (London: EETS S.S. 7, 1981) xiii-xxxiii. The *Menologium* refers to the saint as Aikaterina and includes most of the major elements of her *passio* as we now have it.

[339] Nevanlinna and Taavitsainen 5. Lewis suggests that the Crusades were also a likely vehicle for transporting the cult of St. Katherine to the west. See Lewis 49.

[340] Nevanlinna and Taavitsainen 5; Lewis 52. His version, which may be the so-called Vulgate version, is based on the Metaphrastes text.

[341] For example, poems began to be written about her, and hospitals were dedicated to her. For details, see Lewis 53-63.

common source and, generally speaking, are not revisions of one another. Rather, all the versions of her *passio* are revisions of Jacobus de Voragine's *Legenda Aurea*, which is based on the Vulgate version. The source of the Middle English *vitae* is less certain. The earliest English account of Katherine's life before her martyrdom is in a prose legend composed in the early fifteenth century, and some important speculation about its origins will appear later in the course of discussion. For the present, insofar as all the Middle English narratives agree, the life of St. Katherine is as follows.

The *vita* begins with Katherine, daughter of King Costus, growing up in late third century Alexandria. As a child, she is instructed in all the arts and sciences, and she becomes a learned and studious young woman. For this reason, she is often depicted with a book in her hand. Beautiful, chaste, serious, and highly educated, Katherine has her share of suitors, and after her father dies (and she becomes queen), everyone urges her to marry. Her mother and parliament both beg her to provide the country with a king and produce an heir. Katherine, who has yet to hear of Christ, feels (rather than knows) that she must preserve her virginity for a bridegroom who will be her superior in every way. When her parliament pressures her, she defeats them all in argument, insisting that she will marry only the one who exceeds her in beauty, goodness, and wisdom, which none of her suitors can claim to do. She also demands a husband so chaste that he will always safeguard her virginity, a characteristic not likely to produce an heir to the realm. Upon hearing this requirement, both parliament and the Queen Mother decide that the queen is insane, and Katherine leaves them lamenting her supposed loss of wits. She has won the argument, but she has also fallen passionately in love with a man she has never seen. He is, of course, the man she described, and she feels strongly that he must exist. Having grown up among pagans, she does not know who he is.

While Katherine retires to her rooms to study, the Virgin Mary visits the hermit Adrian at his isolated cell in the woods. After convincing him that she really is the Virgin Mary, which naturally takes some time, she commands him to go to the palace and fetch Katherine, whom her son wants to marry. Adrian brings Katherine back to where his cell ought to be, and in place of it, they find the Heavenly City, where Katherine meets Mary, receives baptism, and joyfully marries Christ, whom she immediately recognizes as the perfect bridegroom she has sought. In a ceremony commonly called her "Mystic Marriage," Christ puts a ring on her finger and tells her she must remain on earth a little longer before she can join Him in Heaven and that she must learn about the true faith from Adrian. Then, to Katherine's sorrow, the Heavenly City vanishes, and she is left in Adrian's cell, without her bridegroom, but with the ring still on her finger. She remains with Adrian and receives instruction in Christian doctrine, during which an angel substitutes for her at the palace, so no one knows she is missing. Afterwards, she returns to the palace and continues for a short time as before, though she suffers with longing for her new husband.

The *passio* begins where the *vita* ends, with Katherine studying in her palace. Hearing a commotion outside, she sends a messenger to find out what it is. He reports that the Emperor Maxentius has ordered a sacrifice in honor of one his heathen gods. Using threats of torture and death, he forces the whole city, including many Christians, to participate in the sacrifice. Katherine rushes to the scene and reproaches Maxentius for worshipping devils. The Emperor, finding himself unable to answer her, sends her back to his own palace, promising to answer her after the sacrifice. When he returns, he tries to argue with her and fails as quickly as her parliament did. Of course, the Emperor could have her tortured and killed on the spot, as some of his followers suggest, but he is much impressed with her beauty and would rather persuade her to his way of thinking than kill her. Therefore, he summons the fifty best rhetoricians in the realm to defeat her in argument and thereby convert her. At first, she fears such an unequal contest, but then an angel appears, urging her to be brave, and she uses her vast amount of learning to defeat all fifty, who confess themselves converted.

The Emperor, of course, is infuriated, and orders them burnt. The only concern they express is that, being so recently converted, they have never been baptized. Katherine assures them that a martyr's blood is sufficient baptism, and when the Emperor's soldiers carry out the order, a miracle happens: the martyrs' souls go straight to Heaven without the slightest damage to their bodies. Even their clothing is unburned.

The Emperor then tries to tempt Katherine with promises of gold, power, and status, but to no effect. Katherine scorns his promises and laughs at his threats. To break her resolve, he has her stripped, beaten, and thrown in prison for twelve days without food, but an angel feeds her with heavenly food. During this time, the Emperor's wife, Faustina, approaches Porphiry, her husband's second in command, and asks him to take her to Katherine. The two enter the dungeon together, and Katherine converts them both, foreseeing martyrdom for the queen. Afterwards, the queen announces her conversion and reproaches her husband for his treatment of Katherine. Maxentius, beside himself with anger and sorrow, orders his soldiers to tear the queen's breasts from her body with iron hooks and to cut off her head. She dies bravely, and Porphiry buries her body— against the Emperor's orders. When the Emperor hears of this crime, he becomes even angrier and orders Porphiry's execution, which his soldiers soon carry out. While the Emperor is still in a rage, one of his minions designs what is still known as the "Katherine Wheel": four wheels lined with spikes and sharp saws, two moving in one direction, and two moving the other, so that anything put between them would be torn and cut to pieces. Katherine, placed naked between the wheels, prays to God to show the gathered mob His power, and an angel smashes the wheel with such force that it kills five hundred heathens. (The number varies somewhat from one account to the next.) At this point, the Emperor gives up all thoughts of persuading Katherine and orders his men simply to behead her. Katherine, delighted to be finally joining her bridegroom, stretches out her neck and hears a voice calling "Come love! Come spouse! The gates of

Heaven are opened to thee!" When her head is cut off, she bleeds milk instead of blood, and angels carry her body to Sinai.

The first Middle English narratives of St. Katherine were composed in the early thirteenth century.[342] They include only the *passio*, as do their sources, the Vulgate and the *Legenda Aurea*. Their authors employ the techniques of romance to appeal to audiences who already enjoy romances. Whether addressing a religious community or the lay public, these writers seek to make their own view of the good life as attractive as the one offered in popular romances. Their criticism of romance, when present, is gentle, and their imitation is unapologetic. Clerical writers were not yet ready to say that knighthood had no legitimate purpose.

A. The Early-English *Seinte Katerine* and the Katherine Group

The early thirteenth-century *Seinte Katerine* is the first known Middle English narrative of the saint. It was composed in the West Midlands for nuns or female recluses, and its literary context helps explain some of the choices its author makes. The time, area, and dialect of *Seinte Katerine* are the same as that of *Hali Meiðhad, Sales Warde, Saint Juliana,* and *Saint Margaret*.[343] This group of texts, known as the Katherine Group, presents a highly personal view of Christ, and *Hali Meiðhad* argues specifically for young women to choose a heavenly husband over an earthly one, which is precisely the choice that Katherine makes and urges the queen to make also. *The Ancrene Riwle*, which is also

---

[342] The earliest of these, *Seinte Katerine*, may have been composed just before the turn of the thirteenth century. However, its most recent editors place it between 1200 and 1210. See D'Ardenne and Dobson xxxix.

[343] See J.R.R.Tolkien, "*Ancrene Wisse* and *Hali Meiðhad*," *Essays and Studies of the English Association* 14 (1929): 114, 122. Editions are as follows: *Seinte Katerine*, ed S.R.T.O. d'Ardenne and E.J. Dobson (London: EETS S.S. 7, 1981); *Hali Meiðhad*, ed. F.J. Furnivall, rev. Oswald Cockayne (London: EETS 18, 1866); *be Liflade ant te Passiun of Seinte Iuliene*, ed. S.R.T.O. d'Ardenne (London: EETS O.S. 248, 1961); *Seinte Marherete*, ed. Francis Mack (London EETS O.S. 193, 1934)

contemporaneous with *Seinte Katerine*, comes from the same Southwestern area of England as the Katherine Group, and it romanticizes the love between the holy maiden and Christ in the same way.[344]

As Karen Winstead has pointed out, the description of Katherine's conduct that appears in *Seinte Katerine*, even before her conversion, closely matches the proper conduct of an anchoress according to *Ancrene Riwle*.[345] The *Seinte Katerine* author says of her, "þeos milde, meoke meiden þeos lufsume lefdi mid lastelese lates ne luuede heo nane lihte plohen ne nane sotte songes. Nalde ha nane ronnes ne nane luue runes leornin ne lustnen."[346] The author of *Ancrene Riwle* repeatedly warns the young anchoresses about the dangers of chatter, songs, diversions, and light looks. For example, he says some might ask, "is it now so yuel forto loken outward and gon to solas z to games and to karoles," and the answer is "ӡe" because of the "yuel þat þere comeþ of."[347] He cautions them not only against talking unnecessarily with men, but also against listening to them, even if their intentions seem honorable.[348] Thus, the author of *Seinte Katerine* presents a heroine whose example other brides of Christ can follow.

The author of *Hali Meiðhad* offers Christ not only as the better or holier alternative to an earthly husband, but as the more appealing choice for a woman who desires love as it appears in the romances. He paints a deliberately sordid

---

[344] The popular view, which appears in many textbooks and translations of *The Ancrene Riwle*, is that its author was gentler, more tolerant, better educated, even more intelligent than the author of *Hali Meiðhad*. For discussion and a contrasting view, see Tolkien 116.

[345] Winstead, *Virgin Maryrs* 37.

[346] *Seinte Katerine*, ed. D'Ardenne and Dobson 73-79. "This mild, meek maiden, this lovely lady with chaste looks, loved no frivolous plays nor foolish songs. Nor would she learn ditties nor listen to love talk." Trans. Eugen Einenkel, *Seinte Katerine* (London: EETS O.S. 80, 1884) 103-110.

[347] *The English Text of The Ancrene Riwle*, ed. A. Zettersten (London: Oxford University Press, 1976) 19. "Is it now so evil to look outward and to enjoy diversions and games and dances?...Yes, for the evil that comes of it." My translation.

[348] *Ancrene Riwle* 34-36.

picture of marriage, implying that even if a woman marries the man she loves, she will still be miserable. She will still have to endure "alle hiƒ fulitohchipef 't hiƒ unhende homeneƒ—ne beon ha neauer ƒwa wið fulðe bifunden, noneliche I bedde."[349] As for the possibility that a woman might find a husband who suits her and makes her happy, he says, "ӡea. Ah hit iƒ ƒelt on eorðe"[350] Thus, the author of *Hali Meiðhad* offers his female readers a dose of reality, arguing that if they truly seek perfect love, they should seek a heavenly bridegroom, not an earthly one.

This view of earthly marriage completely agrees with the one we find in many romances. Isolde does not love King Mark, nor does she have much reason to do so. What Guinevere feels for Arthur may be some combination of admiration and tender regard that passes for love, but it has little in common with the passionate, painful, seemingly uncontrollable love she feels for Lancelot. Marriage in these works, as in the feudal society that produced them, "served the purpose of cementing family alliances and consolidating estates and fortunes."[351] In other words, "love had very little to do with marriage."[352] While "love matches between socially compatible couples were considered charming and appropriate,"[353] love was not the primary reason for marriage among the aristocracy. Nor would a noble lady have had the option of remaining unmarried until she met the man of her dreams. This fact accounts for the unattainability of the lady in the courtly romances, and, of course, for their implicit endorsement of

---

[349] "All his foulness and indecent playings—be they never so accompanied with filthiness, specially in bed." Trans. Furnivall, *Hali Meiðhad* 44.

[350] "Yea. But tis rarely [seen] on earth." *Hali Meiðhad* 37-8.

[351] Kate Mertes, "Aristocracy," *Fifteenth-Century Attitudes: Perceptions of Society in Late Medieval England*, ed. Rosemary Horrox (Cambridge: Cambridge University Press, 1994) 45.

[352] John Moore, *Love in Twelfth-Century France* (Philadelphia: University of Pennsylvania Press, 1972) 89.

[353] Mertes 46.

adultery. Because their happiness depends upon a person they can never really possess, the lovers in these works often do not live happily ever after, and the greatest of them, Lancelot and Guinevere, are far from bringing each other happiness. Their love is a torture, apparently for both of them, and after they have played into Mordred's hands, destroying Camelot, they go their separate ways.

Sad endings such as this one do not necessarily mean that the author is condemning adultery. As any student of this genre knows, some of the most influential medieval romances, especially the French, valorize love outside marriage, presenting it as ennobling to both lovers.[354] Such love inspires knights to great deeds of arms and ladies to great constancy and self-sacrifice. Medieval love-texts, such as Andreas Capellanus' *De Amore*, promote love outside marriage as the only kind of true love. In one of his famous dialogues, Andreas claims to quote Marie, Countess of Champagne, as saying that "love cannot exert its powers between two people who are married to each other. . .[N]o woman, even if she is married, can be crowned with the reward of the King of Love unless she is seen to be enlisted in the service of love outside the bonds of wedlock."[355] The pain, then, is not the wages of sin. Rather, it is inherent in an ideal whose fulfillment depends upon attaining the unattainable.

The suffering of lovers is, in fact, similar to that of martyrs, except that martyrs are, on the whole, happier. Katherine's love-longing for her new husband, whose presence is denied her while she lives on earth, is comparable to that of any long-suffering lover in romance. The similarity is certainly intentional on the part of romance writers. D.D.R. Owen points out the "element of sacred

---

[354] Romances such as *Sir Orfeo* and the Gawain romances depict adultery negatively, when they deal with the subject at all. English writers, as noted earlier, tend to present adultery less tolerantly than do their French counterparts.

[355] Andreas Capellanus, *On Love*, ed. and trans. P.G. Walsh (London: Duckworth, 1982) 106-7.

parody"[356] in Chrétien de Troyes's *Lancelot*. The hero, having to leave Guinevere's bedroom, is described as a "true martyr,"[357] and the pain he endures at his lady's capricious will parallels the martyr's unquestioning acceptance of the will of God. As Roger Boase explains, the lover in medieval romance "regarded himself as a martyr subject to the whims of the person whom he 'adored.'"[358] The result is not only ironic parody, but also (perhaps intentional) humor. Some authors, even in the Middle Ages, found the comparison absurd, and Owen attributes the irony of Lancelot's less-than-holy "martyrdom" to Chrétien's sense of humor. Whatever the purpose of the irony, humor is the natural result of Chrétien's treating secular subjects as if they were sacred.

Thus, courtly romances agree with saints' lives on the basically unsatisfying nature of marriage. However, they offer different solutions to the problem. Many romance writers offer love outside marriage, following the advice of Capellanus, as the easiest route to true love. On the other hand, religious writers offer the love of God, symbolized by marriage between the holy maiden and Christ. Far from opposing the idea of happiness through success in love, they argue, quite logically, that the only way to attain it is to love the perfect man. Suddenly, marriage becomes fulfilling and success in love, which all agree is necessary to happiness, is now possible for anyone who desires it. How could the love of God be unsatisfying? The traditional image of the holy woman as a bride of Christ seems to offer an obvious way to appeal to young girls who might yearn for romance, despite their enthusiasm to serve God. Accordingly, religious literature of the Middle Ages, when trying to attract women to a holy life, often depicts Christ as suffering suitor, lover, and eventually spouse of the holy maiden.

---

[356] D.D.R. Owen, introduction, *Lancelot (The Knight of the Cart), Arthurian Romances*, by Chrétien de Troyes, (London: Orion, 1993) 19.

[357] *Lancelot* 247.

[358] Roger Boase, *The Origin and Meaning of Courtly Love* (Manchester: Manchester University Press, 1977) 85.

The consecration ceremony for nuns, at least from the time it was standardized in the central Middle Ages, contained nuptial imagery, as it does now, including the wedding ring. Understandably, works intended for young women entering or considering a religious life often borrow extensively from romances in their presentation of Christ as the perfect man.[359]

Like *Hali Meiðhad, Seinte Katerine* appeals to images of idealized love whose source can only be courtly romance. Since *Seinte Katerine* contains only the *passio*, the love theme is not as highly developed as in some later narratives, but it appears clearly in Katherine's response to the Emperor's promise of riches and power if she will abandon her belief in Christ:

> ne mei me wunne ne weole,/ne nan worldes wurðschipe,/ne mei me/nowþer teone/ne tintreohe turnen/from mi leofmonnes luue,/Þ ich on leue./He haueð iweddet him to/mi meiðhad mit to ring/of rihte beleaue,/t ich habbe to him/treoweliche itake me./Swa wit beoð ifestnet/t iteiet in an,/t swa þe cnotte is icnut/bituhhen unc tweien,/Þ ne mei hit liste/ne luðer strengðe nowðer/of na liuiende mon/leowsin ne leoðien./He is mi lif t mi luue;/he is Þ gledeð me;/mi soðe blisse buuen me,/mi weole t mi wunne;
>
> ne nawt ne wilni ich elles./Mi swete lif, se swoteliche/he smecheð me t smealleð,/Þ al me þuncheð sauure/t softe Þ he sent me.[360]

---

[359] There is considerable evidence that the women themselves saw their marriage with Christ in passionate, physical terms. One of the most interesting examples is Mechthild of Magdeburg, who wrote, in the thirteenth century, a dialogue between the soul and the senses. When the senses invite the soul to bow down to Mary in hopes of holding the Christ child, the soul responds, "That is a childish joy/To suckle and rock a Babe!/But I am a full-grown Bride/I must to my lover's side." Trans. Lucy Menzies, *The Flowing Light of the Godhead,* Petroff 220.

[360] *Seinte Katerine*, ed. D'Ardenne and Dobson 1020-1041. "neither joy nor prosperity, nor any worldly honour, neither suffering nor torment, can turn me from the love of my beloved in whom I believe. He has wedded himself to my virgin state with the ring of true belief, and I have truly devoted myself to him. So are we united and bound into one, and the knot is so knit betwixt us two, that neither craft nor cruel force of any living man may loosen or slacken it. He is my life and my love; and he it is that gladdeneth me; my true bliss (in the world) above me, my wealth and my joy; nor do I desire anything else. My sweet life, so sweetly doth he taste and smell to me, that all seems to me delicious and soft that he sends me." Trans. Einenkel, *Seinte Katerine* 1501-1528.

This highly sensual description of the holy woman's relationship with her spouse is, to say the least, more appealing than the view of earthly marriage we get in *Hali Meiðhad*. It makes use of the parodic "religion of profane love," which, like the love of God, "demanded patience, humility, abnegation, obedience and fidelity."[361] This is the love of Tristram for Isolde, of Lancelot for Guinevere, which continues, as Malory says, regardless of whether the lovers ever attain the success in love that defines happiness in both romance and hagiography.

In *The Ancrene Riwle*, the romantic imagery is even clearer. The author tells a story about a besieged maiden and the knight who dies to rescue her. Although the maiden previously rejected his love, he still willingly gives his life to save her because "so debonairte wib loue hab ouercomen hym."[362] The author asks whether, in consequence of his sacrifice, the maiden ought to love him, henceforward, better than anyone in the world.[363] The knight, of course, turns out to be Christ and the maiden humanity in general, but also specifically the anchoresses for whom the work is intended.[364] Here, the author depicts Christ as a martyr for love—like Lancelot. After all, if Chrétien could call Lancelot a martyr, this author is no less accurate in calling Christ a lover. In an earlier section, the author of *Ancrene Riwle* presents Christ explicitly as the lover of the holy woman. He reminds his readers of the new wife in the Canticles who hears her lover calling, "Surge propera Amica mea. Columba mea. Formosa mea. Ostende michi famiem tuam. Sonet vox tua in auribus meis. Come to me my lemman. My

---

[361] Boase 85.

[362] *The Ancrene Riwle* 168. "His gentle heart with love had so overcome him." (Translations are mine.)

[363] *The Ancrene Riwle* 169.

[364] Mechthild of Magdeburg shows Love boasting that "I drove Almighty God/From Heaven and it was I/Who took His human life/And gave Him back again/With honour to His Father." Petroff 214-15.

culuer. My schene spense. Schewe me þi loue nebb and þi leuesom leere."[365] Here, the author presents the Church's official interpretation of the Song of Songs, in which the female speaker is a holy woman, and her beloved is Christ.

This idea of a marriage between Christ and holy women dates back to Katherine's own culture. Athanasius the Great, sometime Bishop of Alexandria, who lived from 296-373 AD, "wrote from exile to certain virgins of Alexandria" that "your Bridegroom is Christ."[366] Perhaps for this reason, the Middle English prose life of St. Katherine refers to Athanasius as Katherine's teacher.[367] If Katherine did live at the time the legends say, she and Athanasius would, at least, have been contemporaries and would probably have agreed on most points of doctrine. The way Christ calls Katherine just before her death clearly echoes the Song of Songs. In the *Legenda Aurea*, he says, "Come, love! Come, spouse! The gates of Heaven are opened to thee!" In the Early English *Seinte Katerine*, the resemblance is even stronger. She hears that voice from the heavens, calling,

"Cum, mi leoue leofmon; cum þu, min iweddit, leouest awummon! Low, þe ʒate of eche life abit te al iopened."[368] If the author of the *Riwle* did not write *Seinte Katerine*,[369] their rhetorical situations were certainly very similar. Both of them wrote for a religious community of women, for whom they served an instructional

---

[365] *The Ancrene Riwle* 37. "Arise, my love. My dove. My beautiful one. Show me your face. Let your voice sound in my ears. Come to me, my love. My dove. My beautiful spouse. Show me your lovely face and your fair countenance. Turn to me, you that will speak with none but with me."

[366] Qtd. in Nevanlinna and Taavitsainen 22.

[367] Nevanlinna and Taavitsainen 21 .

[368] *Seinte Katerine*, ed. D'Ardenne and Dobson 1660-1662. "Come, my dearly beloved: come now, my spouse, most beloved of women! Behold the gate of eternal life awaits thee fully opened." Trans. Einenkel, *Seinte Katerine* 2418-2422.

[369] Einenkel argues that each of the works in the Katherine Group was composed by a different author. For discussion, see Einenkel 19.

and devotional purpose.[370]

B. The *South-English Legendary*

Later in the thirteenth century, the author of the *South-English Legendary* uses other techniques of romance to attract a much wider audience to his version of St. Katherine's life.[371] Composed in the London region around 1285, the *South-English Legendary* is a rarely-studied gem, as Carl Horstmann says in 1887, "one of the most important works of medieval literature."[372] I have argued in an earlier chapter that the *South-English Legendary* is an example of what Finlayson calls a "romanticized folktale." Although Finlayson, anachronistically, had fairy tales in mind, the *South-English Legendary*'s prologue indicates that hagiographers were willing to overlay their saints' lives with "a few chivalric elements" in order to enhance their popularity.[373]

---

[370] The authors likely came from the same intellectual circle, and the audience for all the works in the Katherine Group could have been the three anchoresses. An easy, though not a provable, scenario suggested by E.J. Dobson is that the three "dear sisters" addressed in *The Ancrene Riwle* were named Katherine, Margaret, and Juliana. See E.J. Dobson, *The Origins of* Ancrene Wisse (Oxford: Clarendon Press, 1976) 138.

[371] The *South-English Legendary*, along with other collections of saints' lives, was part of a larger effort of the thirteenth-century Church to educate the laity, as discussed in chapter one. Its target audience, though impossible to know for sure, probably consisted of laymen as well as laywomen. Thus, the author's preference for virgin martyr legends is difficult to understand. In what sense could he possibly expect a farmer or carpenter with a wife and children to imitate Katherine of Alexandria? Winstead suggests that the martyred saints of the *South-English Legendary* are intended to represent the clergy, rather than the reader. If this is so, the author may have wanted to inspire respect for Church authority, rather than emulation of the saints. See Winstead, *Virgin Martyrs* 65.

[372] Carl Horstmann, introduction, *South-English Legendary* 7.

[373] See excerpt from the prologue in chapter one, above. The reference to "apostles & martirs . that hardy knightes were" suggests that that the author of the *South-English Legendary* was not averse to borrowing elements from romance when he thought they would appeal to his audience. See Derek Pearsall, "John Capgrave's *Life of St. Katherine* and Popular Romance Style," *Medievalia et Humanistica: Studies in Medieval and Renaissance Culture*, N.S. 6 *Medieval Hagiography and Romance*, ed. Paul Maurice Clogan (Cambridge: Cambridge University Press, 1975) 121.

In the process of doing so, the author of the *South-English Legendary* does what no romance writer would dream of doing. Drawing on the Latin tradition in which the "combat" of martyrdom can turn women into men, he essentially turns a virgin martyr into a knight. Katherine is clearly one of the "martirs . that hardy knightes were," and surrounded with knights and ladies, she makes a creditable hero. Unlike *Seinte Katerine*, the *South-English Legendary* was not written for a religious community. It probably had a wide audience, composed of secular people, both male and female. Therefore, its purpose was probably to both entertain and instruct. In order to give his audience the same elements that the public enjoyed in romances, this author constructs a heroine who seems more like a knight wounded in battle than a martyred saint. For example, in the flogging scene, the Emperor "hire let strepe naked : and to a piler faste hire bounden./With stronge schourges men beoten hire sore : and maden hire harde wounden."[374] This description emphasizes the violence of the clash and is the only one to describe Katherine as "wounded," a term used more often for soldiers in combat than for saints under torture. Then, while Katherine is in prison, Christ appears to her and urges her to be "studefast" through her "tormenz." Not only her physical courage, but also her skill at "verbal jousting" allows her to defeat Maxentius and his fifty greatest rhetoricians. The knightly warrior with God on his side who defeats numerous opponents would be familiar to the audience of romances, and the author of the *South-English Legendary* takes care to show Katherine in this light. The argument scenes are not nearly as lengthy as in later versions, since the scholars never really answer Katherine, but yield after her first speech. While Horstmann, in one of his invaluable summaries, says she "refutes" them, the author says, "heo ne couthen answerie hire of neuere a word: and yeuen hire the maistrie."[375] So, they yield the "maistrie," just as one of Sir Lancelot's lesser opponents would yield to him in Malory's romances or, eventually, as the knight

---

[374] *South-English Legendary* 167-8.

[375] *South-English Legendary* 128.

yields the "maistrie" to the old "wyf"in the *Wife of Bath's Tale*.

The author further appropriates the trappings of romance by including a literal knight, a figure who appears in no other life of St. Katherine. The Emperor's right-hand man, merely Porphyry in most versions, is "sire porfirie," and Maxentius calls him "mi knight." When "sire porfirie" declares himself a Christian, the emperor cries out to his heathen god, "hou schal this beo? : hwat schal ich nou do./Nov Ich habbe mi wif for-lore : and mi knight porfirie al-so?"[376] In Anglo-Saxon literature, the almost passionate relationship between feudal lord and vassal is a common theme. One sees it in the Wanderer's longing for his dead lord and in the refusal of the retainers in *The Battle of Maldon* to abandon their dead leader. This devotion between men in Anglo-Saxon poetry is much more significant and likely to produce noble acts than the love of man for woman. In its curious analogy between the wife and knight of the Emperor, the *South-English Legendary* follows a specifically English romance tradition, which has roots in the epics and sagas of earlier times.

There are other knights in the palace, of course, but "porfirie al min heorte was," and the Emperor will regret the loss of him more than the loss of his wife. This sentiment appears later in the courtliest of English romances. Malory's Arthur tells his knights, "much more I am soryar for my good knyghtes losse than for the losse of my fayre quene; for quenys I myght have inow, but such a felyship of good knyghtes shall never be togydirs in no company."[377] Later, Arthur tells Gawain "that in youre person and in sir Launcelot I moste had my joy and myne affyaunce. And now have I loste my joy of you bothe, wherefore all myne erthely joy ys gone fro me."[378] Never mind Guinevere in the Tower of London, beset by Mordred, who wants to force an incestuous marriage with her in

---

[376] *South-English Legendary* 257-8.

[377] Malory 685.

[378] Malory 709.

order to gain the throne. One can always get another queen. The Emperor Maxentius is no King Arthur, but as Eugen Einekel points out in his introduction to *Seinte Katerine*, we pity his sorrow and confusion—probably more than the narrator intends. This observation is doubly true of the Emperor in the *South-English Legendary Katherine*. He reminds us even more strongly of Malory's Arthur, who knows of the Queen's love for Lancelot, but "wold nat here thereoff, for sir Launcelot had done so much for hym and for the quene so many tymes that wyte you well the kynge loved hym passyngly well."[379] Maxentius also shares with Arthur the wish that he could turn away the law, just for his wife or just for his best friend, but perceives that the law will perish if he starts making exceptions for his own loved ones. The Emperor may deserve his suffering more than Arthur does, but the cause of it links him more closely with the kings of English romance than with the villains of hagiography.

C. The Fifteenth Century

As *Seinte Katerine* and the *South-English Legendary* show, the thirteenth-century lives of St. Katherine often incorporate the trappings and conventions of romance—courtly love, the knightly hero, feudal relationships—to communicate their own message more effectively. Religious writers have to ask themselves the question, "What is to be done with the man who listens impassively to the Gospel account of Christ's Passion but weeps when he hears a reading of *Guy of Warwick?*"[380] The answer, of course, is the "romanticized" saint's life: an already appealing story full of violence and heroism updated with the most popular features of romance. Furthermore, hagiographers and romance writers have an honest disagreement over church reform, which, ironically, produces a type of romance that resembles hagiography in plot, theme, and preoccupations, creating

---

[379] Malory 674.

[380] Crane 95.

an illusion that the two agree much more than they really do. In the fifteenth century, I would argue, the relationship between hagiography and romance changes in subtle ways that speak volumes about the new positions of the Church and the aristocracy in England. To explain what these changes were and how they worked, I shall now return to St. Katherine, whose popularity became even greater in the fifteenth century than it was before, especially in Norfolk and Suffolk, where the cult of Mary was strongest.[381] As the introduction to the present work explains, the large number of narratives about this saint provides a rich laboratory of examples that allow us to see the changing nature of hagiography's engagement with secular forms.

Needless to say, we know more about some of St. Katherine's fifteenth-century biographers than about others, and the lack of information will require some educated guessing. All were probably in religious orders, and they were certainly literate, with resources and leisure time to spend on composition. They had stronger religious reasons than their countrymen to revere the papacy, but they owed most of what they had to the English king or an English noble. Thus, they would likely share the patriotism of their contemporaries and the politics of their patrons. As religious, they might deplore the increase in state power at the expense of the Church. As writers, they would know of the popular taste for romance as well as the less-than-ideal conduct of knights in their time. Unlike their predecessors, they might not regard knighthood as necessary for the defense of Holy Church. They would be aware of the anti-clericalism of their contemporaries, though they need not all respond the same way to it. In short, their work reflects the contradictory, transitional time between the Century of the Devout Layman and the Protestant Reformation.

---

[381] Gail McMurray Gibson, *The Theater of Devotion: East Anglian Drama and Society in the Late Middle Ages* (Chicago: University of Chivago Press, 1989) 137.

D. The *Prose Legend*

The most obvious change in the Middle English Katherine legend that occurred in the fifteenth century is the appearance of the *vita*. This part of her story (summarized above) includes her early education, her debate with parliament over her refusal to marry any of her suitors, her conversion and Mystic Marriage with Christ. All accounts that include it are long and detailed and seem intended for a more specialized audience than the *South-English Legendary* or even the shorter contemporaneous versions. Saara Nevanlinna and Irma Taavitsainen trace the development of the Katherine legend in their invaluable introduction to *Katherine of Alexandria: The Prose Legend in Southwell Minster*, which contains a version of the early fifteenth-century *Prose Legend*, including both the *vita* and the *passio*.[382] The editors believe that the original *vita* was composed in Sinai at the Convent of St. Katherine, where her relics are located. The manner in which it made its way to England is less clear. When Robert, the Abbot of Rouen, became Bishop of London, the version of St. Katherine's life he might have brought with him contained only the *passio*. The actual *Prose Legend*, as we now have it, was composed at the height of not only Katherine's popularity, but also the cult of Mary, whom Katherine resembles in some obvious respects. Mary plays a large role in Katherine's *vita*, instructing the hermit Adrian to bring Katherine to her and preparing Katherine to marry her son. The only woman in the *vita* who is described as more beautiful than Katherine, is, of course, Mary. Both are not only appealing figures to the general public, but also natural role models for holy women. When Katherine's *vita* appeared in Middle English, at the beginning of the fifteenth century, it seems to have circulated

---

[382] Although we do not have a definite date of composition for the *Prose Legend*, Winstead concurs with Kurvinen's opinion that the original version (which does not now exist) was written about 1420. The earliest extant versions date from the second quarter of the fifteenth century. See Winstead, *Virgin Martyrs* 156.

separately from the *passio*. Readers of the *vita* would, of course, already know the *passio*. After all, Katherine was a popular saint, and the story of her martyrdom had been in England for centuries. The laity would certainly have seen visual depictions of her passion, which seems to have interested artists as much as hagiographers.[383]

In Middle English hagiography in general, the *vita* was superseding the *passio* as the important and interesting part of any saint's life. By the fifteenth century, the number and variety of *vitae* far exceed that of stories about martyrdom. The reasons, to some extent, are obvious. Since few Christians suffered martyrdom after the Church became powerful, a saint's claim to sainthood depended less on his death or manner of dying than on his manner of living—and, of course, miracles associated with him before and after death. Later *vitae* also increasingly emphasize Christ's humanity and locate the important action within the self, rather than between the forces of good and evil. In other words, the typical *vita* of the late Middle Ages is "less a battle than a journey—a journey toward God."[384] Therefore, by the time the *Prose Legend* was written, Katherine's conversion and marriage with Christ had become the more interesting parts of her story. In the mid-fifteenth century, Osbern Bokenham apologizes for not including it, pleading a lack of knowledge and poetic skill, and refers the reader to another source. Before the fifteenth century, none of the Middle English Katherine narratives includes her *vita*, and none contains an apology, explanation, or any other sign that the author is aware of omitting anything. Apparently, the

---

[383] Common early portrayals of Katherine's life include her dispute with the philosophers, her beheading and the angels carrying her body to Sinai. In thirteenth-century portrayals, Katherine trampling or sitting on Maxentius begin to appear more often, perhaps as the visual equivalent of her quasi-military victor in the *South-English Legendary*. (See Winstead, *Virgin Martyrs* 90.) Starting in the fifteenth century, depictions of her conversion and Mystic Marriage become more common. For a detailed listing, see Louis Reau, *Iconographie de L'Art Chretien* (Paris: Presses Universitaires de France, 1958) 266-71. In most visual representations, she appears with a book (signifying her great learning) and the wedding ring (signifying her marriage with Christ). Other signifiers that distinguish St. Katherine include the spiked "Katherine Wheel" and the sword which Maxentius finally used to execute her.

[384] Bynum 16.

vita either did not exist or was not in wide circulation before the fifteenth century, when it appeared in the *Prose Legend.*

Some parts of Katherine's *vita* may have originated in a Dominican convent.[385] Dominican friars, also called Preaching Friars, saw their role as much more public than the older monastic orders did.[386] They tended to be highly educated and sought the salvation of society through active evangelism, including preaching and public debate. While Dominican nuns lived in traditional enclosure, St. Dominic himself "was conspicuously successful in his ministry to women."[387] C.H. Lawrence notices a "paradox" in the idea of the Mendicant orders establishing monastic communities for women, since they themselves developed so deliberately outside these older structures of religious life.[388] Yet, as Lawrence points out, the Dominicans filled a need for religious direction that many women felt and other orders were reluctant to meet. Most of them were established "by and for men," and the nunneries that did exist tended to be only for the upper classes.[389] Thus, women who were called to a religious life often sought the counsel and assistance of the Preaching Friars.

The more closely one examines the Katherine of the *Prose Legend*, the more like a Dominican nun she appears. Her Mystic Marriage with Christ is clearly modeled on the consecration ceremony for nuns, which (as mentioned above) includes the wedding ring, symbolizing the marriage between the holy woman and Christ. Katherine's erudition also connects her with the Church and

---

[385] Nevanlinna and Taavitsainen provide the unpublished insights of their mentor, Auvo Kurvinen, who believed she saw Dominican rituals in Katherine's marriage scene. While there is no way to prove or disprove this theory, I find it plausible, judging from what we do know of that order and its ideals. Nevanlinna and Taavitsainen 23.

[386] For a detailed comparison between the mendicants and the monastic orders, see David Knowles, *The Religious Orders in England* (London: Cambridge University Press, 1960) 61-73.

[387] Lawrence 78.

[388] Lawrence 79.

[389] Lawrence 76.

with the Dominicans in particular. Coming from Alexandria, that ancient center of learning, Katherine is first instructed in all seven liberal arts. An apt learner, she "dranke of the well of wysdam" deeply because, the author says, "sho was ordeynyd in tyme to come to be a techer and an informar of the euerlastyng blysse of lyfe."[390] Like the Preaching Friars, whose lodgings always contained classrooms,[391] Katherine has to become educated in order to preach. After her Mystic Marriage, Christ tells Katherine to remain with the hermit for ten days and receive instruction in Christian doctrine, so that she may "parfitely lerne my lawes and my wyll."[392] Having educated herself, Katherine is ready to challenge the pagan emperor and convert his wisest scholars.

Whether or not a Dominican wrote the *vita*, members of that order would surely have found her legend appealing. Even in the *passio*, she shows qualities that would have made her an ideal role model for Dominicans. Her erudition is already obvious there, as is her skill at public debate and preaching. The replacement of the battle by the journey, which Bynum notices in the hagiography of the late Middle Ages, makes female heroes much more common in religious texts than they could ever be in romances. Still, the claim that later religious texts are not concerned with battles can be overstated. The typical heroine of a Dominican narrative is the center of a cosmic war, "a war replete with stunning victories and crashing defeats as the forces of good and evil [fight] over the ground of her body and soul."[393] Clearly, Dominicans saw their mission much more as a battle than a journey. After all, St. Dominic began his order to fight against the heresy of the Cathars,[394] and Dominicans were among the most zealous

---

[390] *Prose Legend* 96-8.

[391] Lawrence 84.

[392] *Prose Legend* 555.

[393] Bell 130.

[394] Lawrence 67.

120

and reliable administrators of the Inquisition, which also began as a thirteenth-century fight against heresy. For this reason, the old stories of martyrdom, in which the soldier of Christ battles against the forces of evil, had a new audience, who would have found Katherine's particular virtues appealing. Because competition between Dominicans and Franciscans "for the hearts and minds of religious women"[395] was creating a need for narratives promoting the ideals of the Dominican order, a *vita* for the St. Katherine legend would be a natural project for a Dominican nun.

Katherine's martyrdom, like Perpetua's, is a quasi-military victory over evil. It is certainly a defeat for the Emperor, who wants to persuade Katherine, not kill her. Gradually, he loses his scholars, his wife, and his best friend, to Katherine and her preaching. Each execution represents a failure for him, starting with the scholars, whom he has charged with converting her because "I had leuer þat scho wer *ouercomyn* by yowr argumentis"[396] than made to do the sacrifice through force. The Emperor does not get what he would "leuer," and the pattern continues longer than he could have believed. Even torture, which he once said he could use to "constrain" her, fails. At that point, the only thing left to do with Katherine's too-able head is to cut it off, and the Emperor's decision to do so is a clear result of his inability to defeat her intellectually.

The relationship between the *Prose Legend* and the romance genre is complex. On the one hand, the *Prose Legend* presents the love between Katherine and her perfect spouse in much more detail than earlier accounts. When Katherine describes to her parliament the only man she will take for a spouse, she is already in love with him. Although she has no idea who Jesus Christ is, he "had kyndelyd hur hert on brennyng fyr of love þat schuld neuer be quenchid"[397]

[395] Bell 127.

[396] *Prose Legend* 680-1.

[397] *Prose Legend* 247-8

This language resembles the discourse of *fin amor* even more closely than the references to the Song of Songs in earlier accounts. The prose *vita* also contains a lengthy nuptial scene in which Christ appears as a handsome youth and Katherine feels joy the like of which has never been felt before "out-take the ioy þat our lady had when scho bar Jhesu."[398] After her mystical lover disappears, the narrative dwells on her sadness and love-longing for her new husband. Finding herself alone in Adrian's cell, "Now ys hur hert in so grete mornyng that scho cowde noþyng do but wepe and weyle."[399] At this moment, she behaves exactly like a lover in a courtly romance, suffering in the absence of the beloved. Undoubtedly, the affinity between her relationship with her heavenly spouse and the conventions of romance made this part of Katherine's life appealing to readers of the *Prose Legend*. Like the Early English *Seinte Katerine*, it served an instructional and devotional purpose, encouraging holy women to love the only truly perfect man, who gave his life to save them.

On the other hand, the first part of the *vita* contains a lengthy defense of virginity and an argument against the need for husbands or lovers that is hardly compatible with the ideals of courtly romance. Courtly love is sexual love, no matter how idealized or sublimated an author wants to imagine it, and Katherine's "ioye was euer to kepe hur body and hur sowle from all corrupcion of synne."[400] In fact, one of her requirements for a husband is that he be "so pur of his modre beyng a virgyn."[401] Of course, such a chaste husband will also safeguard his wife's virginity, a condition that leads Katherine's mother to question whether her daughter's famous wisdom has been overrated. She angrily demands, "ys this

---

[398] *Prose Legend* 542

[399] *Prose Legend* 572-3

[400] *Prose Legend* 141-142.

[401] *Prose Legend* 205.

your grete wysedam þat ys talkyd of so fer?"[402] Yet, Katherine has just eloquently
defended her decision to remain single, claiming that "we schall not nede of a
straunge lord to rule us and our reamus."[403] Considering the wisdom and loyalty of
her parliament, the young queen says, she feels safe ruling alone. Those in
parliament who would argue with her can hardly claim that she should not: to do
so would be to confess themselves unworthy of her trust.

Thus, the *Prose Legend* contains both an elaborate love story and an
equally elaborate defense of maidenhood. Crane believes that romances borrow
"the models of conduct" from religious texts, while they "resist or subvert the full
implications of the same religious material."[404] They appropriate elements of
religious texts to give depth and seriousness to their own claims. In other words,
they borrow elements from the rival genre for the same reason religious writers
do: to make their work more appealing to the public. Yet, the chivalric ideal that
informs the courtly romances seems based upon the idea that one can reconcile
the two ideals, that holiness is not only compatible with courtliness, but essential
to it. Religious writers are much more likely to claim these ideals cannot be
reconciled. As Ferguson observes, Malory saw "no conflict between the
knighthood of this world and the demands of the life everlasting."[405] The great
lovers of courtly romance may displease God, as everyone does, but even Sir
Lancelot disobeys Guinevere to participate in the Grail Quest. A sinner but no
scoffer, he is finally allowed to look at the Holy Grail.[406] Even Andreas
Capellanus, who seems to be proffering an alternative to the Church's views on
carnal love, lists "blasphemy against God or his saints" and "mockery of the

---

[402] *Prose Legend* 216.

[403] *Prose Legend* 155.

[404] Crane 102.

[405] Ferguson 56.

[406] Ferguson endorses the idea of a "triple scale of values" in Malory, consisting of the
bad (King Mark), the good (Lancelot), and the best (Galahad). See Ferguson 54.

ceremonies of the Church" among the "things which weaken love."[407] On the other hand, the Katherine of the prose *vita* makes a clear choice between the true religion and the parody of it that characterizes love in courtly romances. Her rejection of earthly love is what allows her access to the superior love of God: to both the Virgin Mary and her son, Katherine's willingness to fight for her virginity makes her the most beloved of women. As Mary tells Adrian, Christ "desyryth hur beaute and louyth hur chastity among all the virgynys in erþe."[408]

E. John Capgrave

To view Katherine's *vita* in its most developed form, one has to consider *The Life of St. Katherine*, composed in Norfolk around 1445 by the Austin friar John Capgrave. Capgrave's situation is perhaps easier to imagine than that of Katherine's other biographers because we know the most about him. Clearly one of the *litterati*, he attended Cambridge and probably Oxford as well.[409] Being an Austin friar, he needed no excuse or special leave for higher education: the order had a close relationship with Oxford, whose classrooms they often used, and "cultivate[d] a real interest in book-collecting."[410] In this, the Austins followed the example of the Dominicans, who saw education as essential for their effectiveness as preachers and teachers.[411] Capgrave was apparently one of the

---

[407] Capellanus 155.

[408] *Prose Legend* 280-1.

[409] Furnivall mentions some sources which say he went to Cambridge and others which say Oxford, offering the "probability" that he went first to Cambridge, which was nearest his home, and then completed his Doctorate of Divinity at Oxford. Since he met Osbern Bokenham at Cambridge, he must have gone there for at least part of his education. F.J. Furnivall, intro. *Life of St. Katherine of Alexandria*, by John Capgrave, ed. Carl Horstmann, (London: EETS O.S. 100 1893) vii..

[410] Dickinson 300.

[411] Lawrence 99.

order's "most prominent scholars," who, a contemporary recalled, "clung to his books like a limpet to his rock."[412] He wrote numerous biblical commentaries, saints' lives in Latin and English, a vernacular *Abbreuiacion of Cronicles* running, incredibly, from Adam and Eve to 1417, and *De Illustribus Henricis*, which Dickinson accurately describes as "a curious rag-bag concerning men called Henry."[413]

During the rigorous education of an Austin Friar, he read Chaucer, Lydgate, Gower, and other important secular writers in addition to religious works. He also may have been aware that he lived near the mystic, Margery Kempe. Pearsall thinks he would have approved of her, and not without reason. St. Katherine, as Capgrave presents her, does share with Kempe a passionate, personal relationship with God. Kempe herself identified closely with St. Katherine and used the saint to refute the common argument that women should not preach.[414] The two women also have a similar problem, in that they must resist the demands of earthly men, who want them to be wives, in order to keep themselves chaste for God. Kempe, who is already married, must resist her husband's legal claim to her body, while Katherine must resist the demands of numerous subjects that she take a husband and start producing heirs. As shown above, this kind of problem has been common to religious women since Katherine's own time and does not necessarily mean that Kempe influenced Capgrave, although some critics contend that she did.[415]

Capgrave's passion for books and learning explains his attraction to the life of St. Katherine. He discusses at length the city of Alexandria, where "There

---

[412] Dickinson 300.

[413] Dickinson 300.

[414] *The Book of Margery Kempe*, ed. Sanford Brown Meech (Oxford: Oxford University Press, 1940) 111-112.

[415] Winstead, "John Capgrave and the Chaucer Tradition" *The Chaucer Review* 30 (1996) 397.

was the fyrste excersyse of dyuyne scole,/Whech is a scyens that longeth to noo foole."[416] The young princess Katherine is "set to book"[417] at an early age, and Capgrave spends nearly two hundred lines describing the nature and extent of her learning. Like Capgrave, she is attached to books: solitary study in her garden is "all hir dysporte."[418] Capgrave explains the purpose of all this learning as any Austin or Dominican would. Referring to her as "Goddys scolere,"[419] he tells us:

> whan that His chyrche was at gret neede,
>
> He ordeynd this lady for to geve batayle
>
> Ageyn al the world; thei schall hir not ovyre lede,
>
> Ne alle her argumentis schal not avayle.
>
> Sche schal so be lerned that alle her assayle
>
> Schall fayl, and falle bothe cunnyng and bost,
>
> Sche shall by myty with strength of Goost.[420]

So, God's scholar, in perfect solitude and chastity, prepares to do battle with the world, which she will win because her learning makes her mighty. As noted above, by Capgrave's time, the Austin friars had come to resemble the Dominicans in their passion for study. Like the Dominicans, the Austins realized that their "pastoral mission to the literate and relatively sophisticated people of the cities, as well as disputation with the elite of the heretical sects, demanded both mental agility and theological learning."[421] A friar would easily see Capgrave's Katherine as a shining example of what all mendicant preachers strove to become: God's perfect weapon in the war against heresy.

---

[416] John Capgrave, *The Life of Saint Katherine*, ed. Karen Winstead (Kalamazoo, MI: Medieval Institute Publications, 1999) 1.125-6. References are to books and line numbers.

[417] Capgrave, *The Life of Saint Katherine* 1.247.

[418] Capgrave, *The Life of Saint Katherine* 1.349.

[419] Capgrave, *The Life of Saint Katherine* 1.285.

[420] Capgrave, *The Life of Saint Katherine* 1.295-301.

[421] Lawrence 84.

126

Anti-clerical, fifteenth-century England was certainly full of heretics. Capgrave himself spent time at Oxford where the friars and the Lollards met, first as allies, then as opponents.[422] Wycliffe, who encountered many friars at Oxford,[423] initially admired them and attracted some admirers among them. After all, they worked outside the established Church hierarchy and lived by mendicancy precisely to avoid the necessity of owning property. Nevertheless, for some unknown reason, he soon began to include friars in his attacks on the clergy. His criticisms of friars included "that charge of sexual immorality which is part of the stock-in-trade of anti-clericals down the ages."[424] They also included the equally common charge that friars lived luxuriously on money and food beguiled from the poor.[425] Chaucer's "wontowne" friar, who gives easy penance to attract clients,[426] illustrates the anti-clerical opinion, which Wycliffe emphatically shared.

Apparently, the feeling was mutual. Capgrave calls Wycliffe "þe orgon of þe deuel, þe enmy of þe Cherch, þe confusion of men, þe ydol of heresie, þe merour of ypocrisie, þe norcher of scisme."[427] He reports Wycliffe's death in 1384 with relish: this organ of the devil "be þe rithful dome of God was smet with a horibil paralsie þorwoute his body. And þe venjauns fel upon him on Seynt Thomas day, in Cristmasse, but he deyed not til seynt Siluestir day. And worþily was he smet on Seynt Thomas day, ageyn whom he had gretely ofended,

---

[422] McFarlane 17.

[423] There were about 270 friars at Oxford in 1360, of whom about were students. See McFarlane 17.

[424] Dickinson 302.

[425] Dickinson 303.

[426] Geoffrey Chaucer, *General Prologue*, *Canterbury Tales*, *The Riverside Chaucer*, ed. Larry Benson, 3rd ed. (Boston: Houghton-Mifflin, 1987) 208-269.

[427] John Capgrave, *Abbreuiacion of Cronicles*, ed. Peter J. Lucas (Oxford: Oxford University Press, 1983) 188.

letting men of þat pilgrimage; and conueniently deied he in Siluestir fest, ageyn whom he had venemously berkid for dotation of þe Cherch."[428] Throughout the *Abbreuiacion of Cronicles*, he mentions, with apparent approval, the burning of Lollards. For example, in 1416, he says, "In þis tyme on Benedict Wolleman, a citecyn of London, a gret Lollard, whech had set up billes of grete erroure, was takyn, hanged, and drawe on Myhilmasse Day."[429] Oldcastle, of course, is "that satellite of the devil" who, "as a blasphemer and abandoned abetter of heretics. . .suffered the disgrace of death as he deserved."[430] Since Oldcastle had not only spread Lollard heresy, but also plotted against the life of his beloved Henry V, Capgrave would naturally consider death too good for him.

At the time he wrote his *Life of St. Katherine*, probably between 1438 and 1446, Capgrave was Prior of Lynn monastery and probably Provincial (Controller) of all the friaries in the province.[431] As such, he had good reason to be "wholly devoted" to his king. In *Henricis*, under 1446, he reports that the following took place:

> In the twenty-fourth year of his reign, this most devout king
> [Henry VI], in the course of the solemn pilgrimage which he made
> to the Holy Places, received into his favour the place of the Hermit
> Friars of S. Augustin in the town of Lynn, promising to his priests
> who dwelt there, by his own mouth, that from thenceforth that
> place should be regarded as closely connected with himself, and
> also with his successors lawfully begotten of his body. That he
> himself, also, and his successors, as before, should be regarded as

---

[428] Capgrave, *Abbreuiacion* 188.

[429] Capgrave, *Abbreuiacion* 248.

[430] John Capgrave, *Liber Illustribus Henricis*, ed. and trans. Francis Charles Hingeston, Rolls Series (London: Her Majesty's Treasury, 1858, rpt. Kraus-Thomson Organization Ltd., 1970) 141-2.

[431] Furnivall x.

> its true founders, or founders, not in name only, but in deed and in truth. These events occurred in the feast of S. Peter ad Vincula, in the year of our Lord 1446, and in the twenty-fourth year of the reign of our illustrious lord king, as we said above.[432]

Thus, Capgrave's patriotism, as well as his Lancastrian politics, make perfect sense with the founder and patron of Lynn priory on the throne.[433]

Accordingly, Capgrave implies a surprising parallel between Katherine and Henry VI. After the great King Costus, her father dies, Katherine is crowned in opulent splendor. She treats her guests liberally and afterwards rules with faultless holiness and justice. Nevertheless, the lords grumble because she will not marry, asking "Wythowte a kyng how schuld a cuntre stand?"[434] While recognizing the virtues of their queen, they desire a king to lead them into battle, punish evildoers, etc. Their concerns echo those Capgrave heard at the coronation of the child, Henry VI: "Many persons of a malignant disposition, interpreting amiss this coronation of our king, continue to sow among the people such murmuring words as these,--'Alas for thee, O land, whose king is a boy.'"[435] In his discussion of this passage, Furnivall gives the whole proverb: "Often reuithe the realme, where chyldren rule, and women gouerne."[436] These "murmurers" have the same worries as Katherine's nobles: Who will lead them into battle? Who will punish criminals? Surely, foreign powers will now see their chance to

---

[432] Capgrave, *Henricis* 158-9.

[433] As for Capgrave's change of heart, Furnivall offers the sensible conjecture that "Capgrave had still to be Prior of Lynn, and Provincial of his province"(16). In other words, with a Yorkist king on the throne, the Austins of Lynn had lost their patron, and Capgrave was responsible for their survival in the changed landscape. Moreover, since so many of Austin friars were Yorkist from the outset, the prior's best option, in the political sense, was to profess devotion to Edward IV.

[434] Capgrave, *The Life of Saint Katherine* 1.860.

[435] Capgrave, *Henricis* 148.

[436] Furnivall xix.

invade, and there will be no king to defend the realm.[437]

Thus, Katherine's elaborate defense of her ability to govern alone could easily be a defense of the child king who became the pious Henry VI, patron of Lynn priory. Her argument is not a defense of women in particular, but of any ruler who cannot personally serve as a military chief. She reminds the nobles that her father was often absent from the country, and yet they managed to defend themselves well enough under a chosen captain.[438] They know as well as she does that traitors and other criminals were punished in her father's absence while he was alive. She asks why, then, "[m]ay it not now in the same case be wrowte?"[439] To the charge that she is not physically strong enough to lead men or punish criminals, she notes that kings often pay soldiers and deputies to do such things, and so can she.[440] This talk of captains and deputies applies equally well to a young king who must rely on the trusted officers of his father to serve him loyally.

Regarding the importance of loyal nobles, Katherine's rhetoric becomes impassioned. She argues that even a wise king cannot rule alone: "His lordes must help to his governayle."[441] Therefore, she urges the lords in her parliament to

> [H]elpe ye on youre syde as I shal on myn!

---

[437] Winstead sees Capgrave's *St. Katherine* as a "chronicle of the fall of a once great empire under the stewardship of a virtuous incompetent" (*Virgin Martyrs* 168). Given Capgrave's devotion to a king who was clearly a generous patron of his priory, I cannot agree with this characterization. There is a close resemblance between the two monarchs, but it suggests the opposite politics (see below).

[438] Capgrave, *The Life of Saint Katherine* 2.288-295.

[439] Capgrave, *The Life of Saint Katherine* 2.308.

[440] Capgrave, *The Life of Saint Katherine* 2.400-434; This argument, more than any other, shows that medieval England was in its autumn. The professionalizing of both the justice system and the military made the successful rule of a Virgin Queen appear possible over a hundred years before England actually had one.

[441] Capgrave, *The Life of Saint Katherine* 2.496.

> Loke ye be trew onto my crowne and me,
>
> Lete no treson in youre hertys lyn,
>
> Than schal this lond ful wele demened be
>
> O noble God, who grete felicite
>
> Shuld be with us if we were in this plyth!
>
> We myth sey than, oure levyng were ful ryght.[442]

Again, she could be speaking to the lords in Henry VI's parliament, whose disloyalty his supporters had reason to fear. He would be well able to rule, Capgrave seems to say, if his nobles did not have treason in their hearts, if they would help him instead of misleading him.[443]

Accordingly, Capgrave's Katherine has more reverence for royalty than most scholars of hagiography would believe possible. During the debate with parliament, a certain duke argues that a woman will not be able to quell dissension in the kingdom. Katherine reproaches him, pointing out that the duke himself has a duty to end quarrels, and if he does not, "ye be ontrewe to me,/Not to me oonly but to the mageste/Of my crowne and gylty for to deye."[444] In other words, a powerful lord who does not do anything in his power to end dissension is guilty of treason and deserves death. The implications for Henry's disloyal lords could scarcely be clearer. Then, she must defend herself against the charge that she despises the idea of a king. Since this is the last thing Capgrave wants to imply, he gives Katherine's response the extra emphasis. Coming as she does from royal stock,

> Shuld I than dyspyse that hye degre
>
> Whech that is ordeynd be Goddys providens,

---

[442] Capgrave, *The Life of Saint Katherine* 2.498-504.

[443] Lewis (following Bray) notes that both Capgrave and the *Prose Life* feature Katherine as an English-style monarch. The debate with parliament is "a uniquely English addition," apparently designed to identify the heroine with fifteenth-century English royalty. See Lewis 79.

[444] Capgrave, *The Life of Saint Katherine* 2.711-13.

> Whech is eke come be descense to me?
>
> Godd forbede in me that gret offens,
>
> Or that I were founde in swech neclygens!
>
> I wot full weele, a kyng is al above
>
> Ovyr his ligys, bothe in fere and love.[445]

She follows this statement with another observation about the weakness of any king who does not have the support of loyal lords. Apparently, she believes in hereditary right to rule and in the nobles' responsibility to assist the king in any way they can. Certainly, Capgrave believed in such a responsibility. To Furnivall, this makes him a "flunkey by nature," but to Francis Hingston, editor of *Henricis*, he is "honest old John Capgrave" who "loved and revered the King of the time being, whoever he might happen to be, simply because he was the King."[446] He admonishes his readers to do the same.

A reader familiar with the *Legenda Aurea* or the *South-English Legendary* might well wonder when the loyalty of nobles in parliament became vital—or even relevant—to the legend of St. Katherine. As noted above, although no one knows when the *vita* first appeared, recent scholarship suggests that it was circulating (separately from the *passio*) by the end of the thirteenth century.[447] Auvo Kurvinen believes that the Parliament theme was added to it in England, perhaps in the early fourteenth century, but no earlier.[448] Unless the *Prose Legend* in Southwell Minster differs greatly from other versions, the marriage theme is much more important than the debate with parliament, as anyone might expect. If Katherine's *vita* did originate in a Dominican convent, its writer would probably

---

[445] Capgrave, *The Life of Saint Katherine* 2.792-8.

[446] Hingeston 16.

[447] Nevanlinna and Taavitsainen 23.

[448] Nevanlinna and Taavitsainen, working with Kurvinen's unpublished papers, say that she bases this conclusion on a version of the *vita*, translated from Latin in the late thirteenth or early fourteenth century, which does not include the Parliament theme. The *Prose Legend* is the earliest Middle English version that does include it. See Nevanlinna's and Taavitsainen.23.

have had more interest in Katherine as a bride of Christ than as a temporal queen. In any case, her marriage with Christ affects the basic story of her martyrdom. Even the early accounts of her *passio* take care to mention this marriage because it determines what Katherine's attitude will be when the Emperor gives her the chance to be his wife. It also explains the joy with which she greets death when it finally comes: she hears her spouse calling. Apparently, the protracted debate between Katherine and her own parliament is original with Capgrave. Admittedly, Capgrave also expands every other part of the story, including the wedding scene. However, his version of her debate with parliament emphasizes a new point. Queen Katherine's sharp reproach of her nobles, whose faith she has no reason to suspect, does not affect the story and makes no sense unless Capgrave actually intends it for the nobles in a real parliament, who undeniably do have treason in their hearts.

Her reproach of the lords in parliament and praise of kingship suggests a natural audience among the English nobility. If the author did intend *St. Katherine* for them, his audience would then be the same as Chaucer's, whom we know Capgrave read and admired.[449] His apostrophe to Katherine, "Therefor lern sore, thou yonge Goddys scolere!"[450] sounds clumsy next to Chaucer's apostrophes, but it would not be out of place in his earlier poems. For example, *The House of Fame* begins, "God turne us every drem to goode!"[451] This possibility would also explain the difference that Pearsall has pointed out between *St. Katherine* and Capgrave's other work. As shown in Chapter Two, the audience must have had a fairly high level of education, probably at a university, to appreciate the endless dialectical debate in *St. Katherine*. Yet, Capgrave also borrows techniques from romance, including the passionate, emphatic language,

---

[449] See discussion of Pearsall in Chapter Two.

[450] Capgrave, *The Life of Saint Katherine* 1.285.

[451] Geoffrey Chaucer, *The House of Fame*, *The Riverside Chaucer*, ed. Larry Benson, 3rd ed. (Boston: Houghton-Mifflin, 1987) 1.

as well as a meter similar to that of *Havelok the Dane*. If he simply admired Chaucer and popular romance writers and wanted to imitate them, surely he would have done so in other works. Yet, his *Life of St. Norbert* contains few such devices and fewer exclamation points. An audience with a high level of education and secular tastes in literature would likely be the nobility, Chaucer's audience. If this conclusion is accurate, his development of the Parliament theme becomes understandable. In the context of a much larger work, Capgrave is gently reminding the great lords of their duty to their king.

This version is certainly the largest and most elaborate ever written in English and includes both the *vita* and the *passio*. Perhaps for this reason, it receives more critical notice than any other version.[452] Capgrave's handling of the flogging scene well illustrates the scale on which he worked. In the *Legenda Aurea*, which is, at least indirectly, a source for all the Middle English versions, the Emperor simply orders Katherine to be stripped and beaten. He gives the order in a single line, and the reader is left to assume that order was carried out. In the *Prose Legend*, which is much longer, the scene is much the same: he "commaundyd that sho shuld be dispoylyd and betyn wyth scharpe scourgis."[453] In Capgrave's version, the same event takes seventy lines. Much of it consists of Katherine and Maxentius taunting one another, as follows:

> The tyraunt aske among this byttir peyne,
>
> Whan all was blode, and the beters wery were all;
>
> "What sey ye, mayden, will ye yete susteyne
>
> Youre elde heresye in whech ye be falle?

---

[452] For discussion of Capgrave's rhetoric, see Crane 102 and Pearsall 123. For an investigation of Capgrave's source, see Auvo Kurvinen, "The Source of Capgrave's Life of St. Katherine of Alexandria," *Neuphilologische Mitteilungen* 61 (1960): 268-324; For a comparison with the *Prose Legend*, see Winstead, *Virgin Martyrs* 147-180; For discussion of of Capgrave's rhetorical situation, see Karen Winstead, "Piety, Politics, and Social Commitment in Capgrave's *Life of St. Katherine*," *Medievalia et Humanistica* N.S. 17 (1991) 59-80; See also Winstead, "John Capgrave and the Chaucer Tradition," 389-401.

[453] *Prose Legend* 830.

134

> If ye will mercy of oure goddes calle,
>
> Ye shall it have, and ellys new game—
>
> Or that ye goo, I trow ye shal be tame."
>
> Sche answerd thus: "Sere, know this wele:
>
> That I am strenger in body and in goost
>
> Than evyr I was to sufferne every dele
>
> Al maner turment, wheyther thu wolt fry or roost.
>
> But thu, my schamful dog ful of boost,
>
> Do what thu wilt, for I shall stronger be
>
> In my sufferauns than thu in thi cruelte."[454]

Apparently, the advice of the *Ancrene Riwle* author about the proper way to handle insults is still meaningful in the mid-fifteenth century. To Katherine, Maxentius represents the rod of the Lord, whom God will throw in the fire when he ceases to be useful as a rod, and His beloved daughter "schulle ben ypayed."[455]

Pearsall, arguing that Capgrave was influenced by popular romance, calls attention to the highly literate and literary nature of Capgrave's work, which may also account for the relatively great critical interest in it. Pearsall shows many similarities in meter and use of metaphor between *St. Katherine* and secular romances that continued to be popular in Capgrave's time, including *King Horn* and *Havelok the Dane*. These apparent borrowings from romance are conspicuously absent from Capgrave's other saints' lives, such as the *Life of St. Norbert*, which is considerably dryer than *St. Katherine* and lacks the moments of high tension that distinguish *St. Katherine*, such as the burning of the wise men, in which Capgrave exclaims, "Well is him that may a fagott bere/To brene the clerkys!"[456] Whether this difference is attributable to the greater drama and

---

[454] Capgrave, *The Life of Saint Katherine* 5.638-51.

[455] "shall be payed." *The Ancrene Riwle* 82.

[456] Capgrave, *The Life of Saint Katherine* 5.286-7.

excitement of Katherine's story or whether, as Pearsall believes, Capgrave was trying to reach a wider audience with *St. Katherine* than with his other works, it certainly showcases Capgrave's literary and rhetorical skills. In some ways, it displays these more than it does the virtues which the life of St. Katherine is supposed to teach. For example, in a scene reminiscent of the devil's temptation of Christ, Maxentius offers not only to make Katherine queen, but also to have a statue of her erected in the public square if she will only sacrifice to his gods. Her response is bitingly sarcastic:

> Of what matere schall my legges be?
>
> What manere werkman that dare undyrtake
>
> To make hem to meve and walke in her degre?
>
> My handys, eke, I wolde wete how that he
>
> Shuld make to fele, and of what matere—
>
> Or we goo ferther, this wold I lere.
>
> The eyne eke whech this ymage schall have,
>
> If thei schul loke ryght as I do in dede. . .[457]

Until the Emperor finds a workman who can create such a moving, seeing, feeling person, she will remain loyal to the only creator who can. Not content to show the saint resisting temptation, Capgrave has her ridicule it, as cleverly as possible.

The *vita*, in Capgrave's hands, both incorporates and criticizes the "romantic" love in courtly literature. Katherine's love-longing for her as-yet-unknown future spouse, her subsequent marriage to Christ, and her longing for him after she wakes up in the hermit's cell are all highly romantic and often eroticized in ways reminiscent of the

earlier *Seinte Katerine*. As she tells the Emperor, "I am His mayde. I wil do that I can/To haven His love; He is al my swetnesse,/He is my joye, He is my gentilnesse."[458] Even at the beginning, before she knows Christ, "the fyre of

---

[457] Capgrave, *The Life of Saint Katherine* 5.450-55.

[458] Capgrave, *The Life of Saint Katherine* 5.523-5.

charite and of love/Brennyth in hir, so that evyre more and more/Hir hert is sette on oon that sytte above."[459] Although she marries the one she loves, she suffers as much as any courtly lover, being deprived of his presence as long as she lives in the world. When she wakes up in Adrian's cell without her bridegroom, she weeps and swoons[460] until Adrian fears she may die. On the other hand, Katherine expresses her disdain for sexual love as eloquently as she celebrates the chaste love of God. Capgrave says her innate virtue "made hir hate these fleschly lustys alle."[461] She wonders why her parliament would want their queen to have her mind on such trivial things. She assures them that "My wyttess, I telle you, nothing besy been/In swech matere, neythir to lust ne to love/Fy on tho hertes that evyr on swech thing hove!"[462] One of her suitors uses a device common in amatory verse when he urges her to do as her mother did, asking how she would be here if her mother had been as stubborn as she is. In response, Katherine points to everything that makes love in courtly literature so painful. If she loved her husband, surely a best-case scenario, he might die or stop loving her, and then her heartache would be great indeed. Therefore, she asks the prince why he should counsel her "swech game to begynne/Whech is not stedfast in lowe ne in astate."[463] This argument about the instability of earthly love resembles the much earlier one in *Hali Meiðhad*, but the purpose of it is less clear. In a sense, Capgrave is following a long tradition of religious literature which argues for the superiority of God's love over that of an earthly man. The complication is that, in this version, Katherine's love for God causes no less pain than the love of Isolde or Guinevere for their earthly knights. Clearly, Capgrave's engagement with romance is much more direct than that of earlier religious writers. It is worth

---

[459] Capgrave, *The Life of Saint Katherine* 2.16-18.

[460] Capgrave, *The Life of Saint Katherine* 3.1353.

[461] Capgrave, *The Life of Saint Katherine* 2.43.

[462] Capgrave, *The Life of Saint Katherine* 2.913-915.

questioning why this should be so.

Hagiographers had long used the techniques of romance to make religious texts more appealing to the public, but a careful reader of Capgrave will probably wonder how religious his purpose really is. *St. Katherine* is clearly a conscious work of art which "can be seen as a continuation of the Chaucer-Lydgate tradition of embellished rhetorical hagiography."[464] In addition, the interest in dialectic, which had been strong at the universities since the Twelfth-Century Renaissance, seems to have greatly influenced Capgrave. As an educated man, he would have studied rhetoric and would know all about Abelard's process of *sic et non*, and the lengthy argument scenes are among the most striking feature of his *St. Katherine*. The life of St. Katherine lends itself to masterful displays of dialectic. She argues with her parliament when they want her to take a husband; she argues with the Emperor when she approaches the scene of the sacrifice; most importantly, she argues with the fifty best scholars in the empire about whether her religion or theirs is the true one. Katherine, the patron saint of Christian philosophers and female scholars, always triumphs. If the author really wants to show Katherine's learning and skill, he has no choice but to show his own.

Nevertheless, most of the Katherine narratives present a very short version of each debate, often omitting the contents of the arguments altogether. For example, in the *South-English Legendary* version, the scholars attribute her victory to the Holy Ghost and make no real attempt to refute her. There are only two possible reasons for this choice. Either the author has no skill at dialectic or he has it and chooses not to display it. I have difficulty believing that someone who shows as much understanding of audience and genre as the *South-English Legendary* author lacks the sophistication to include a lengthy debate in his narrative, if he had seen a reason to do so. Possibly, he fears boring an audience whose taste for adventure stories he so keenly realizes. Perhaps, too, he hesitates

---

[463] Capgrave, *The Life of Saint Katherine* 2.1107-8.

[464] Pearsall 123.

to present the arguments against Christianity to a lay audience who might never have thought of them. If the *South-English Legendary* is a product, as it seems to be, of efforts by the thirteenth-century Church to reform the laity, the last thing the author would want to do is suggest arguments against the faith he is promoting.

Capgrave, who obviously is learned enough to produce a theological discussion of the type Katherine has with the wise men, makes a different decision. He reports the whole argument in detail, and it takes about a thousand lines for Katherine to hear and refute each of the philosophers individually. Throughout the narrative, Katherine out-maneuvers the Emperor with a cleverness and erudition that necessarily displays the cleverness and erudition of Capgrave. When the Emperor threatens to burn her to death, Katherine warns him that, long after her pain is over, "thu with fendes in helle shal be brent."[465] When the Emperor offers to marry her and make her queen, she asks whether she ought to choose a mortal, flawed husband and temporal power or a peerless husband and eternal kingdom. This argument recalls the argument she has with her parliament in the *vita*, where she refutes individually all the lords who want her to choose one of them for a husband. When they praise her beauty, wisdom, and high birth, she observes that she really ought, in that case, to choose a husband who exceeds her in all these qualities.

---

[465] Capgrave, *The Life of Saint Katherine* 5.588.

Naturally, none can be found. During this early argument, she shows great skill, but not nearly as much as she shows in the exchange quoted above, when the Emperor offers to put the statue of her in the public square. His promise to make everyone show reverence to this statue shows an ironic misunderstanding of Katherine's position. He makes the worldly assumption that a woman who will not be compelled by threats or torture to sacrifice at someone else's altar will consent to have others sacrifice at hers.

This argument is not only long, but also subtle and sophisticated as well. Its allusions to biblical events imply a reasonably high level of education, not only in the author but also in the intended audience, who would have needed a specific knowledge of Scripture to appreciate what the author was doing. To enjoy Capgrave, one would also have to love good scholastic argument for its own sake. Thus, while his audience for *The Life of St. Katherine* may have been wider than the scholars and clerics he had in mind for *St. Norbert* or *St. Augustine*, it could not have include every layman who enjoyed *Havelok*. Probably, then, Capgrave did not share the *South-English Legendary* author's goal of reforming the laity. Nor does his *Life of St. Katherine* appear intended for the instruction of religious women, as some earlier versions are. If the work is intended for his own intellectual circle, consisting of other Cambridge-educated Austin friars, we must return to the question of its purpose.

F.J. Furnivall, in his colorful introduction to Horstmann's edition, remarks on Capgrave's patriotism, indeed his devotion, to whoever happened to be in power:

> Capgrave, being an Englishman, was of course by race and nature a flunkey, and had an inordinate reverence for kings and rank. This vice or quality is ingraind in the nation. While Henry VI was alive, Capgrave was his profound admirer, and "wholly devoted to his service" (*Henries*, p. 144); and his grandfather Henry IV, "gained the crown *by the providence*, as we believe, *of God*, who is

mighty to put down the mighty from their seat, and to exalt the humble" (*Henries*, p. 115, quoting Luke i.52). But as soon as York has turnd-out Lancaster, and Edward IV is on the throne, Capgrave dedicates his *Chronicle* to him, and then—"He that entered be intrusion was Herry the Fourte. He that entered *by Goddis provision* is Edward the Fourt. . .We trew loverers of this lond desire this of oure Lord God, that al the erroure whech was browte in be Herry the Fourte may be redressed be Edward the Fourte. . ." (p. 40). . .In the matter of kings, dukes &c., we are a poor lot.[466]

Whether such blind loyalty to the king makes the English a poor lot, I would not presume to say. However, the English definitely were, by the time of Capgrave, a patriotic lot, and the clergy had, perhaps, more reason than most to be devoted subjects of the king. Their reasons had little to do with race or nature and everything to do with the king's patronage. In 1445, when Capgrave was writing *St. Katherine*, Henry VI was ruling, and he was a strong supporter of the Austin friars in general and of Lynn priory in particular. Although concerned about the future of the realm, Capgrave disliked the old proverb that "often ruithe the realme, where chyldren rule, and women gouerne."[467] Since he supported the king with what Furnivall calls "inordinate reverence," he had to refute this saying, which he heard more often than he wished at the time of Henry's accession. Thus, we can understand Capgrave's elaborate defense of Katherine's fitness to rule as a defense of Henry VI.

F. Osbern Bokenham

A very different political agenda underlies the work of Capgrave's friend and protégé, Osbern Bokenham. Bokenham, also an Austin friar, was acquainted

---

[466] Furnivall xv-xvi.

[467] Furnivall xix.

with Capgrave at Cambridge. Shortly after Capgrave wrote his *Life of St. Katherine*, Bokenham wrote an all-female hagiography collection called *Legendys of Hooly Wummen*, which includes a *passio* of St. Katherine. If the reader is interested in Katherine's *vita*, Bokenham directs him to "My fadrys book, maystyr Ioon Capgraue."[468] As suggested above, Bokenham's need to explain this decision shows the importance of *vitae* in the later Middle Ages as well as Bokenham's regard for his colleague. In Capgrave's work, says Bokenham, the reader may find the whole story of Katherine's life "In balaadys rymed ful craftyly."[469] Bokenham himself, he claims, is not "crafty" enough to recount the whole story. However, Bokenham's stated reasons are suspect, since he claims ignorance of the *vita* directly after summarizing it and praising Capgrave's handling of it. More likely, then, he apologizes for this lack of skill and knowledge, a commonplace among romance writers, to avoid doing something he does not wish to do. He sets a precedent in the introduction, where he praises Chaucer elaborately and, with Chaucer-like self-deprecation, apologizes for his inability to write like that "crafty clerk."[470] What Bokenham does wish to do, according to him, is console two Katherines of his acquaintance, Katherine Howard and Katherine Denstoun. He leaves unsaid what the two Katherines need consolation for, but he calls on St. Katherine in her capacity as patron saint of virgins. Unlike most of the Katherine narratives intended for women, this one only mentions her espousal to Christ, and avoids characterizing it in the extremely sensual terms used in other versions. Instead, Bokenham focuses on the honor of being "chosyn" by "My lord Ihesu cryst hys spouse to be."[471]

---

[468] Osbern Bokenham, *Legendys of Hooly Wummen*, ed. Mary Serjeantson (London: EETS 206, 1938) 6356. Sheila Delany translates "fadry" as "spiritual father." See introduction, *A Legend of Holy Women*, by Osbern Bokenham, trans. Sheila Delany (Notre Dame: University of Notre Dame Press, 1992) 126. References are to line numbers.

[469] Bokenham, 6359.

[470] Bokenham 85.

[471] Bokenham 6883-4.

142

The issue of Katherine's worthiness is prominent in Bokenham's narrative, and it relates to the larger political concerns surrounding women in public life. At the time Bokenham wrote his *Legendys*, the Yorkist claim to the throne depended, at least partly, upon the female line. Both Richard, Duke of York and Henry VI, the Lancastrian king, could trace their ancestry back to Edward III. On his mother's side, Richard was descended from Lionel, second son of Edward III. On his father's side, he was descended from Edmond, who was only the fourth son. Richard's rival, King Henry VI, was descended from John of Gaunt, Edward's third son. Consequently, Richard would be ahead of Henry if the succession could pass through his mother's side and behind him if it could not. For this reason, the right of women to participate in public life was a subject of much debate in 1445.[472] As anyone would expect, Lancastrians denied the right of women to play a role in politics and Yorkists defended it. As the ruling house during the Wars of the Roses, the Lancasters had no shortage of talented spokesmen. They included such established figures of the Lancastrian court as Sir John Fortescue, whose misogynist railings[473] become perfectly understandable in light of the succession issues just mentioned.[474]

The Austin friars, who lived very much in the thick of political life, were generally Yorkist.[475] Even Capgrave, who supported Henry VI at the time of his accession, followed others of his order "when Yorkist turned-out Lancaster,"[476] in

[472] Sheila Delany, *Impolitic Bodies: Poetry, Saints, and Society in Fifteenth-Century England* (Oxford: Oxford University Press, 1998) 130.

[473] Here is an example: "An artificer is not so inconsiderate as to cleave wood with a mattock, nor a sailor so careless as to entrust the oar to the hands of one with the palsy. . . Behold, then, a sufficient cause why a woman cannot succeed in a kingdom" (Qtd. in Delany, *Impolitic Bodies*, 155-6).

[474] See also Delany, introduction, *A Legend of Holy Women* 27-29.

[475] Delany, *Impolitic Bodies* 130. A popular story from the Wars of the Roses tells of an Austin friar who spent an exciting night firing a canon at a Lancastrian camp, allowing the Yorkist army to sneak away without detection. See Dickinson 300.

[476] Furnivall xv.

praising the new king. The attraction of Austin friars to the Yorkist cause has not been definitively explained. David Knowles mentions an important house of Austin friars at York, "no doubt a centre of the order's northern activity."[477] So, perhaps, the Duke of York was an important patron of the mendicants there.

Fortunately, the reason for Bokenham's politics is not a matter of speculation. First of all, in 1432, Richard, Duke of York came into possession of Clare Priory, where Bokenham resided. This made Richard his patron and overlord.[478] Secondly, Bokenham's literary patroness also belonged to the House of York. In *Poets and Princepleasers*, Richard Firth Green refers to the *Legendys* as one of many "bespoke hagiographies written for aristocratic patrons by journeyman authors like Osbern Bokenham."[479] In this case, the aristocratic patron is Isabel Bourchier, older sister of Richard, Duke of York. In the prologue to his *Lyf of Marye Maudelyn*, he explains how he was prevailed upon to write it from

> lady bowsere,
>
> Wych is also clepyd þe countesse of hu,
>
> Doun conueyid by þe same pedegru
>
> That þe duk of york is come, for she
>
> Hus sustyr is in egal degre,
>
> Aftyr þe dochesse of york clepyd Isabel.[480]

He was apparently at the home of his patroness, the Duchess of York, when they began discussing the lives of holy women he had written so far, and she asked him "for my sake"[481] to write a life of Mary Magdelene in English. Given the

[477] Knowles 343,347.

[478] Delany, *Impolitic Bodies*, 130.

[479] Richard Firth Green, *Poets and Princepleasers: Literature and the English Court in the Late Middle Ages* (Chicago: University of Chicago Press, 1989) 62.

[480] Bokenham 5004-9.

[481] Bokenham 5073.

144

debate about Richard's claim to the throne, his sister had good reason to commission a series of biographies about intelligent, strong, capable women who would be entirely worthy to speak on political matters. Katherine is probably the best example, considering her great erudition and skill at public argument. Delany mentions, for example, the scene in which the Emperor sneers at Katherine, asking why he should listen to a woman. He echoes the words of Lancastrian writers of Bokenham's day in saying a woman is "a frele creatur,/Wych is euere uaryaunth & vnstable,/Fykyl, fals and decyuable,/As we wel knowyn by experyence."[482] Katherine's response is quick, but calm:

> Syr emperour. . .I you beseche,
>
> Suffre not yur-self of credultye
>
> Ner of woodnesse ouyrcome to be,
>
> For in the soule of a whys man
>
> No passyoun of trouble aboyde can.
>
> Wher-fore, syr, beth reulyd by equyte
>
> If ye lyst to reioyse yu to lyberte.[483]

No other teller makes Katherine's gender an issue between heroine and antagonist as Bokenham does. Like any legend of a martyred saint, Katherine's story has a clear villain, and only in Bokenham's version is that villain so pointedly misogynist. Even in Capgrave's version, where both sides seem to produce every possible argument, they do not debate about whether the sex of the arguer makes her less likely to be right. The idea seems to be original with the "uncrafty" Bokenham, whose patroness was probably well pleased with the politics it implied. Indeed, if the succession really took no account of gender, Isabel Bourchier herself would be closer to the throne than her younger brother, Richard.[484]

---

[482] Bokenham 6630-3

[483] Bokenham 6636ff.

[484] Delany, *Impolitic Bodies* 198.

One might have expected Capgrave to argue that women are fit to govern, considering the subject of Katherine's debate with Parliament. However, since Richard of York's claim to the throne depended upon the right of women to rule (or rather to transmit that right to their descendents), Capgrave, as a supporter of Henry VI, cannot directly defend it. If he did, he would be claiming that the greatest patron of Lynn priory had no right to rule. It is true that Capgrave shows the emperor's fifty scholars sneering at the prospect of debating a woman and finding their possible defeat at her hands intolerably shameful. [485] However, Capgrave ultimately treats Katherine's rhetorical skill as proof of God's limitless ability to exalt the low and strengthen the weak. The first philosopher who counsels that they "leve. . .now oure elde scole" and "Geve entendauns at this tyme to this dame,"[486] does so because he believes her God must be as powerful as she says. Why has he decided this? In his words, "I wold a supposyd. . .that the hevyn schuld falle/Rather than woman swech sciens schuld atame."[487] In short, Katherine's learning says nothing about the worthiness of women. It is the equivalent of God giving learning and eloquence to a horse: the lower the animal, the greater the miracle. It does not mean that horses should (or for that matter, should not) participate in politics.

Whereas Capgrave steers away from the subject of women's worthiness, Bokenham raises it pointedly, making the evil emperor misogynist, along with his other failings. Although Bokenham does not include Katherine's *vita*, he finds space in her *passio* to emphasize the selflessness, wisdom, humbleness, and piety that she shows when she inherits her father's throne.[488]

Bokenham also adds a lecture by Katherine on the issue of who deserves

---

[485] Delany, *Impolitic Bodies* 170.

[486] Capgrave, *The Life of St. Katherine* 5.1640, 1641.

[487] Capgrave, *The Life of St. Katherine* 5.1638-9.

[488] Bokenham 6404-6414.

146

to call himself a king. The Emperor wants to convert Katherine and let her live because she is beautiful, and even the earliest narratives imply that he is motivated by lust. According to her, whoever "is reulyd by resoun/And not by hys senswal felyng/Hath wurthyly pe name of a kyng," but whoever "folwyth pe lust of senswalyte,/Thow he emperour, kyng, or kayser be,/He ne may for al hys ly lynage/The tytyl auydyn of seruage."[489] This sentiment was common enough in religious literature before Benjamin Franklin secularized it to the familiar proverb, "He is a governor that governs his passions, and he is a servant that serves them." However, when Bokenham introduces it into the Katherine legend, where it never before appeared, the political implications are clear: some people, although they may sit on thrones, have no right to rule because they are servants of their passions.

Bokenham's Katherine clearly does not share the reverence for hereditary royalty that Capgrave's Katherine displays. First of all, he avoids the parliamentary debate by leaving out the *vita* altogether, pleading ignorance and encouraging readers to seek it in "My fadrys book, maystyr Ioon Capgraue."[490] There, he says, they will find the story of her youth and conversion "In balaadys rymyd ful craftyly."[491] Apparently, he has read Capgrave's version. He even tells some of the features of the story which "for ingnorance"[492] he cannot tell. For example, he claims not to know "hou she fyrst began/To be crystyne, & how oon clepyd Adryan/Hyr conuertyd & crystnyd in hyr youthe."[493] In short, his claim of ignorance rings false. I would suggest that he prefers not to emphasize Katherine's position as unmarried queen who depends on the loyalty of the lords

---

[489] Bokenham 6644-52.

[490] Bokenham 6356.

[491] Bokenham 6359.

[492] Bokenham 6360.

[493] Bokenham 6350-52.

in Parliament.[494]

Bokenham's Katherine takes no pride in her birth. She tells the Emperor that "by my kunnyng ryht not at al/I set, ner by þe greth honour/Of my byrth, wych at þis our/Wyth al myn hert I her forsake/And set at nouht for crystys sake."[495] Capgrave's Katherine would never be "founde in suche neglygens" as to "despyse that heigh degree,/Which þat is ordeyned be goddys prouydens/Which is eke come be descens on-to me."[496] Bokenham's Katherine does not believe that a person becomes a true king simply by lineal right. When the Emperor finishes raving about the instability of women, Katherine admonishes him:

> Who þat is reulyd by resoun
>
> And not by hys senswal felyng
>
> Hath wurthyly þe name of a kyng;
>
> And þer-ageyn who-so ne wyl
>
> By resoun be reulyd & by skyl,
>
> But folwyth þe lust of senswalyte,
>
> Thow he emperour, kyng, or kayser be,
>
> He ne may for al hys hy lynage
>
> The tytyl auoydyn of seruage.[497]

Henry VI was far too pious for anyone rightly to say he was ruled by sensuality. However, he was always weak and easily influenced by his councilors, as the 1448 appointment of Lumley (see Chapter Two) shows. After a serious illness in 1453, he became truly insane, and the queen tried in vain to cover up the fact "for

---

[494] Delany rightly points out that many of the arguments in favor of Katherine's marrying, especially in Capgrave, are good ones. Thus, Bokenham may limit himself to Katherine's *passio* to avoid the "antiwoman potential" of the Parliament scene. See Delany, *Impolitic Bodies* 172.

[495] Bokenham 6594-6598.

[496] Bokenham 796,792-4.

[497] Bokenham 6644-6652.

148

fear of a regency under York."[498] Clearly, Henry's mental fitness to rule had been
in dispute long before 1453. Thus, if the rule of reason is necessary for true
kingship, Henry's true kingship could well be questioned. In this matter,
Bokenham appropriates Katherine as an articulate speaker for the Yorkist cause.

This adaptation and use of a saint's life not only differs from the
traditional purpose of hagiography, i.e. instructing the reader in proper Christian
conduct, but it validates a sphere of human achievement that sacred writing of the
earlier Middle Ages, almost by definition, rejected. In the thirteenth century, as
shown in Chapter One, the dichotomy between hagiography and romance was not
really between the sacred and the secular, or even Church and state. It centered
on the question of whether "a devotion to God that is compatible with pursuing
earthly and secular well-being"[499] is a legitimate possibility. Romances, as Crane
points out, do not exactly speak for the state. (With a Lancastrian king on the
throne, is the Yorkist claimant "the state"?) They do address issues of state.
They concern themselves with "the relations between personal autonomy and
social engagement."[500] In Bokenham's hands, the passion of St. Katherine looks a
lot like a conflict between the individual and the state.[501] Bokenham's Katherine
is certainly far from dismissing the importance of earthly politics. Rather, she
discourses on what kind of person has the right to call himself a king, i.e. one who
is himself ruled by "resoun" and by "skyl" and not "by hys senswal felyng."[502]
Bokenham then alludes to the "tyrannye"[503] that results when a ruler refuses to be

---

[498] Jacob 508.

[499] Crane 97.

[500] Crane 101.

[501] It has even been described as a "minimirror for magistrates." See Delany, *Impolitic Bodies* 172.

[502] Bokenham 645,648.

[503] Bokenham 6666.

"reulyd by equyte."[504] Rarely do hagiographers use such terms as "liberty" and "equity," but Bokenham gives them a central place in the argument.[505] Then, of course, the fact that God chooses a woman to present His cause in public debate implicitly supports the Yorkist position. Bokenham's *Lyf of Seynte Kateryne* is not exactly a romance, but its concerns are far closer to those of romance than to those of traditional hagiography.

G. *S. Kateryne*

Not all clerical writers shared the political motivations of Capgrave and Bokenham. Some looked askance at the increasing involvement of their colleagues in secular matters and employed the techniques of romance in order to show its shortcomings. One anonymous passion of St. Katherine, written around 1420, adopts the meter and conventions of romance, only to admonish those it attracts by doing so. This version is generally ignored in favor of works with known authors, whose motives are easier to divine. There is neither criticism on it nor references to it in recent scholarship. Perhaps this vacuum is the result of an assumption that *S. Kateryne*[506] lacks both literary merit and historical significance, and is therefore not worth studying. In the context of the politicized hagiography of Capgrave and Bokenham, the *S. Kateryne* looks and feels like a throwback to the days of the *South-English Legendary*. Furthermore, we know nothing of the author, the audience, or the circumstances under which it was written. Thus, the lack of scholarship on it is understandable but does not mean that it has nothing worthwhile to tell us about the viewpoint of religious writers in the fifteenth century. A close analysis of *S. Kateryne* reveals a subtle, intelligent

---

[504] Bokenham 6641.

[505] Delany, *Impolitic Bodies* 173.

[506] *S. Kateryne, Altenglische Legenden, Neue Folge*, ed. Carl Horstmann (New York: Hildescheim & Olms, 1881).

150

critique of the romance genre it seems to imitate.

The romances of the thirteenth and fourteenth centuries are usually recognizable by meter, as well as theme and character. *King Horn*, with its three-stress, rhyming couplets, is a good example of a popular metrical romance, and the fact that hagiographers adopted the same style might imply no more than the traditional competition between two popular genres. The opening of *S. Kateryne* resembles the beginning of Chaucer's parodic *Sir Thopas* so strikingly that its author appears, like Chaucer, to be imitating tale-rhyme romances that were popular in East Anglia. *Sir Thopas*, which is now more familiar than the works it parodies, begins like this:

> Listeth, lordes, in good entent,
>
> And I wol telle verrayment
>
> Of myrthe and of solas,
>
> Al of a knyght was fair and gent
>
> In bataille and in tourneyment;
>
> His name was sire Thopas.[507]

S. Kateryne, also composed in the London region some thirty years later, begins similarly:

> All tho that be crystenyd & dere,
>
> Lysteneth, and ye may here
>
> The lyfe of a swete vyrgyne:
>
> Hur name ys clepydde Kateryne.[508]

Containing only the *passio* with no apologies and a meter like *Sir Thopas*, *S. Kateryne* does not seem to beg for explanation, as the works of Capgrave and Bokenham do. Clearly, *S. Kateryne* was written, like the *South-English Legendary*, for a wide mixed audience. The meter, as shown above, is like that of

---

[507] Geoffrey Chaucer, *Sir* Thopas, The *Riverside Chaucer*, ed. Larry Benson, 3rd ed. (Oxford: Oxford University Press, 1987) 712-717.

[508] *S. Kateryne* 1-4.

popular songs.

Yet, the narrative contains elements of religious instruction that appear in no other narratives. For example, when Maxentius announces his wife's punishment for converting to Christianity, Porphiry takes up a spear and shield and threatens him. Like a good knight, he wants to defend both the Queen and the Church. In a sense, Porphiry is a one-man crusade, fighting the heathen in defense of Christians and their faith. One would expect the unknown author to approve of his actions. If this were a pious romance, in the tradition of *Guy of Warwick*, he undoubtedly would. However, here, the hagiographer condemns the values of the genre he has been imitating. Katherine reproaches the knight, saying, "Parfory, let be thy fyghtyng!. . ./Yf thou wylt wyth me martyred be,/Fyghtynge thou must leve. . ./And take lyghtly thy payne."[509] Instantly, Porphiry throws down his weapons and begs Katherine to pray for him. The saint's rebuke, which echoes Christ's in the Garden of Gethsemane, seems pointedly critical of chivalric romances and their glorification of violence. Porphiry could easily be a hero in such a romance (as the *South-English Legendary* author shows), and Katherine's admonition comes when he is behaving the most chivalrously. Thus, the author demonstrates the incompatibility of chivalry (even at its best) and genuine holiness. Using the tropes of romance to attract romance readers, he frustrates their expectations in an oddly Chaucerian way, perhaps in an attempt to make them question those expectations.

The criticism of knighthood that one finds in *S. Kateryne* is understandable if one keeps in mind the knight's changing position. The *South-English Legendary*, whose presentation of knights is so much more positive, was written before the fall of Acre, and "Sir Porphiry," the converted knight, has a legitimate role to play. He gives the martyred queen proper Christian burial and

---

[509] *S. Kateryne* 262-5.

152

faces the Emperor's wrath for doing so.[510] Even Katherine, the female knight, hurries to rescue the oppressed Christians whom the heathen Emperor forces to worship his gods: "And forth anon to be Aumperour : baldeliche heo gan gon."[511] Both of these knightly figures act decisively to rescue Christians from heathen oppression, obviously with the author's approval. The difference is that the later hagiographer no longer sees a use for chivalry. Indeed, he has good reason not to. He sees knights becoming businessmen, mercenaries, or outright brigands, just as Malory does. He also sees them becoming unnecessary either to keep law and order or to defend Holy Church. Without these two functions, the violence that naturally accompanies the warrior profession no longer has a redemptive purpose. Therefore, Porphiry—no longer "Sir Porphiry"—finally converts when he obeys Katherine's command to put away his sword. Katherine herself does not rush to the scene of the sacrifice, but must be found by the Emperor, when he hears that one maiden refuses to attend.[512] She no longer actively defends other Christians from oppression, but shows through her own example that each person must suffer for the good of his own soul.

This view of the warrior profession as sinful by nature has, of course, a long and respectable history, going back to the very early Church. As late as the ninth century, Agobard of Lyons still urged *"milites Christi* to bear witness to their faith not by killing but by dying."[513] Porphiry's cause makes no difference: Like Peter, he must learn that he cannot draw a sword in defense of Christ. As scripturally sound as that point is, few churchmen would have advanced it at any time from the first crusade to the fall of Acre. By 1074, Pope Gregory VII was

---

[510] *South-English Legendary* 249-255.

[511] *South-English Legendary* 14.

[512] *S. Kateryne* 35.

[513] Russell 30.

offering to lead troops himself to aid Christians in the East.[514] While denying any "legitimate purpose for secular warfare," Gregory allowed knights to "fight to defend justice on the advice of their bishops."[515] A clerical writer could not very well have demanded that his readers beat their swords into ploughshares while the pope was preaching crusade.

However, by 1420, England and France had been at very secular war, on and off, for nearly seventy-five years. The Avignonese popes had tried and failed to act as peacemakers, perhaps because their situation made them far from objective from an English point of view. Anti-papal and anti-clerical feeling increased from the mid-fourteenth century to the schism because the papacy appeared to the English so blatantly and unaccountably pro-French.[516] During and after the schism, the same forces that limited the power of the papacy to use patronage also limited its ability to promote peace between France and England. An increasingly patriotic and jingoistic England simply would not listen to papal demands.[517] Thus, the war also placed English clerics in the unpleasant position of having to choose between the king and the pope. By this time, given the usual source of patronage and the relative weakness of the papacy, many would choose the king. Nevertheless, an English cleric in 1420 might well long for the days when the Church could compel the nobles to cease killing one another. In 1431, even the patriotic Capgrave says, a little mournfully, "I trust in the Lord that I shall see our borders in peace and prosperity, and our days happy, before the day of my death."[518] Katherine's unknown biographer may hope the same.

S. Kateryne breaks with tradition in another respect: it includes no

---

[514] Riley-Smith 2.

[515] Russell 34.

[516] Pantin 82.

[517] Pantin 82.

[518] Capgrave, *Henricis* 19.

mention of Katherine's marriage with Christ. The tendency among Katherine's biographers had long been to romanticize her life, either by filling it with knights in shining armor or by emphasizing the romance between Katherine and Christ. Every version of her *vita* has an elaborate wedding scene, and every version of her martyrdom echoes the Song of Songs just before her death, when she hears Christ calling her.[519] However, the *S. Kateryne* author rejects this convention. Instead, Christ sends an angel down to tell Katherine that "Jesus hath herde prayere thyne/And the hath grauntyd sekyrly/Owt of payne anone þou hye--/Thy yoye ys dyght rychely."[520] Again, having created the sound and feel of popular romance, the author refuses to fulfill expectations.

While *S. Kateryne* includes no specific condemnation of sensuality, many lives of St. Katherine do. They ignore the apparent contradiction, just as they ignore the contradiction between serving Christ and slashing people with swords. After all, both sexual love and armed combat had long coexisted with Christian morality in chivalric literature. Not surprisingly, they become truly incompatible in hagiography before they do so in romance—but not long before. Eventually, Malory comes to the same conclusion, as Ferguson explains:

> To Malory,. . .there could be no conflict between the knighthood of this world and the demands of the life everlasting. Only when the search for "worship" had degenerated into pride, the play of arms into mere homicide, and love into lechery, only that is, when the virtuous life which was common to both the chivalric and the Christian traditions had become compromised through the weakness of the flesh or the promptings of the devil could the

---

[519] In the *South-English Legendary*, he says, "Cum forth. . .mi suete leman : mi leue spouse al-so" (288). In the *Prose Legend*, he says, "Come on, my feyr love and my der love and spowse" (924). Even in the Early-English *Seinte Katerine*, she expresses her love for Christ in sensual, almost sexual terms. See above for other versions.

[520] *S. Kateryne* 420-4.

chivalric life be held to imperil the soul.[521]

A better description of the fifteenth century would be hard to find. As Malory himself says, "whether [Lancelot and Guinevere] were abed other at other maner of disportis, me lyste nat thereof make no mencion, for love that tyme was nat as love ys nowadayes."[522] Perhaps for the same reason, the author of *S. Kateryne* does not feel as comfortable as his predecessors did, depicting a courtly romance between an earthly woman and God.

H. Conclusion

The development of the St. Katherine legend, from the thirteenth century to the fifteenth, demonstrates how, in the later Middle Ages, hagiography began to resemble romance. The earlier narratives borrow techniques from romance, as romances borrowed from hagiography, in order to enhance their own popularity. Later, the sacred literature begins to engage with the secular literature more pointedly, either to critique it or to usurp is function as a vehicle for secular polemic. In the case of the 1420 passion of *S. Kateryne*, the author's quarrel with popular romance ironically leads to a saint's life that resembles the genre it critiques more closely than any of its models did.

In general, St. Katherine's fifteenth-century biographers, instead of making sinners less worldly, make Katherine more so. They represent, as Malory's Grail Quest does,[523] an attempt to reinvigorate a vanishing ideal. The saint's perfect devotion to God, her contempt for worldly goods and temporal power, made her a good example of everything that seemed to be lacking in late medieval England. Yet, the very methods that her clerical biographers employed

---

[521] Ferguson 56.

[522] Malory 676.

[523] See Chapter 5, below.

show the impossibility of their project. As the embodiment of someone's idea of perfection, she becomes a Lancastrian or a Yorkist, a person with the politics. Attempts to remove her from the political realm do so at the cost of nearly everything that makes her legend appealing. Since love and glory are no longer innocent concepts, the author of *S. Kateryne* removes them, but ultimately has nothing with which to replace them. In every case, instead of real life coming closer to the ideal, the ideal moves drearily closer to real life.

In the final analysis, the construction of hagiography to resemble romance did not occur because authors or audiences wanted it to occur. It began long before the medieval Church even considered relinquishing its influence over the daily lives of the laity. In fact, the Church itself began the process while its power was still increasing. By appropriating romance techniques—just to make the spiritual medicine easier to swallow—perfectly orthodox hagiographers made Katherine's life sound so much like a romance that the same people who loved romances would love her story, too. From that point, the transition must have been imperceptible when writers of the late Middle Ages began presenting secular, political themes through fictional stories that, incidentally, had a saint for the central character. Thus, by the end of the Middle Ages, her own biographers had done what the Emperor could not: they secularized St. Katherine.

Chapter Five:

Thomas Malory and the Grail Quest

The most influential of the fifteenth-century English "hagiographic romances" is Thomas Malory's *Tale of the Sankgreal*, which is a much-abbreviated translation of the Old French *Queste del Saint Graal*. Compared to the amount of scholarship that Malory's other works have attracted, his Grail Quest has received relatively little critical attention. Many critics consider it a simple translation and therefore unworthy of serious analysis.[524] Eugene Vinaver, while acknowledging that Malory's Grail Quest differs somewhat from its source, calls it "the least obviously original of [Malory's] works."[525] Another more practical reason for the relative lack of scholarship on Malory's version of the Grail Quest is the impossibility of classifying it, an issue that the present chapter hopes to resolve. It does not slip neatly into the category of chivalric romance, or even of exemplary romance, where the rewards for right conduct are earthly as

---

[524] For an example, see William Ryding, *Structure in Medieval Narrative* (The Hague: Mouton, 1971) 158.

[525] Eugene Vinaver, ed., *The Works of Sir Thomas Malory*, 2nd ed. (Oxford: Oxford University Press, 1971) 758.

158

well as heavenly.[526] Galahad, the most successful knight on the quest, desires—
and receives—only the saint's reward of immediate departure from this
"unstable" world.[527]

Discussions of Malory's treatment of his source necessarily focus on the
key distinction (drawn repeatedly by the French *Queste*) between *chevalerie
celestiel* and *chevalerie terriene*. The French *Queste*, like a thirteenth-century
saint's life, consistently argues that earthly success must be abandoned, if one
wishes to achieve spiritual success, i.e. salvation. Scholars disagree on what
Malory does with this distinction. Most agree that his interest in knighthood is
much keener than that of his French predecessor.[528] Thus, the idea that he would
abandon earthly chivalry as a worthy goal seems unlikely. Vinaver believes that
his one desire is "to secularize the Grail theme as much as the story will allow."[529]

---

[526] This difficulty of classification is not unique to Malory. The origins of the romance
genre—in epic, hagiography, or folktale—have been the subject of much controversy, and even
the basic characteristics of romance are impossible to state with much certainty, due to the national
and regional variations mentioned in chapter one. For the details of the controversy, see Nancy M.
Bradbury, *Writing Aloud: Storytelling in Late Medieval England* (Urbana and Chicago:
University of Illinois Press, 1998) 7-14; Paul Strohm, "The Origin and Meaning of Middle English
Romance," Genre 10 (1977) 1-28 and "Storie, Spelle, Geste, Romance, Tragedie: Generic
Distinctions in the Middle English Troy Narratives," *Speculum* 46 (1971): 348-59.

[527] Most recent scholarship on Malory's Grail Quest tends to deal with issues of
character, rather than genre. See Sandra Ihle, "Invention of Character in Malory's Grail Book,"
Medieval Studies in Honor of Douglas Kelly, ed. Keith Busby and Norris J. Lacy (Amsterdam:
Rodopi, 1994) 181-192; Ginger Thornton and Krista May, "Malory as Feminist? The Role of
Percival's Sister in the Grail Quest," *Sir Thomas Malory: Views and Re-Views*, ed. D. Thomas
Hanks (New York: AMS, 1992) 43-53; Victoria Weiss, "Grail Knight or Boon Companion? The
Inconsistent Sir Bors of Malory's *Morte Darthur*," *Studies in Philology* 94 (1997): 417-27.
Despite the awkwardness of the task, a few scholars have written insightfully on the subject of the
Malory's "translation." My own analysis is much indebted to Sandra Ness Ihle, *Malory's Grail
Quest: Invention and Adaptation in Medieval Prose Romance* (Madison: University of Wisconsin
Press, 1983), which includes an extensive discussion of Malory's abbreviation techniques. All
subsequent references to Ihle will be to this edition.

[528] P.E. Tucker remarks on the "fervour behind Malory's belief in chivalry," which he
shows in passages such as this one: "'What?' seyde sir Launcelot. 'is he a theff and a knyght?
And a ravyssher of women? He doth shame unto the Order of Knyghthode, and contrary unto his
oth. Hit is pyte that he lyvyth!'" See P.E. Tucker, "Chivalry in the *Morte*," *Essays on Malory*, ed.
J.A.W. Bennett (Oxford: Clarendon Press, 1963) 269. See also Ihle's discussion of Vinaver and
Brewer, pp. 184-5.

[529] Vinvaver 758.

Even some who consider this an overstatement of the case[530] agree with Vinvaver
that Malory's Grail Quest is "primarily an *Arthurian* adventure,"[531] whereas the
Queste del Saint Graal is "primarily a theological treatise on salvation."[532] This
view holds that Malory ignores the dichotomy between heavenly and earthly
chivalry to focus on his real interest, which is secular knighthood.

The opposite position is articulated most thoroughly by Stephen Kraemer,
who sees Malory's Grail Quest as much closer to hagiography than to romance,
and therefore closer to its source than is generally argued. According to Kraemer,
the most important requirements for sanctity in fifteenth-century England were
"aristocratic or royal lineage, virginity or chastity, and participation in miraculous
events."[533] For Kraemer, Malory's successful grail knights exemplify saintly
behavior, as understood by Malory and his audience. If Malory needed to change
his source, according to this view, he did so because the essential characteristics
of a saint were not the same in fifteenth-century England as in thirteenth-century
France. Thus, Kraemer sees Malory as translating the *Queste* into terms
appropriate for his own culture, but with the original message intact.

In this, Kraemer follows Dhira Mahoney, who argues that Malory does
"not so much secularize it as Anglicize it."[534] Here, Anglicizing means treating
earthly and spiritual ideals as compatible and even necessary to one another.
While Mahoney associates this view with fifteenth-century England, as Chapter
One of the present work establishes, a certain type of romance (the hagiographic

---

[530] See Ihle 184 and Charles Moorman, "'The Tale of the Sankgreal': Human Frailty,"
Malory's Originality: A Critical Study of Le Morte Darthur, ed. R.M. Lumiansky (Baltimore:
Johns Hopkins Press, 1964) 187.

[531] Vinaver 758.

[532] Moorman 186.

[533] Kraemer 12.

[534] Dhira Mahoney, "The Truest and Holiest Tale: Malory's Transformation of *La
Queste del Saint Graal*," *Studies in Malory*, ed. James W. Spisak (Kalamazoo, MI: Medieval
Institute Publications, 1985) 110.

160

or exemplary type) had been doing this for some time. Thus, if Malory is treating the two ideals as equally valid, but different pursuits, "not to be led concurrently,"[535] he is romanticizing, rather than Anglicizing, "the truest and holiest tale." In any case, Mahoney reasons that *chevalerie celestiel*, whose exemplar is Galahad, requires withdrawal from the active life. Therefore, a knight may not pursue it while bearing arms in the service of a feudal overlord. Yet, he may (as many do) abandon the comfortable, courtly life in his old age to become a holy hermit.[536]

On the other hand, Stephen Atkinson sees Malory as advocating a "balanced" respect for *chevalerie terriene* along with the reverence for *chevalerie celestiel* that his subject demands.[537] Atkinson argues that, regardless of the order in which Malory composed his tales, his grail quest was never designed to stand alone, but must be viewed in the context of his other tales.[538] Thus, Lancelot, whose excellence in *chevalerie terriene* and aspirations to *chevalerie celestiel* make him the crucial figure in both quest narratives,[539] need not be regarded as a complete failure simply because he fails at this quest. In Atkinson's reading, Malory can treat Lancelot's attempt at *chevalerie celestiel* as a serious failure, while giving him credit for his other accomplishments, as well for the progress toward salvation that he makes on the quest.[540]

Each of these interpretations will be addressed later in this chapter, as all have much to recommend them. However, it seems to me that, individually and

---

[535] Mahoney 123.

[536] Mahoney 123.

[537] Stephen Atkinson, "Malory's Lancelot and the Quest of the Grail," *Studies in Malory*, ed. James W. Spisak (Kalamazoo, MI: Medieval Institute Publications, 1985) 133.

[538] Atkinson 129.

[539] Mahoney 118.

[540] Atkinson 148.

collectively, they raise an important question that none of them answer. Why does Malory choose a source text with which he disagrees so seriously,[541] and what is he attempting to do with it? While accepting Malory's *Tale of the Sankgreal* as falling within the expansive medieval definition of translation, I cannot agree with Kraemer that Malory simply updates his material while preserving the doctrinal implications of the original. Rather, I see him purposely and systematically reversing its central argument. I do agree with Kraemer that Malory makes extensive use of hagiographic techniques, including a source text that makes Galahad an uncanonized saint. However, I would argue that he does so to critique his source text, not to interpret its message for his own time. In the same way that religious writers of the fifteenth century imitated the popular romances of their day in order to critique them, Malory reworks an essentially religious text in order to correct its message.

In this chapter, I shall argue that Malory is performing, in reverse, the same operation as the author of the 1420 *S. Kateryne*. Whereas that author uses the methods of romance to critique its values, Malory "adheres closely to the plan of his French source"[542] to reverse its otherworldly, anti-chivalric message. In the French work, the quest for the Holy Grail is "a failure resulting from man's inability to exchange temporal, courtly values for a religious principle which transcended them."[543] Its hero, Galahad, is essentially a saint, who abandons earthly chivalry for heavenly chivalry and receives the saint's reward of departure from this sinful world. However, Malory "does not agree with his source that the chivalric ideal is anti-Christian."[544] Rather, he believes that Christian morality (of an admittedly earthly sort) is an essential part of knightly behavior. The result is a

---

[541] By all accounts, he had other choices. See discussion in Mahoney 112.

[542] Moorman 186.

[543] Moorman 186.

[544] Derek Brewer, "the hoole book," *Essays on Malory*, ed. J.A.W. Bennett (Oxford: Clarendon Press, 1963) 58.

"hagiographic romance," promoting the chivalric code in direct contradiction with his anti-chivalric source.

The Grail Quest occupies a pivotal position in Malory's Arthurian cycle, and Atkinson rightly observes that we must view it in context.[545] It follows the story of Lancelot and Elaine, in which Elaine uses magic to seduce Lancelot and conceives Galahad, whom she expects to "preve the beste man of hys kynne excepte one."[546] In this rare case, the mother's expectations are far too modest. Galahad grows up to be the best knight in the world and the only one completely to achieve the Grail. Galahad's success illustrates, as saints' lives do, how a great spiritual achievement can bring earthly disaster. As soon as Arthur's Round Table—with all its passion, prowess, and idealism—produces Galahad, its decline begins. The first step in the disintegration of the Round Table fellowship is, ironically, the highest quest to which Arthur's knights have ever been called: the Quest for the Holy Grail. As Arthur fears at the outset, many good knights do not return. The worst return first because they fail soonest, and their return confers little benefit on Camelot. The best knight, Galahad, wishes to die as soon as he achieves the Grail. Thus, his success renders him completely useless for the Round Table. After everyone who is willing or able finds his way back, the division and strife among the knights steadily increases. Arthur's illegitimate son, Mordred, now fully grown, enters the court with no other goal than to break the Round Table and depose his father. The affair between Lancelot and Guinevere provides Mordred with a convenient wedge to drive between Arthur and his best friend, and Arthur dies on the battlefield in a war he wanted only to prevent. The Grail Quest thus marks the beginning of the end of Camelot.

The Cistercian monk who wrote the Old French *Queste* did not consider the demise of the Round Table a tragedy. For him, it earns its downfall through its sins and has no further purpose after the triumph of Galahad. However, Sir

---

[545] Atkinson 129.

[546] Malory 505.

Thomas Malory regrets deeply the passing of what he sees as chivalry's golden age. While recognizing the faults of the Round Table knights, he values the institution of which they were the shining example. For Malory, knighthood is a real institution, so real that he will not demand perfection from it.

Malory, who was barely old enough to remember the glory days of Henry V and Agincourt, saw a High Order of Knighthood badly in need of a King Arthur. He saw men of noble lineage refusing knighthood, preferring to pay fines rather than to incur the responsibility. As Chapter Two of the present work shows, actual dubbed knights were becoming businessmen, bankers, lawyers, and professional politicians.[547] Like Chaucer, who lived through the transition, he mourned the replacement of feudal obligation with money and contracts. Arthur Ferguson, among others, has pointed out the medieval tendency to view all change as decay: Malory's nostalgic longing for a Golden Age of chivalry was certainly nothing new.[548] After all, those who saw the major institutions of medieval Europe declining had no way of knowing that they stood at the dawn of the Renaissance. To Malory, the inevitable collapse of the Round Table explained, in the familiar terms of human frailty, the state of chivalry as he found it. Yet, he was far from giving up on knighthood and its potential for bringing out man's better nature. Like the religious writers of his day, who saw Christian principles losing their influence, Malory blamed humans for their inability to live up to an ideal, rather than blame an ideal that was no longer workable.[549] Moreover, chivalry constituted the only standard of ideal conduct Malory knew, religious perfection being out of most people's reach.

---

[547] Ferguson 113-115.

[548] Ferguson 57. While Malory's "choice of chivalric subjects was not. . .an exercise in nostalgia" (Mahoney 110), since the fifteenth century did take chivalry seriously, his references to a time when knights were true and lovers were faithful certainly is nostalgic.

[549] Ferguson 57.

164

A. Sir Thomas Malory, Knight

Malory's own life seems to provide a good example of everything that disturbed him about late medieval chivalry. Born into the knightly class, he served in the military and in parliament. Nevertheless, court records show him accused of various crimes, from theft to rape to murder. As Ferguson notes laconically, "his relations with women were not notable for their courtesy."[550] Vinaver points out that people could be accused of crime for political reasons, but that the charges against Malory are too numerous and various to ignore completely. He is accused of lying in wait "with other malefactors" to rob passengers along the highway[551] and of robbing a man and raping his wife on two separate occasions. According to the same records, he not only stole from a monastery, but then returned two days later to abuse the abbot.[552] In other words, if the Malory named in the court record is the same one who wrote the King Arthur tales,[553] he was everything that he said brings shame on the High Order of Knighthood: a thief, a murderer, and a ravisher of women. After fighting (apparently on both sides) in the War of the Roses, he was back in prison when he wrote "the hoole book of Kyng Arthur and of his noble knyghtes of the Rounde Table," curiously excluded from the pardons Edward IV extended to many other

---

[550] Ferguson 50.

[551] Vinaver 5.

[552] Vinaver 5.

[553] The claim that the Thomas Malory mentioned in the court records is the same one who wrote the Arthurian tales remains controversial. For the original argument, see George Lyman Kittredge, *Sir Thomas Malory* (Barnstable: Priv. print, 1925). For the opposing view, see William Matthews, *The Ill-Framed Knight: A Skeptical Inquiry Into The Identity Of Sir Thomas Malory* (Berkeley: University of California Press, 1966). For a more recent perspective on the controversy, see also P.J.C. Field , *The Life And Times Of Sir Thomas Malory* (Rochester, NY : D.S. Brewer, 1993). The present discussion does not require that one accept the full story of Malory's criminal career, although I do take seriously Malory's plea that his readers "praye for me whyle I am on lyve that God sende me good delyveraunce" (726).

Lancastrians.[554] This fact gives particular poignancy to one of the few direct addresses in all of Malory's work, in which he condemns the "instabylite" of his countrymen. Describing the shift of popular support from Arthur to Mordred, Malory says the following:

> Lo ye all Englysshemen, se ye nat what a myschyff here was? For he that was the moste kynge and nobelyst knyght of the worlde, and moste loved the felyshyp of noble knyghtes, and by hym they all were upholyn, and yet myght nat thes Englyshemen holde them contente with hym. Lo thus was the olde custom and usayges of thys londe, and men say that we of thys londe have nat yet loste that custom. Alas! Thys ys a greate defaughte of us Englysshemen, for there may no thynge us please no terme.[555]

The reference to the Wars of the Roses could scarcely be clearer. Since one of the most important chivalric virtues was loyalty,[556] Malory must have seen a failure of knighthood in the rebellion of so many good knights against their king.

The "felyship" which is the strength of the Round Table is rooted in the feudal loyalty whose decline Malory so deplores. When Arthur accuses Lancelot of having a guilty relationship with Guinevere, Lancelot exclaims that "excepte youre person of your hyghnes and my lorde sir Gawayne, there nys no knyght undir hevyn that dare make hit good uppon me that ever I was traytour unto your person."[557] Lancelot seems stung at the idea of being thought a traitor to his lord, but he will not fight either Gawain or Arthur about it. Lancelot's greatness is determined by his service to Arthur, and even when the two meet on the

---

[554] Malory fought on the Yorkist side with the Earl of Warwick in the early 1460s. He appears to have joined the Lancastrians when Warwick did, following a break between Warwick and the king. Malory's grave near Newgate suggests that he died in prison. See Vinaver 6.

[555] Malory 708.

[556] Matthew 358.

[557] Malory 688.

battlefield, Lancelot refuses to strike his lord. Defining the three knightly ideals, Arno Borst describes the "courtly knight," Malory's specialty, as one who "perform[s] purposeless tasks in enchanted forests, not for his own profit, but for the good of King Arthur's chivalric round table."[558] For Malory, loyalty is always the proper motivation. Even in adulterous love, which is not Malory's favorite subject, he is willing to praise a quasi-feudal loyalty between lovers. Of Guinevere, he says, "that whyle she lyved she was a trew lover, and therfor she had a good end."[559]

While his French source uses hagiography in writing the Grail Quest, Malory, in reminding Englishmen of their duties, appropriately uses romance, the only place where the knightly ideal still thrived. Yet, his own representations of knighthood do not show its best days, but the dying chivalry of his own day. The idea that knights should be loyal to the king was by no means an original part of the chivalric ideal, and its currency in the late Middle Ages both responded to and facilitated the rise of the court-centered Renaissance state. The early barons of the ninth century that seized control after the fall of the Carolingian empire "defended their fortresses...against the king" and anyone else who wished to limit their power.[560] The force that transformed this "wild horde of daredevils" into the High Order of Knighthood was not the king, but the Church.[561] When the feudal system did evolve, along with the chivalric code that defined the obligations of the ruling warrior class, European "countries" were far from united under a monarch. Indeed, they did not become completely united under a king until the very late Middle Ages, when the feudal system was giving way to the nation-state. Thus, the knight whose claim to virtue lies in his loyalty to his king (e.g.

---

[558] Borst 150.

[559] Malory 649.

[560] Borst 146-7.

[561] Borst 148. See also Chapter Three of the present work.

Malory's Lancelot) is a feature of chivalry in decline, about to be replaced by new ideals. The connection that developed in the late Middle Ages between knighthood and service to a monarch therefore contributed immeasurably to the creation of the Renaissance gentleman, in whom chivalric loyalties had been completely converted into patriotism.[562]

As shown in Chapter Three, the transition occurred more quickly and easily in England than on the Continent. First of all, the English barony was accustomed to a more centralized political structure. Unlike France, where "the fragmentation of power and the complicated, often conflicting oaths of fealty. . .made administration difficult,"[563] England had a clearer political structure with the king at the top. Established after 1066 under William the Conqueror and his heirs, English feudalism was a much simpler, more logical system than the older ones on the Continent that evolved over centuries. Furthermore, when Henry II outlawed private war among the barons and required that they all swear an oath of fealty to the king, he instituted an effective court system where they could have their grievances resolved without resorting to bloodshed.[564] For this reason, the English barony was always more tranquil than its counterparts on the Continent.

Having never had the autonomy that the French barons enjoyed, English barons lost little in the transition to the centralized state. Furthermore, since their real power had come to depend more on land than on military might, they moved easily into their new role as administrators of land. As such, they welcomed the protection of the courts.[565] Most importantly, since there were fewer noblemen in England than in France, knights who found themselves overburdened by their traditional responsibilities welcomed a growing number of government

---

[562] Ferguson 128.

[563] Crane 7.

[564] Crane 7.

[565] Crane 7.

168

professionals to relieve them of administrative tasks that they could no longer manage. In other words, the state in England had to become larger to fill an administrative gap. Whereas the French barony saw a growing state as usurping their privileges, the English barony saw it as serving their interests.[566] Loyalty to the king easily became a knightly virtue, replacing loyalty to a feudal overlord. Thus, the chivalric ideal in England survived the breakdown of feudalism through "the absorption of feudal loyalties into a rudimentary sense of patriotism."[567]

Thus, Sir Thomas Malory came of age in a country where doing his knightly duty as the sword-arm of the commonwealth was no longer enough. Like other men of his class, he found himself unable to meet his expenses without pursuing careers not previously considered knightly.[568] Most of his peers accordingly abandoned their nobler roles and devoted themselves to making money. Malory himself, rather than go into business, finance, litigation, or politics, may have preferred to make his living by "robbery, theft, and raiding on an extensive scale.[569] His looting of the abbey of Blessed Mary[570] shows not only the decline of knightly behavior, but also the rift between chivalry and the Church that characterizes Malory's age as well as his writing.

His rejection of the dichotomy between heavenly and earthly chivalry bespeaks an ideal that is in the process of secularization. While Malory regarded knighthood as a Christian vocation, he had little use for Galahad's kind of virtue, which "does not in any way affect the fate of the Round Table."[571] Galahad's

---

[566] Crane 7-8.

[567] Ferguson 128.

[568] Ferguson 115.

[569] Jacob 656.

[570] As previously acknowledged, our Sir Thomas Malory may not have been the guilty party. Even if he was not, the perpetrator's knightly title illustrates the point equally well, albeit less ironically.

[571] Moorman 196.

behavior, like that of other saintly figures, is motivated more by the goal of personal spiritual perfection than by helping a political cause. Thus, Winstead's claim that Capgrave's St. Katherine's was "ineffective"[572] in her temporal role could be made more accurately about Galahad. His perfection, though admirable, does no good to the commonwealth,[573] and Malory takes this problem much more seriously than Capgrave. On the other hand, Lancelot, who truly acts as Arthur's sword-arm, is much more important. When Arthur poignantly pleads with the knights of the Round Table not to go on this quest, he forces them to choose between pleasing their king and pleasing God.[574] Their choice, of course, proves as disastrous to the Round Table as Arthur feared it would be. While Malory believes that a knight should behave consistently with Christian morality, he clearly agrees with many of his countrymen who now see the knight's purpose in society as predominantly secular.

B. Malory and His Source

The radical nature of Malory's departure from his original is perhaps not apparent until one looks at the two texts side by side. Malory himself, untroubled by the modern concern for originality, describes his work as "briefly drawn out of French."[575] Nevertheless, as Ihle has effectively shown, Malory's abbreviation of the Old French *Queste* required him to make value judgments about what was most important in his original. What he leaves out is, thus, as revealing as what he changes. Furthermore, Malory makes numerous changes in the story that his

---

[572] Winstead, "Piety, Politics, and Social Commitment" 59-80.

[573] Several critics have noticed this fact about Galahad. For example, Moorman refers to him as "a supernatural object lesson in heavenly chivalry, as a knight whose deeds do not in any way affect the fate of the Round Table" (196).

[574] Malory 522.

[575] Malory 513.

desire to abbreviate does not explain. Sometimes, he adds characters and events, making certain sections even longer than they are in the original. Other changes do not alter the length, but change the message of the original substantially. All of these changes follow discernible patterns, which several recent critics have helped to show, but have not completely explained. Perhaps the most important difference between Malory's version and his source lies in their respective views of the Grail itself.

C. The Holy Grail

The author of the French *Queste* treats the Grail as unknowable, at least by earthly sinful men. The messenger of the hermit Nascien refers to the object of the quest as "que cuers mortex ne porriot penser ne langue d'ome terrien deviser" ["what mortal hearts could never imagine or human tongue describe"].[576] When the Grail makes its first appearance in Arthur's court, covered by a silken cloth, the food that each man most desires appears on his plate. The king observes that everyone present should "avoir grant joie de ce que Nostre Sires nos a mostre si grant signe d'amor au'il de sa grace nos volt repaistre a si halt jor come le jor de la Pentecouste" ["be very happy that our Lord showed us a sign of such great love that he would nourish us with his grace on such a solemn day as Pentecost"].[577] So, the source of Arthur's happiness is not the sight of the Holy Grail, but the proof of God's love in the form of literal nourishment. Neither Arthur nor his knights saw the Grail, and most are incapable of ever seeing it. Gawain compares the event he has just witnessed to a similar event that occurred in the Maimed King's court. On that occasion, as Gawain recalls, "de tant sont il engignie qu'il

---

[576] *La Queste del Saint Graal*, ed. Albert Pauphilet (Paris: Librairie Honore Champion, 1984) 19; Trans. E. Jane Burns, *The Quest for the Holy Grail*, ed. Norris J. Lacy (New York: Garland Publishing, 1995) 8.

[577] *Queste* 16; Trans. Burns 7.

nel porent veoir apertement, ancois lor en fu coverte la vraie semblance" ["the observers were so deceived that they couldn't see the Grail clearly; its true form remained hidden from them"]. [578] The implications for Arthur's court are obvious: the observers there, too, are so blinded by sin that they are incapable of seeing the sacred mysteries which the Grail represents. When Galahad is allowed to look into the Holy Vessel, he sees "ce que langue ne porroit descrire ne cuer penser. Ici voi ge l'a comencaille des granz hardemenz et l'achoison des proeces; ici voi ge les merveilles de totes autres merveilles!" ["what no tongue could describe and no heart could imagine. I see here the source of great deeds and the cause of all prowess. I see mysteries that surpass all other mysteries"].[579] In short, then, the Holy Grail is a mystery, which earthly, sinful men can never fully understand. When the one elect knight gains a clear view of it, he ceases to be a part of this world, and his soul is soon carried away by angels.[580]

Malory, on the other hand, assigns to the Grail the more material function of being the Eucharistic vessel and systematically "transforms the hazy symbols of the French *Queste* into tangible, concrete parts of a real quest."[581] When the Grail appears in Arthur's court, the king urges his knights to thank Jesus Christ for what "he hath shewed us this day at the reverence of this hyghe feste of Pentecost."[582] Here, "showed" clearly refers to the Grail, the tangible vessel itself, rather than the "nourishment" which God provides as a sign of His love. While essentially the same event occurs in both narratives, the author of the *Queste* does not regard the Grail as "shown," i.e. visible, in Arthur's court, whereas Malory does. In both versions, Gawain then embarks upon a quest for

---

[578] *Queste* 16; Trans. Burns 8.

[579] *Queste* 278; Trans. Burns 87.

[580] *Queste* 279.

[581] Moorman 190.

[582] Malory 522.

172

the Holy Grail and vows not to return until he has "seen" it more clearly. However, Malory's Gawain interprets the problem more concretely than the Gawain of the *Queste*. He leaves out the Maimed King altogether and observes that "we myght nat *se* the Holy Grayle: hit was so preciously coverde."[583] Thus, those present were unable to *see* the Grail, not because they were incapable of seeing it, but because it was "covered." This distinction, of course, raises the possibility of the Grail's being uncovered for those who prove worthy.

In Malory's Grail Quest, Galahad's final triumph differs from its source in ways that Malory's desire for brevity does not explain. First of all, Malory has Christ himself emerge from the vessel with his wounds still bleeding. He brings the Grail to Galahad, asking, "Sonne, wotyst thou what I holde betweyxte my hondis?"[584] Galahad answers, "Nay...but if you telle me." Christ answers, "Thys ys...the holy dysshe wherein I ete the lambe on Estir Day."[585] At that point, Galahad is allowed to gaze into the Grail and thereby fulfill his greatest wish. In the French *Queste*, Christ does show the Grail to Galahad, but he complicates its meaning, thus: "Ce est, fet il, l'escuele ou Jhesucriz menja l'aignel le jor Pasques o ses deciples. Ce est l'escuele qui a servi a gre toz cax que j'ai trovez en mon servise; ce est l'escuele qu onques hons mescreanz ne vit a qui ele ne grevast molt" ["It is the platter from which Jesus Christ ate the lamb with his disciples on Easter. And it is the platter that has generously fed all those in My service. It is the platter that no faithless man has beheld without suffering for it"].[586] Galahad is not allowed, at this point, to gaze into it. He does so only when he receives it later, not from Christ, but from Joseph of Arimathea. In both versions, Galahad looks into the Grail, sees its secrets, trembles violently, and begs for death.

[583] Malory 522.

[584] Malory 603.

[585] Malory 603.

[586] *Queste* 270; Trans. Burns 85.

However, in the *Queste*, he claims to see "ce que langue ne porroit descrire ne cuer penser" ["That which no tongue could describe and no heart could imagine"].[587] While Malory accurately translates "espiritex choses"[588] as "spirituall thynges,"[589] he omits the statement that these things are indescribable. Again, Malory removes abstraction wherever possible and systematically deletes "references to the Grail wherein its nature is not clearly defined, or at least not presented as readily accessible to human understanding."[590]

By simplifying the Grail's meaning, Malory changes the nature of the quest. Malory's Grail Quest is not about "the search for the great mysteries that the Almighty will reveal openly to the special knight he has chosen from among all others to be his servant,"[591] as the *Queste* is. Rather, it is about "how earthly knights, with the Christian vocation that knighthood implies, ought to act to be worthy of seeing the Eucharist unveiled in this world."[592] Thus, the *Queste* is about the Holy Grail in a much more direct sense than Malory's Grail Quest, which is mostly about the knights themselves. In the *Quest*, the responses of different knights to the Grail reveal "various aspects of the Grail's meaning."[593] The knights are there to reveal the qualities of the Grail, and not the other way about.

D. Heavenly and Earthly Chivalry

---

[587] *Queste* 278; Trans. Burns 87.

[588] *Queste* 278.

[589] Malory 606.

[590] Ihle 45.

[591] Ihle 8.

[592] Ihle 113.

[593] Ihle 110.

174

The *Queste* author draws a careful distinction between heavenly and earthly chivalry—a distinction Sir Meliant learns the hard way when he insists on accompanying Galahad through the forest. After traveling together for a week or so, they encounter a fork in the road, marked by a wooden cross. Inscribed in the wood is this message: "OZ TU, CHEVALIERS QUI VAS AVENTURES QUERANT, VOIZ CI DEUS VOIES, L'UNE A DESTRE ET L'AUTRE A SENESTRE. CELE A SENESTRE TE DEFENT JE QUE TU N'I ENTRES, CAR TROP COVIENT ESTRE PREUDOME CELUI QUI I ENTRE SE IL EN VELT ISSIR; ET SE TU EN CELE A DESTRE ENTRES, TOST I PORRAS PERIR" ["To the knight who seeks adventure, you find here two paths—one to the right, the other to the left. I forbid you to take the left path. Only a very worthy man can enter there and escape alive. If you take the path to the right, death awaits you"].[594] Faced with a choice between a forbidden path on the left and death on the right, Meliant chooses the left path, wishing "esprover ma force et conoistre s'il avra ja en moi proesce ne hardement par quoi je doie avoir los de chevalerie" ["to test my strength and discover whether I have sufficient prowess and bravery to become known as a praiseworthy knight"].[595] Meliant encounters, among other things, an evil knight who nearly kills him before Galahad comes to his rescue. Meliant has clearly failed the test of worthiness, and the monk who heals his wounds explains why: "li escriz parloit de la chevalerie celestiel, et tu entendoies de la seculer, par coi tu entras en orgueil; et por ce chais tu en pechie mortel" ["the inscription spoke of celestial knighthood, and you understood it in a secular sense. This is how you fell into pride and mortal sin"].[596] In other words, Meliant interpreted "worthiness" as "prowess and bravery," the essential elements of earthly chivalry. He failed to realize that the requirements for *chevalerie*

---

[594] *Queste* 41; Trans. Burns 15.

[595] *Queste* 41; Trans. Burns 15.

[596] *Queste* 45; Trans Burns 16.

celestiel are different; therefore, he fell into pride and mortal sin. Meliant did make a confession before he was knighted, but the devil, seeing this, was "dolenz et pensa que il wos corroit sus, si tost come it verroit son point" ["sorely disappointed and decided to attack [him] at the first opportunity"].[597] He therefore tempted Meliant to choose a route where "n'estoit si fondez en l'amor Jhesucrist que por aventure ne peust chaoir en pechie" ["only a knight sufficiently well grounded in Jesus Christ's love could avoid falling, by mishap, into sin"].[598] Here, Meliant is in an impossible situation. He acts virtuously by confessing, but his virtue provokes the devil to attack him and lead him into a temptation that is beyond his ability to resist. In other words, Meliant cannot succeed in this quest no matter what he does. He seems to be, somehow, the wrong person, not the elect knight that God has chosen to succeed.

For Malory, on the other hand, success in this quest is theoretically possible for any worthy knight. As Brewer observes, Malory sees "no essential incompatibility between the values of Christianity and those of the High Order of Knighthood."[599] Since knighthood is a Christian vocation, Christian conduct is an essential part of knightly conduct. Malory frequently acts on this assumption when he abbreviates his source. For example, at the end of the Castle of Maidens episode, the hermit in the French *Queste* tells Gawain that he was inducted into the order of knighthood "por ce qu vos servissiez a nostre criator et defendissiez Sainte Eglise et rendissiez a Dieu le tresor que il vos bailla a garder, ce est l'ame de vos" ["to serve our Creator, to defend Holy Church, and to return to God the treasure that he entrusted to your protection: your soul"].[600] Malory, showing "the characteristic English tendency to turn other-worldly and ascetic religion into

---

[597] *Queste* 45; Trans. Burns 16.

[598] *Queste* 45; Trans. Burns 16.

[599] Brewer 58.

[600] *Queste* 54; Trans. Burns 19.

this-worldly morality,"[601] abbreviates this list into "knyghtly dedys and vertuous lyvyng."[602] Apparently, for Malory, "knyghtly dedys" covers a lot of ground that has nothing to do with warfare. Malory also interprets Gawain's refusal to do penance differently from his source. In the *Queste*, Gawain "dist que de pinitance fere ne porroit il la piene soffrir" ["replied that he could not bear the burden of doing penance"].[603] In Malory, Gawain makes the curious objection that "I may do no penaunce, for we knyghtes adventures many tymes suffir grete woo and payne."[604] Of course, Gawain is wrong in both versions.[605] Malory is far from accepting Gawain's excuse that, as a knight, he suffers enough and is therefore exempt from penance. However, instead of simply lacking the fortitude to do penance, Malory's Gawain misunderstands (perhaps willfully) the meaning of knighthood as a Christian vocation. Thus, his "sins are against the ideal knightly code,"[606] including Christian morality. Since being a good Christian is, for Malory, an essential part of being a good knight, success in any knightly enterprise will demand the same combination of "knyghtly dedys and vertuous lyvyng." Thus, being the most chivalrous knight in the quest for the Holy Grail means the same thing as it does when Arthur outlines the code of conduct he expects from his knights:

> never to do outerage nothir mourthir, and allwayes to fle treson, and to gyff mercy unto hym that askith mercy, uppon payne of forfiture [of their] worship and lordship of kynge Arthure for

---

[601] Brewer 58.

[602] Malory 535.

[603] *Queste* 55; Trans. Burns 19.

[604] Malory 535.

[605] One can profitably contrast Gawain's refusal with Lancelot's willingness to do penance. See Atkinson 138.

[606] Moorman 190.

evirmore; and allwayes to do ladyes, damesels, and jantilwomen and wydowes [socour:] strengthe hem in hir ryghtes, and never to enforce them, upon payne of dethe. Also, that no man take no batayles in a wrongefull quarell for no love ne for no worldis goodis."[607]

Naturally, then, Malory interprets Meliant's failure far differently from his source. In his telling, the inscription on the cross reads: "NOW YE KNYGHTES ARRAUNTE WHICH GOTH TO SEKE KNYGHTES ADVENTURYS, SEE HERE TWO WAYES; THAT ONE WAY DEFENDITH THE THAT THOU NE GO THAT WAY, FOR HE SHALL NOT GO OUTE OF THE WAY AGAYNE BUT IF HE BE A GOOD MAN AND A WORTHY KNYGHT. AND IF THOU GO ON THE LYFTE HONDE THOU SHALL NAT THERE LYGHTLY WYNNE PROUESSE, FOR THOU SHALT IN THYS WAY BE SONE ASSAYDE."[608] Here, both roads appear difficult, but possible for "a good man and a worthy knight," whereas in the French *Queste*, the right path meant death. Malory's monk does draw a distinction between two kinds of knightly deeds, but they are "knyghtly dedys in Goddys workys" and "knytes dedys in worldly workis,"[609] as opposed to the *chevalerie terriene* and *chevalerie celestiale* of the source. In Malory's Grail Quest, the two arenas do not require two different codes of conduct. When Meliant takes the golden crown, he sins "in covetyse and in theffte. . .All this," says the monk, "was no knyghtly dedys."[610] Clearly, Malory's concept of knightly deeds includes good Christian conduct as well as prowess and bravery. Thus, for Malory, "to do 'knyghtly dedys in Goddys

---

[607] Malory 75; The keeping of this oath proves not only difficult, but also charged with contradiction when Sir Pedyvere cuts off his wife's head and then begs the incensed Sir Lancelot for mercy (See Malory 171). Lancelot handles the situation as befits the "best knyght of the worlde," i.e. he finds a way to support the rights of the lady while still giving mercy to the knight who asks it. For a detailed discussion of chivalry in the *Morte*, see Tucker 64-103.

[608] Malory 529.

[609] Malory 531.

178

workys' appears to be synonymous with knightly behavior according to the chivalric code."[611]

Since this code is possible for any good knight to follow, the requirements for success in this adventure are much more reasonable in Malory than in his source. Ironically, most of the knights still fail, despite these more reasonable demands. Again, Meliant takes the left path and is wounded by an evil knight. When the monk explains why, he marvels, "how ye durste take uppon you so rych a thynge as the hyghe Order of Knyghthode ys withoute clene confession. That was the cause that ye were bittirly wounded."[612] So, in this version, unlike the French source, the devil tempts Meliant because he did not confess before he was knighted. Making a proper confession would have shielded Meliant from the Devil's machinations, instead of provoking them, as in the original *Queste*. The monk describes Meliant's joining the quest as "presumption," not because Meliant is ill-equipped for success, but because the Quest "may nat be echeved but by vertuous lyvynge."[613] For Malory, the quest for the Holy Grail is not fundamentally different from any other quest. It is simply the highest quest, with the greatest reward. Knights such as Meliant fail because of their "failure to maintain normal Christian morality,"[614] not because their brand of chivalry is inadequate for the task.

E. Predestination

One reason for this difference is that the French *Queste* contains a strong

---

[610] Malory 531.

[611] Ihle 129.

[612] Malory 531.

[613] Malory 531.

[614] Brewer 58.

element of predestination, which Malory systematically removes. The hermit Nascien sends a messenger to warn all knights preparing for the quest that "nus en ceste Queste ne maint dame ne damoisele qu'il ne chiee en pechie mortel" ["anyone taking a lady or young lady along on the Quest will fall into mortal sin"].[615] Indeed, on a religious quest, where avoiding sin is essential to success, bringing one's sweetheart would be a great mistake. Since yielding to lust for one's wife is, in the medieval view, no less a mortal sin than lust for any other woman, the prohibition of all women is easy to understand. Yet, the avoidance of sin does not seem to be the only reason that knights must leave their ladies at home. He explains that this quest is different from others in that "n'est mie queste de terriennes choses, ainz doit estre li encerchemenz de grans secrez et de privetez Nostre Seignor et des grans repostailles que lit Hauz Mestres mostrera apertement au boneure chevalier qu'il a esleu a son serjant entre les autres chevaliers terriens" ["This is not a quest for earthly goods. Rather, it should be understood as the search for the great secrets of Our Lord and the great mysteries that the Almighty will reveal openly to the special knight he has chosen from among all others to be his servant"].[616] Apparently, the search for the Grail, like the search for salvation, is a lonely business in which sweethearts are less a temptation than a distraction. Yet, success or failure in it seems already to be a foregone conclusion. The one knight, already chosen by God, will succeed, and all the others will fail.

Moreover, the identity of the chosen knight is hardly a mystery. Galahad has just earned the title of "mieldres chevaliers del monde" ["World's best knight"][617] by removing the sword from the stone and sitting in the Perilous Seat. The other knights at the Round Table honor him because "bien pensent que ce soit cil par cui les merveilles dou Saint Graal doivent faillir, et bien lou sonoissent par

[615] *Queste* 19; Trans. Burns 8.

[616] *Queste* 19; Trans. Burns 8.

[617] *Queste* 5; Trans. Burns 4.

l'esprueve del Siege, ou onques hom ne s'estoit assis a cui il n'en fust mescheu, ne mes a cestui" ["they felt sure he was the one destined to put an end to the adventures of the Holy Grail. They knew this because of the trial of the Seat, which no one had occupied previously without misfortune befalling him"].[618] After the knights depart together on the quest, Galahad receives a shield predestined for him. The white knight, in telling the story of the shield, emphasizes the great harm that "avenues as chevaliers pleins de fol hardement qui sor cestui deffens en voloient porter l'escu qui a nului n'esoit otroiez fors a vos" ["befell those foolishly audacious knights who, despite fair warning, tried to wear the shield destined only for you"].[619] Galahad's next project is to banish the devil from a cemetery, where he has been so frightening sinners with his "voiz horrible et spoantable que il en perdoient le pooir del cors" ["horrible and terrifying voice that they lose all bodily control"].[620] The devil becomes powerless in the face of Galahad's purity and flees. Afterwards, the monk explains that "li pecheor n'I fussent toz jors entrepris, se Diex ne vos I eust amene por la mener a chief" ["the sinners would have remained captive to this day if God had not sent you to deliver them"].[621] Once again, Galahad easily accomplishes something that has been deadly for everyone else who has tried it. The reason for his success is always the same: God intended the sword, the shield, or the victory only for him. Thus, there is no doubt who the special knight God has chosen from among all others must be. The only wonder is that the other knights begin the quest at all, given that they know the outcome. They must all be, like Meliant, presumptuous.

This is a major difference between Malory's version and his French source. For Malory, success in this quest is theoretically possible for all the

---

[618] *Queste* 9; Trans. Burns 5.

[619] *Queste* 35; Trans. Burns 13.

[620] *Queste* 39; Trans. Burns 14.

[621] *Queste* 39; Trans. Burns 14.

knights who undertake it. When Nacien's messenger admonishes them not to
"lede lady nother jantillwoman" on the quest with them, he explains that "hy that
ys nat clene of hys synnes he shall nat se the mysteryes of oure Lorde Jesu
Cryste."[622] Here, too, a knight who brings his sweetheart with him will certainly
fall into sin, and only those who are free of sin will succeed on this quest. At this
point, Malory cuts the message short. He omits the difference between this quest
and all others—for Malory, there is no difference, at least not a fundamental one.
He also omits the part about the knight God has chosen.

Throughout his "translation," Malory consistently removes references to a
predestined outcome of the Quest. While the shield is still intended for Galahad,
Malory does not dwell on the sufferings of those others who were so foolishly
audacious as to try to carry it. The white knight simply quotes Joseph of
Arimathea, claiming that those who try to bear the shield before the coming of
Galahad "shall repente hit,"[623] and he omits the final warning.[624]

The scene where Galahad drives the devil from the cemetery is in Malory
as well, but greatly shortened. Here, again, Malory makes a change that has
nothing to do with abbreviation. When the monk explains the significance of the
event, he implies that Galahad's coming is symbolic of Christ's coming to rescue
sinners from the devil:

> Sir, that that coverde the body, hit betokenyth the duras of the
> worlde, and the grete synne that oure Lorde founde in the worlde.
> For there was suche wrecchydnesse that the fadir loved nat the
> sonne, nother the sonne loved nat the fadir. And that was one of
> the causys that oure Lorde toke fleysh and floode of a clene
> maydyn; for oure synnes were so grete at that tyme that well-nyghe

[622] Malory 523.

[623] Malory 527.

[624] Ihle 112.

all was wyckednesse.[625]

Here, Malory departs from his usual method of abbreviation, which is to remove the exegetical interpretations from each episode.[626] In this case, he retains the anagogical meaning, omitting the more immediate reason for Galahad's seemingly accidental appearance, i.e. his being sent by God to free those sinners from the devil. Some things, such as the sword, are clearly destined for Galahad and no one else, but observers do not conclude, as they do in the *Queste*, that he is therefore the only one chosen to succeed. Therefore, the admonition to leave the ladies at home makes much more sense in Malory than in his source. While the chance that Galahad will remain free of sin is greater than, for example, the chance that Gawain will do so, each knight has the ability to succeed. While perfection in action and understanding might be out of the reach of most of Arthur's knights, "knyghtly dedys and vertuous lyvyng" are not.

F. Galahad

This altered standard for success on the Grail Quest shows a fundamental difference between Malory's definition of ideal conduct and that of his source. The *Queste* has many of the elements of a saint's life and, despite the Arthurian context, asks to be treated as one. Aside from being a fictional character, Galahad fills all the requirements for sainthood.[627] The devil, as we see in the graveyard

---

[625] Malory 528.

[626] The author of the *Queste* often explains an episode two or more times. The second time, he has a holy person explain its allegorical significance, etc. Malory usually eliminates this "repetition" by retaining only the literal meaning of events or objects. The best example is the Grail itself, for which Malory gives only its literal meaning, as the Eucharistic vessel. As shown above, his elimination of other meanings not only shortens his story, but also substantially changes the meaning of the quest. For an analysis of Malory's abbreviation, see Ihle 110-160.

[627] In a sense, even fictionality has not always been a drawback. As noted in Chapter Two, above, the Church has removed St. Katherine's November 25 feast from the calendar due to a lack of historical evidence. However, controversy about the real existence of some officially canonized saints is a subject for another analysis.

episode, has no power over him and begs him to leave, calling him "serjant Jhesucrist" and "Sainte chose" ["holy thing"].[628] The monk who interprets the adventure explains that the devil, "qui vos savoit a virge et a net de toz pechiez si come hons terriens puet estre, n'osa atendre vostre compaignie, ainz s'en ala et perdi tot son pooir par vostre venue" ["who knew you to be a virgin and as free of sin as an earthly man can be, became powerless and fled"].[629] The same monk goes so far as to "vostre venue comparer pres a la venue Jhesucrist, de semblance ne mie de hautece" ["compare [Galahad's] coming to the coming of Jesus Christ, in form if not in significance"].[630] Apparently, the holy men of this place have waited many years for Galahad to arrive drive out the devil. When he performs this task, his first act is thank God, whom, of course, he credits for all his victories.

Being a soldier of Christ, Galahad does not fight for personal glory or bloodlust, and he wins his battles with as little bloodshed as possible. For example, when he saves Meliant from the evil knight, "Galaad ne l'enchauce plus, come cil qui n'a talent de fere lui plus de mal que il a eu" ["Galahad did not pursue his opponent, since he had no desire to harm him further"].[631] Instead, he attends to the injured Meliant, "et ne resgarde plus le chevalier qu'il avoit abatu" ["without a glance in the direction of the defeated knight"].[632] Afterwards, the "moine ancien, qui chevaliers avoit este" ["elderly monk who had once been a knight"] explains to Meliant that God "envoia il Galaad, cest saint chevalier, as deus chevaliers qui senefioient les deus pechiez qui en toi estoinet herbergie, et n'i porent durer por ce que il estoit sanz pechie mortel" ["sent Galahad, the holy

---

[628] *Queste* 36.

[629] *Queste* 39; Trans. Burns 14.

[630] *Queste* 38; Trans. Burns 14.

[631] *Queste* 43; Trans. Burns 16.

[632] *Queste* 43; Trans. Burns 16.

knight, to fight the two knights who represented the sins lodged within you. They could not resist him, since he was free of sin"].[633]   Unlike Meliant, Galahad understands the difference between *chevalerie terriene* and *chevalerie celestiel* is therefore able to take either the right or the left path without falling into temptation. In the religious literature of the Middle Ages, only one kind of person is free of sin and immune from the power of the devil: a soldier of Christ, i.e. a saint.[634] Galahad also performs miracles, as saints also do, not only by defeating numerous opponents at the same time, but also by healing the wounds of King Mordrain and making the waters of the fountain in the Perilous Forest cease to boil.[635]

The true mark of a saint is, of course, a miracle after his death. As soon as Galahad's prayer for death is answered, Perceval and Bors see a hand reach down from above, seize the Grail and the Lance "et l'enporta tot amont vers le ciel" ["and carried them both up to heaven"].[636] The Grail has obviously served its purpose, and no one on earth sees it again.

Certainly, Galahad's attitude toward death is saintly. While Galahad, Perceval, and Bors are aboard the ship with the Holy Grail, Perceval is astonished to hear Galahad praying that "de quelle hore qu'il Li requeist le trespassement de cest siecle, qu'Il li envoiast" ["Our Lord to allow him to leave this world at the moment he might request it"].[637] Eventually, a voice from heaven answers, "Ne t'esmaier, Galaad, car Nostre Sires fera ta volente de ce que tu requiers: de quelle hore que tu demanderas la mort del cors, tu l'avras et recevras la vie de l'ame et la joie pardurable" ["Do not worry, Galahad; Our Lord will grant your request.

---

[633] *Queste* 46; Trans. Burns 16.

[634] For a fuller discussion of sainthood, see Chapter One.

[635] *Queste* 263.

[636] *Queste* 279; Trans. Burns 87.

[637] *Queste* 273; Trans. Burns 86.

Whenever you ask for bodily death, you will receive the life of the soul and eternal joy"].[638] While the villains of the saints' lives can never kill their victims until God decides they should, the saints themselves greet death joyfully and often pray for it. In this respect, St. Perpetua, dreaming about her "victory," is typical, as is St. Katherine, stretching out her neck for the executioner. Like Katherine, Galahad actually decides when he will die, and he cannot be killed before then. Recall that, when the Emperor tries to execute Katherine on her Wheel, God sends an angel to smash it, in answer to her prayer. Yet, in the final beheading scene, she hears her bridegroom calling and wishes to go. Galahad also is a sinless virgin who has seen the secrets of heaven and has no reason to cling to the earth. After gazing into the Grail, he makes his request for death and says goodbye to his companions. After his "saintly death,"[639] Galahad bypasses purgatory and goes straight to heaven.

The similarities between Galahad and actual saints are too pointed to be coincidental. If the French *Queste* is "a romance of chivalry, firmly set in the *Lancelot-Grail* cycle of which it is a part,"[640] it differs sharply from contemporary Middle English chivalric romances.[641] In fact, it differs most from the sub-genre to which it appears to belong. "Hagiographic" or "exemplary" romance, as established in Chapter One, explicitly argues for the compatibility of earthly and spiritual success. Yet, in the *Queste*, *chevalerie celestiel* and *chevalerie terriene* are two different paths, and being a perfect knight, a saintly knight, removes Galahad from practicing *chevalerie terriene*. Thus, the achievement of perfection in knighthood, ironically, will mean a loss for knighthood. Arthur, knowing that he will lose many of his best knights to the ultimate quest, wishes to keep them

---

[638] *Queste* 274; Trans. Burns 86.

[639] Ihle 76.

[640] Ihle 54.

[641] For a description of these, see Chapter One.

from leaving. However, they have already sworn an oath and cannot renounce the quest, even to please him.[642] Thus, the *Queste* explores conflicts not only between chivalry and holiness, but also within the High Order of Knighthood, between one's duty to God and to one's king.

Such conflicts had long characterized French romances. In this respect, the French *Queste* has much in common with the romances of Chrétien de Troyes, whose knights are constantly having to choose between two chivalric duties, such as keeping an oath and rescuing a maiden (Yvain) or serving the queen without betraying the king (Lancelot). English romances, as shown in chapter one, remain relatively free of such conflicts until *Sir Gawain and the Green Knight*, whose complexity tempts one to say that English romance was simply maturing. Yet, late in the fifteenth century, Malory's works, which are far from simple or immature, deny the existence of conflicting obligations within the chivalric ideal. He differs from his Middle English predecessors in that he acknowledges the possibility of such conflict sufficiently to argue against it. His Lancelot must walk a fine line among duties to his God, to his king, and to his lady, and sometimes, of course, he fails to make the right choices. However, for Malory, he fails because he is "unstable" and cannot always order his feelings in accordance with proper knightly conduct. For example, even on the Grail Quest, he cannot stop thinking of Guinevere. Thus, he fails because he is not perfect, not because the ideal for which he strives contains irreconcilable conflicts. Malory does not agree with his source that these are part of the knightly code, and he consistently removes them from the French work he is "translating."

First of all, he removes Galahad's sainthood. I cannot agree with Moorman's claim that "Malory regularly elevates and dehumanizes Galahad."[643] Kraemer, who recognizes the saint-like qualities in the most successful grail knight, describes Malory's Galahad without reference to the source:

---

[642] *Queste* 22.

[643] Moorman 196.

Even taking into account the almost magical nature of the Grail quest world, Galahad is fully realized from start to finish, is never stretched either morally or physically, and thus always presents to a reader the face of a saintly being whose human needs and desires rarely suface. Using the three key generic attributes of saints in fifteenth-century hagiographies identified earlier, Malory shows us a knight at once Heaven-bound but personally distant.[644]

However, as shown above, Galahad's saintly qualities are not created by Malory, but firmly established in the *Queste*. In fact, the changes Malory makes have the consistent effect of rendering Galahad less saintly and more human. Though Malory's Galahad is no less virtuous, he is a much less exalted figure, more subject to human passions and more affectionate towards his father.

Malory's decision not to make him a saint becomes obvious as early as the graveyard scene. When the Devil calls Galahad "serjant Jhesucrist," Malory, as a translator, had a choice. The Old French *serjant* could mean either *soldier* or *servant*.[645] Although Galahad is a knight, presumably a professional soldier, Malory translates the phrase as "servaunte of Jesu Crist,"[646] a distinction to which any Christian may aspire, and leaves out "sainte chose" altogether. By making Galahad a "servant" rather than a "soldier of Christ," Malory deftly avoids a term synonymous with sainthood. After Galahad drives out the devil, the monk explains what the event "betokenyth" without directly comparing the coming of Galahad to the coming of Christ. Malory also omits the literal explanation, that the devil became powerless and fled, because of Galahad's purity. While Malory must remove some things in the interest of abbreviation, his decision here to keep the symbolic explanation at the expense of the literal is a departure from his usual practice. In effect, Malory has removed from this scene the exaltation of Galahad

---

[644] Kraemer 70.

[645] *A Medieval French Reader*, ed. C.W. Aspland (Oxford: Clarendon Press, 1979) 408.

[646] Malory 528.

188

to quasi-sanctity.

He does the same soon afterward with Galahad's rescue of Meliant. In Malory, as in his source, Galahad stabs the first attacker through the shoulder, knocking him off his horse, but breaking his own lance. However, when the second attacker appears, Malory has Galahad cut off his whole arm, rather than just his hand, as he does in the *Queste*. More importantly, after he does so, Malory says the evil knight "fledde and sir Galahad sewed faste aftir hym."[647] This renders Galahad more gratuitously violent, and therefore less saintly, than he is in the *Queste*. Since the *Queste* author makes such a point of Galahad's not even looking in the direction of the defeated knight, let alone chasing him, Malory has clearly made a decision, the effect of which is to make Galahad virtuous in terms of the High Order of Knighthood, while falling short of the ideal of *chevalerie celestiel*. While both demand good Christian conduct, Malory's view of "knightly deeds" includes showing the kind of physical prowess that Galahad shows against Meliant's attacker. A soldier of Christ, on the other hand, would be concerned only with avoiding further bloodshed and would not care at all about gaining what Malory approvingly calls "worship." By de-sanctifying Galahad, Malory turns the story of the Grail Quest from quasi-hagiography to romance. Once again, we should remember that "hagiographic romances" such as Malory's Grail Quest are actually further from real hagiography than other chivalric romances because they specifically oppose the otherworldly values promoted in religious literature. Malory presents his Grail Quest as a translation of a religious text, but the resulting story valorizes the chivalric code at the expense of the Christian ideal. Thus, Malory quarrels with, and ultimately transforms, his source.

Accordingly, Malory consistently expresses his praise of Galahad in terms of ordinary Christian morality, not *chevalerie celestiel*. When his monk interprets

[647] Malory 530.

Meliant's adventure, he translates "saint chevalier" as "holy knyght."[648] This is a reasonable translation, and Burns adopts it as well. However, the word *saint* in Old French is a stronger word than the modern English *holy*. *Saintly* would be at least as accurate, but Malory chooses the milder word. Once again, where his source elevates Galahad to something resembling sainthood, Malory reduces him to simply an exemplary Christian.

Malory's King Mordrain wishes to die in Galahad's arms, as he does in the French *Queste*, but in Malory's rendering, the virginal knight does not perform the saintly miracle of healing his wounds. Kraemer says that "Malory puts Galahad at the center of two major miracles, one involving his earthly tasks—his arming for the coming battles—and the second involving his heavenly one—the possession of the Grail."[649] However, once again, the miracles are already present in the *Queste*. Malory's changes, if anything, reduce their impact. While the hand does come down from heaven after Galahad's death and seize the Grail, the event has less significance for Malory. It brings the quest to a decisive end, but Malory does not connect it with Galahad's death as explicitly as the French *Queste* author does. Instead of seeing the hand "Si tost come Galaad fu deviez avint illuec" ["at the moment of Galahad's death"],[650] Perceval and Bors see the hand at the same time as they see angels bearing Galahad's soul to heaven. Thus, the taking of the Grail does not constitute, for Malory, a miracle *following* a saint's death. Instead, both the death and the simultaneous taking of the Grail signify the end of the quest.

Malory also adds a line to Galahad's leave-taking. In the French *Queste*, he tells Bors to "saluez moi monseignor Lancelot mon pere si tos come vos le verroiz" ["give my greetings to Sir Lancelot, my father, when you see him"].[651]

---

[648] Malory 531.

[649] Kraemer 77.

[650] *Queste* 279; Trans. Burns 87.

[651] *Queste* 278; Trans. Burns 87.

Malory has him say, "salew me unto my lorde sir Launcelot, my fadir, and as sone as ye se hym bydde him remembir of this worlde unstable." Malory's Galahad can give advice that his predestined-for-sanctity counterpart of the *Queste* cannot give because the nature and source of his success are much more accessible to other good knights, especially Lancelot, whose worthiness is second only to Galahad's. Moreover, the words about reminding his father of the world's instability make Galahad (in Malory) more humanly capable of recognizing that the world can provide its destabilizing temptations and distractions. The French Galahad, knowing nothing of temptation, would have no reason to recognize this fact.

Galahad certainly sees Lancelot as worthy, and his filial affection is much stronger in Malory's version than in the *Queste*. When the two meet on the ship and Lancelot identifies himself, Galahad kneels and asks his blessing.[652] This gesture of high regard is entirely Malory's invention and serves to render Galahad less "personally distant" than he is in the *Queste*.[653] Then, after half a year, when father and son must part, Malory's Lancelot says, "I pray to the Hyghe Fadir, conserve me and you bothe." To this, Galahad responds, "no prayer avaylith so much as yours."[654] In the *Queste*, when Lancelot takes his leave, sobbing, he begs Galahad, to "prie le Haut Mestre por moi, qu'il ne me lest partir de son servise, mes en tel maniere me gar que je soie ses serjanz terriens et esperitiex" ["implore the almighty on my behalf not to abandon me, but to keep me in His service as His earthly and spiritual soldier"].[655] Lancelot seems to feel unable to pray for himself, and asks the help of his virtuous son. Galahad answers, "nule proiere n'I

---

[652] Malory 594.

[653] Atkinson also makes this observation. For additional analysis of the Lancelot-Galahad relationship in Malory, as compared to his source, see Atkinson 142-4.

[654] Malory 595. Atkinson (143) points out that Lancelot's offer to pray for Galahad increases the respect due Lancelot and alters the meaning of Galahad's reply.

[655] *Queste* 252; Trans. Burns 79.

vaut autant come la vostre. Et por ce vos soveigne de vos" ["No prayer will carry as much weight as your own. So think about yourself"].[656] Here, instead of praising his father, Galahad admonishes him, reminding him that salvation is a lonely business, and no one can help except oneself. Malory's Galahad implies almost the opposite: not only can one man's prayers help another, but Lancelot's prayers may actually help Galahad, who in the French *Queste* does not seem to need such help, as he is, like a saint, sinless. Clearly, for Malory, the "best knyght of the worlde" (Galahad) and the best "of ony synfull man of the worlde" (Lancelot) are much nearer to equality than they are in the *Queste*.

G. Lancelot

To make them so, Malory must elevate Lancelot at the same time he diminishes Galahad, a task he executes with enthusiasm. For Malory, as well as for most readers, "Lancelot is the most interesting character."[657] Unlike Gawain, who is clearly a failure, or Galahad, who is clearly a success, Lancelot's achievement is open to interpretation. Thus, how charitably an author judges Lancelot reveals much about how he sees the whole nature of the quest. Especially in the context of "the hoole booke of Kyng Arthur," as the "finest knight the Round Table has to offer...Lancelot is Malory's hero."[658] He remains so even in the Quest, where, by the logic of the plot, the hero ought to be Galahad. By this, I do not mean to say that Malory tries to make Lancelot a better man or even a better knight than Galahad. I do mean to say that Lancelot's struggle for salvation is the focal point of Malory's narrative and that his success is important

---

[656] *Queste* 252; Trans. Burns 79.

[657] Brewer 58. Mahoney (118) also points out that Lancelot is the focus of most scholarly discussion on the Grail Quest. This, as Mahoney also notes, is because one's reading of the *Queste* or of Malory's *Sankgreal* is largely determined by how one sees its treatment of Lancelot.

[658] Moorman 191.

192

to Malory. For him, Lancelot represents the best that the High Order of Knighthood has ever produced, and as a defender of that Order, he vigorously defends Lancelot.

Malory's first clear attempt to make Lancelot more appealing occurs at the beginning of the *Tale of the Sankgreal*, when Galahad pulls the sword out of the stone. Almost immediately, a lady approaches on a white horse and asks for Sir Lancelot. When he answers, she begins weeping about his change of "luck" and explains that, since the coming of Galahad, Lancelot can no longer consider himself the world's best knight. In the French *Queste*, Lancelot "dist qu'il nel cuidera ja mes, car ceste aventure l'en a mis tot fors del cuidier" ["answered that he would never make that mistake, because this adventure had convinced him otherwise"].[659] This answer is meek and proper enough, but Malory increases its appeal by quoting Lancelot directly: "'As towchyng unto that,' seyde sir Launcelot, 'I know well I was never none of the beste.'"[660] The modesty of this answer draws a protest from the lady: "Yes...that were ye, and ar yet, of ony synfull man of the worlde."[661] This exchange is actually longer in Malory's "abbreviated" version than in the source, and it arouses more sympathy for Lancelot than the *Queste* author would have wished to do.

Atkinson sees this change as referring to the new spiritual ideal of *chevalerie celestiel*, which Lancelot admits he fails to meet. In this reading, "the best" does not refer "to prowess or to chivalric courtesy, in both of which his excellence is established."[662] However, Atkinson's reading cannot be entirely corrrect because the maiden insists that he was the best and still is, "of ony synfull man," which is to say any man except the saintly Galahad. Therefore, the lady

---

[659] *Queste* 13; Trans. Burns 7.

[660] Malory 520.

[661] Malory 520.

[662] Atkinson 132.

says, "there ys now *one* bettir than ye be."[663] While Lancelot may be second in prowess to Galahad, he is far from second in the spiritual arena. Atkinson himself quotes the old man at Pelles' castle as saying "in this spyrytuall maters he shalle have many hys bettyrs"[664] In fact, on the Grail Quest, we learn that Percival and Bors, as well as Galahad, are Lancelot's spiritual superiors. Thus, Malory's system, by which Galahad ranks first and Lancelot second, must include physical prowess and knightly courtesy, as well as holiness. If it did not, Lancelot would have to acknowledge more than one superior. Therefore, Malory appears to be measuring his knights by a single standard, which includes both earthly and spiritual greatness. By this standard, Lancelot, with his prowess, his courtesy, his humility, and his willingness to accept penance, may even be a close second to his saintly son.

By contrast, in the French *Queste*, the finest that the Round Table has to offer is far from being good enough. Although the Lancelot of this version sees the Grail in Corbenic Castle, he agrees with the people around him that he has failed in the quest. When he awakens from his trance, he exclaims, "Ha! Diex, por quoi m'avez vos si tost esveillie? Tant je estoie ore plus aeise que je ne sere hui mes! Ha, biax peres Jhescriz, qui porroit estre tant bons eurez ne tant preudons que il veist apertement les granz merveilles de vos secrez, et la ou mes regarz pechierres et ma veue conchiee de la tres grant ordure dou monde fu essorbee" ["Dear God! Why did You wake me so soon? I was resting more peacefully than I ever will again! Dear Lord Jesus Christ, who could be so fortunate and so worthy that he might see clearly the great wonders of Your mysteries, there where my sinful gaze and my sight defiled by the endless filth of the world were sorely diminished"]?[665] Although he has finally seen the Holy

---

[663] Malory 520 (emphasis mine).

[664] Malory 484.

[665] *Queste* 257-8; Trans. Burns 81.

194

Grail, he regrets not having the complete vision, which God has denied to his sinful gaze. Naturally, his attendants clamor to know what he did see, and again he acknowledges failure:

> Je ai, fet il, veu si granz merveilles et si granz beneurtez que ma langue nel vos porroit mie descovrir, ne mes cuers meismes nel porroit mie penser, com grant chose ce est. Car ce n'a mie este chose terriane, mes esperitel. Et se mes granz pechiez et ma grant maleurtez ne fust, j'eusse encor plus
> veu, se ne fust que je perdi la veue de mes euz et le pooir dou cors, por la grant desloraute que Diex avoit veue en moi. [666]
> ["I have seen such wonders and blessings that my tongue could not reveal them to you. Even my heart cannot imagine them, they were so overwhelming. Indeed, they were not earthly but spiritual things. If it had not been for my sins and misfortune, I would have seen more, but I lost my sight and the strength of my body, because of the great treachery that God saw within me."] [666]

Again, he emphasizes not what he saw, but what he was not allowed to see. The passionate tone of his speech suggests that Lancelot judges himself a failure because of the agonizing sense of loss he feels upon awakening. He has experienced the equivalent of having his greatest desire fulfilled in a dream: the more beautiful the dream, the greater the pain of waking.

Observers in the castle confirm his sense of failure. When he tries to put on the hair shirt back on, they say, "Sire chevaliers, vos poez bien lessier la here, car vostre queste est achevee; por noient vos travailleroiz plus por quierre la Saint Graal; car bien sachiez que vos n'en verroiz plus que veu en avez. Or nos ameint Diex cax qui plus en doivent veoir" ["Sir knight, you can leave the hair shirt aside, for your quest is now over. Further efforts in search of the Holy Grail will be in vain, for you will certainly see no more than you have already seen. May

---

[666] *Queste* 258; Trans. Burns 81.

God send us others who are destined to see more"].[667] Without responding, Lancelot dons the hair shirt anyway and prepares himself to meet King Pelles.

The remainder of the story only increases Lancelot's sadness. King Pelles tells him of Elaine's death, which saddens Lancelot "por ce que si gentil fame estoit et estrete de si haut lignage" ["because she had been such a noble woman, born of a distinguished family line"].[668] More bad news follows, including the humiliation of his brother and the murder of King Bademagu by none other than Gawain. Disconsolate, Lancelot returns to court, where he receives a "warm welcome," but learns that few knights have yet returned, "Et cil qui revenu estoient n'avoient riens fet en la Queste, don't il ont grant honte" ["And those who had returned had done nothing on the quest, to their great shame"].[669] Clearly, Lancelot is included in their number.

Malory disagrees. Without altering the events of the quest, he does the nearly impossible by transforming "Lancelot's experience in the quest from one of failure to one of almost complete success."[670] His approach within sight of the Grail at Corbenic Castle appears in Malory about the same as it does in the original. Yet, when Lancelot awakens from his twenty-four day trance, both he and the castle residents interpret his experience with the Grail in much more positive terms. He still feels sorrow at waking from his dream, but he blames the folk of the castle, rather than God: "Why have ye awaked me?" Instead of resting more peacefully than he ever will again, he "was more at ease than I am now."[671] This view of the future is certainly more hopeful. When he does address God, he asks "who myght be so blyssed that myght se opynly Thy grete

[667] *Queste* 259; Trans. Burns 81.

[668] *Queste* 259; Trans. Burns 81.

[669] *Queste* 261; Trans. Burns 82.

[670] Ihle 141.

[671] Malory 597.

mervayles of secretnesse there where no synner may be?"[672] Some might argue that being a sinner is the same as having one's sight defiled by endless filth and that Malory is simply shortening the speech in accordance with his ongoing effort to be brief. Yet, the term "sinner" applies, for all practical purposes, to everyone (except the truly saintly, such as Galahad). Thus, Lancelot's admitting that it applies to him is hardly an admission of exceptional guilt. Also, Malory adds an assessment by Lancelot: "Now I thanke God…for Hys grete mercy of that I have sene, for hit suffisith me. For, as I suppose, no man in thys worlde have lyved bettir than I have done to echyeve that I have done."[673] The source contains no such expression of self-satisfaction and contentment. Malory has temporarily suspended his attempt to abbreviate in order to shift the emphasis to what Lancelot has been allowed to see, which, as Lancelot himself observes, is more than anyone else so far.

The castle residents also evaluate his effort much more positively than they do in the source. When offered linen clothes, Lancelot reaches for his hair shirt, which the residents allow him to do without protest. They then tell him that "the queste of the Sankgreall ys echeved now ryght in you, and never shall ye se of Sankgreall more than ye have sene."[674] Such a statement would be unimaginable in the original *Queste*, where the quest of the Holy Grail is certainly not achieved in Lancelot and everyone laments his failure. Malory simply removes the statement of hope by the castle folk that God will send them someone destined to see more. When King Pelles tells him about the death of Elaine, Lancelot honors her memory much more generously than in the original. He recalls that "she was a full fayre lady, freyshe and yonge. And well I wote she bare the beste knyght that ys now on erthe, or that ever was syn God was

---

[672] Malory 597.

[673] Malory 598.

[674] Malory 598.

borne."[675]   Thus, for Elaine as well as himself, Lancelot allows praise to overshadow sorrow.

Malory also lessens his brother Ector's humiliation. In both versions, Ector fails to gain admittance to the castle. However, in the original, when the residents of the castle see Ector ride away in shame, they "crient tuit apres lui et le vont huiant et maudisant l'ore qu'il fu nez, et le cleiment mauves chevalier et recreant" ["shouted after him, hooting and cursing the hour of his birth and proclaiming him to be a failed knight and a coward"].[676]   The wretched Ector is "en a si grant duel que il volsist bien estre morz" ["so mortified that he wished he were dead"].[677]   Malory allows Ector to ride away, certainly with shame and sorrow, but without being taunted or ridiculed.

Finally, Malory reduces the sorrow with which Lancelot returns to court. In both versions, King Bademagus's death saddens him, but the feeling lasts much longer in the original. There, "Celui jor remest Lancelot Laienz molt dolenz et corrociez" ["Lancelot spent the day there [at the tomb], saddened and dismayed"].[678]   He wanders at random "come aventure le menoit" ["[l]ed only by chance"] until he finds "tombes la ou les espees estoient dreciees" ["some tombs surrounded by upright swords"].[679]   Thinking he sees an adventure, he musters some energy and races toward them for a closer look, but nothing comes of the effort. Eventually, "se parti d'ilec et erra tant qu'il vint a la cort le roi Artus" ["he departed and wandered farther until he came to King Arthur's court"].[680]   There, despite the warm welcome, the overriding sense is one of shame, sorrow, and

---

[675] Malory 598.

[676] *Queste* 260-261; Trans. Burns 82.

[677] *Queste* 261; Trans. Burns 82.

[678] *Queste* 262; Trans. Burns 82.

[679] *Queste* 262; Trans. Burns 82.

[680] *Queste* 262; Trans. Burns 82.

198

failure.

Malory reverses this. As soon as he expresses his sorrow at King Bademagus's death, "he departed and cam to the abbey where sir Galahad dud the aventure of the tombis and wan the whyght shylde with the red crosse. And there had he grete chere all that nyght, and on the morne he turned to Camelot where he founde kynge Arthure and the quene."[681] Suprisingly, Kraemer claims that, "Lancelot's part in the quest is over, and sadly he heads back to the court having seen all he ever will."[682] This statement would have been undeniable, had Kraemer been describing the *Queste*. However, Malory adds not only the "grete chere," but also the identification of the graveyard as the place where his son won such glory. Moreover, his journey back to the court is much more purposeful in Malory. Instead of wandering aimlessly, as if his pain is so great he no longer cares where he goes, he "departed" Bademagus's tomb and "turned to Camelot."

Once he arrives at the court, he assumes the role of "spokesman for the elect who do not return."[683] He tells not only of his own adventures, but of "sir Galahad, sir Percivale, and sir Bors whych that he knew by the lettir of the ded mayden, and also as sir Galahad had tolde hym."[684] When Arthur expresses the wish that the three of them would come back, Lancelot answers prophetically: "That shall never be...for two of hem shall ye never se. But one of hem shall com home agayne."[685] This is another scene which Malory expands instead of abbreviating, and its effect is to increase the importance of Lancelot.

As Ihle has shown, Malory actually includes Lancelot "among the elect

---

[681] Malory 599.

[682] Kraemer 99.

[683] Ihle 157.

[684] Malory 600.

[685] Malory 600.

knights"[686] by altering Bors' version of the story. In the original, Bors "contees les aventures del Seint Graal telles come il les avoit veues" ["recounted the adventures of the Holy Grail, as he had seen them"], and they are "furent mises en scrit et gardees en l'almiere de Salebieres" ["recorded and kept in the archive at Salisbury"].[687] In Malory's Grail Quest, Bors tells the king "of the hyghe aventures of the Sankgreall such as had befalle hym and his three felowes, which were sir Launcelot, Percivale and sir Galahad and hymselff."[688] For Malory, Lancelot is part of the elect fellowship of those who have seen the Grail. Accordingly, when Bors finishes his story, "sir Launcelot tolde the adventures of the Sangreall that he had sene. And all thys was made in grete bookes and put up in almeryes at Salysbury."[689] There seems to be no question in Malory's mind that Lancelot has seen the Grail and therefore deserves to have his story included in that great book at Salisbury.

H. Malory's Purpose

As noted in the beginning of this chapter, contemporary scholarship has moved beyond the assumption that Malory "content[ed] himself with a brutal reduction of the symbolic and allegorical commentary that made the Old French text more a didactic than a narrative work."[690] My own analysis of Malory has supported the conclusion of more than one critic, that the story's "entire 'shape' has been altered, and consequently the meaning also has undergone a radical

---

[686] Ihle 158.

[687] *Queste* 279-80; Trans. Burns 87.

[688] Malory 607.

[689] Malory 607.

[690] Ryding 158.

transformation."[691] Malory has turned the Grail itself from the ineffable symbol of divine mystery to the Eucharistic vessel, still holy, but entirely knowable. More importantly, he has altered the purpose of the quest itself. The purpose of the Old French *Queste* is to "contrast...earthly and divine chivalry and condemn...the former."[692] Malory's purpose is to show "how earthly knights, with the Christian vocation that knighthood implies, ought to act to be worthy of seeing the Eucharist unveiled in this world."[693] Consequently, Malory greatly changes the requirements for success in the Grail Quest. Instead of living up to the demands of heavenly chivalry (as opposed to earthly), his Grail knights must meet the requirements of the High Order of Knighthood. This is still a difficult task, but conceptually, it is a much clearer one. As several critics have observed,[694] Malory judges his knights on their actions, not their understanding. For this reason, Lancelot, who tries hard to keep his knightly vows and accepts penance willingly when he fails, has the right to consider himself almost successful on the quest.

Moorman agrees with Vinaver that Malory simply ignored his source wherever it conflicted with that purpose. Moorman makes the point that Malory has to fit the Grail story into the "Arthurian cycle of growth, decay, and fall" and therefore "pares away from the hermits' comments the purely religious commentary which is alien to his purpose."[695] In other words, Moorman agrees that Malory regards the Grail Quest as an Arthurian story and therefore omits the homilies of the hermits because they seem to him irrelevant. Ihle makes the same

---

[691] Ihle 4.

[692] Vinaver 758.

[693] Ihle 113.

[694] See Larry Benson, *Malory's* Morte Darthur (Cambridge, MA: Harvard University Press, 1976) 222; Derek Brewer, *Malory: The Morte Darthur*, ed. Derek Brewer (Evanston, IL: Northwestern University Press, 1974) 34-5; Ihle 163.

[695] Moorman 187.

argument when she says that "Malory systematically eliminates narrative that takes attention away from his major interest: how earthly knights, with the Christian vocation that knighthood implies, ought to act to be worthy of seeing the Eucharist unveiled in this world."[696]

Atkinson takes this argument further by noting that Malory has to make the Grail Quest fit into "the hoole book" and therefore uses other information to judge his characters. However, as noted earlier, Atkinson disagrees with the assumption that Malory is not interested in heavenly chivalry. Rather, Atkinson takes the "balanced" position that the spiritual ideal replaces the earthly one, and Lancelot shows his virtue by bowing to this change.[697] Mahoney likewise sees earthly and heavenly chivalry as different ideals, appropriate to different stage in an individual's life.[698] She agrees with Atkinson that Malory did understand the distinction his source was drawing between heavenly and earthly chivalry. However, she notices that Malory alters or removes the doctrinal implications of that distinction and seems unsure why he would choose a source that he so pointedly disagrees with.[699] Kraemer agrees with Mahoney that Malory is not trying to challenge the message of the *Queste*, but to translate it, culturally as well as linguistically, for fifteenth-century England. Yet, as this chapter has shown, many of Kramer's observations about Malory's grail quest could be made with as much, if not more, justice about the old French *Queste*.

If, then, we must reject Kraemer's explanation, how shall we understand Malory's project? The most common view is that Malory developed the aspects of the *Queste* that he found interesting and removed or drastically shortened the

---

[696] Ihle 113.

[697] Atkinson 133.

[698] Mahoney 123.

[699] Mahoney speculates that this version might be "purer, less adulterated by the wider chivalric narrative" than other available sources (112). Yet, the version he does choose seems to require much revision, in meaning, as well as content, to suit Malory's purpose. It therefore seems unlikely that he found the Old French *Queste* easier to work with.

rest. For example, in his much-quoted explanation of Malory's purpose, Vinaver has this to say:

> [T]hroughout the story Malory is primarily concerned with "erthly worship" and the consequent attempt to secularize the Grail theme as much as the story will allow. Ignoring the contrast between *la chevaillierie celestiale* and *la seculiere*, Malory replaces the former by 'virtuous living', and even uses the phrase "knyghtly dedys and vertuous lyvyng" to describe the duties of a good Christian. Naturally enough, when he comes to assess Lancelot's virtues and vices he finds himself unable to follow either the spirit or the letter of the French.[700]

Another answer, which the first partially implies, is that Malory did not understand his source. P.E. Tucker expresses this position best:

> Malory was confused by the two senses of "chivalry" in the French *Queste*. In the first place, chivalry had no courtly implications for him, and it was in itself a high moral ideal. He was therefore at a loss to understand why the French writer persistently condemned *la chevaillierie terriene*, quite apart from his difficulty in grasping the exact nature of *la chevaillierie celestiale*. For, in the second place, he did not follow the theological expositions of his source, and the result was that he never fully grasped the purpose of the *Queste*.[701]

In truth, these two positions are not very far removed from one another. After all, the issue on which Malory disagrees from his source is not a minor detail which a translator (particularly one who wishes to be brief) can simply omit if he finds it less than interesting. The main point of the Old French *Queste* is to explain the

---

[700] Vinaver 758.

[701] P.E. Tucker, "Chivalry in the *Morte*," *Essays on Malory*, ed. J.A.W. Bennett (Oxford: Clarendon Press, 1963) 84.

difference between *la chevaillierie celestiale* and *la chevaillierie terriene* and to condemn the latter. If Malory sees no difference between these two and regards the Grail Quest as "an opportunity offered to the knights of the Round Table to achieve still greater glory in this world,"[702] then he disagrees with his source on the basic lesson of the Grail Quest. To say that Malory is not interested in the main point of his original and therefore produces a "translation" whose point is diametrically opposed to that of the original is, essentially, to say that Malory misunderstood his source. Only Brewer raises all the possibilities, observing "that Malory rejects, or is not interested in, or does not understand, the transcendent quality of the Grail legend, and of its underlying theology, for he denies their lesson."[703]

However, Malory must have seen the distinction his source was drawing. The dichotomy between earthly and heavenly chivalry was everywhere in the literature of his time. Kraemer rightly points out that Malory and his readers would have been familiar with fifteenth-century hagiography,[704] which makes exactly this distinction. In 1447, not long before Malory, Bokenham's St. Christina speaks of being "clepyd to heuenly cheualrye."[705] If "heuenly cheualrye" meant the same thing as Malory's "knyghtes dedys in Goddys workys,"[706] then fair ladies like Christina could not very well speak of being called to it. Yet, female saints do speak of being called to it, at least as often as male saints do. *S. Kateryne*[707] makes an even clearer case for heavenly chivalry. When Porphiry draws his sword to protect a Christian lady (the queen) against the

---

[702] Vinaver 758.

[703] Brewer, "the hoole book" 58.

[704] Kraemer 15-29.

[705] Bokenham 67.

[706] Malory 531.

[707] See Chapter 4 for details.

204

evil Emperor, he acts in full accordance with the High Order of Knighthood. Therefore, Katherine's rebuke of him sends a clear message that the demands of true holiness are incompatible with earthly knighthood. Malory must have understood the concept—he simply disagreed with it. As Brewer explains, "Malory does not agree with his source that the chivalric ideal is anti-Christian."[708]

Proceeding, then, from the assumption that Malory understood, but disagreed with his source, we can now focus more specifically on how he was using the quasi-hagiographic *Queste*. As with the true hagiographers' use of romance, the answer is largely historical.[709] By Malory's time, neither authors nor audiences were interested in Christ-like knights. The issues that seemed so pressing to the French *Queste* author—the true meaning of heavenly chivalry, the quest for spiritual perfection—mattered not at all to Malory. For him, this Christ-like ideal was not only unattainable, but ultimately useless. Malory had a much more immediate problem: the general collapse of knighthood in all its forms. In prison, Malory had ample time to reflect on the inability of a knight such as himself to succeed in the traditional way, by pursuing the profession of arms in the service of a lord, so glorified in romances, yet suddenly so impossible in reality. Malory's England did not need Galahad, and since the fall of Acre, neither did anyone else. What England seemed to need was the chivalry of Lancelot, the imperfect knight who tries to live by the code and be of practical service to the commonwealth. Thus, Malory, from his prison cell, undertook its defense, although he may have been living proof that the code was no longer workable. He pays dutiful homage to Galahad and his perfection, but welcomes Lancelot home with an enthusiasm his source has no reason to feel. Malory, of

---

[708] Brewer, "the hoole book" 58.

[709] Mahoney rightly points out that the theological lessons of the *Queste* would be "alien to the temper of [Malory's] time" (117). I would go further, to argue that Malory considered his source not only outdated, but dangerously wrong, considering the political and social problems of fifteenth-century England.

course, recognizes the sins that brought down the Round Table, as he would recognize the sin that cost man Paradise, and with the same sadness. The fall of the Round Table explained for Malory the sorry state in which he found English chivalry. If he is indeed the Malory of Newbold Revell, his decision to become a criminal and a soldier of fortune was a response to the same forces that drew other knights into business and banking. It was certainly no more an abandonment of chivalric idealism than these other options, and in some ways, it was less so.[710]

Furthermore, the decline of the military religious orders helps explain Malory's rejection of the distinction between "celestial chivalry" and "earthly chivalry." By Malory's time, the only real use for knighthood was the service of a king—not a feudal lord, and certainly not the Holy Church. Yet, historically, knighthood was a feudal institution with religious underpinnings. If celestial knighthood no longer had a meaning, even less so did earthly knighthood. If one subtracts both piety and feudal loyalties from knighthood, one is left with the warrior profession as it existed before the crusades and the Peace of God. Malory may not have understood the return of many knights to the robber baron profession as the throwback it was. Yet, he clearly did understand that there was something inadequate about knighthood as practiced in his time, perhaps as he himself practiced it. It is also true that the courtliness and gallantry which came to characterize the knightly ideal, when stripped of their military and religious implications and employed in the service of a strong king, created the Renaissance gentleman. However, Malory could see only the decay of knighthood—he had no way of seeing what was going to replace it, and I am not sure he would have liked it if he had.

Malory was certainly not the first to argue that the knightly ideal was itself a Christian ideal, nor even the first to do so in a romance. All the thirteenth-century "sacred romances" discussed in Chapter One make this argument, often

---

[710] Traditionally, knights, by definition, did not pursue professions like these. See Bloch's discussion of knights as businessmen, bankers, etc., pp. 288-292.

directly opposing the hagiographers' argument that worldly success is incompatible with salvation. Moreover, a certain school of critical thought maintains that all medieval romances were intended to justify the continued rule of the knightly class.[711] If this is so, then romance writers had another compelling reason to present the chivalric ideal as a Christian ideal.

However, Malory differs from his predecessors in a crucial way. Instead of writing a romance of his own that quarrels with the values of the French *Queste,* he transforms the French *Queste* itself from an anti-chivalric religious text, which comes

close to constructing Galahad as a saint in a hagiographical text, to a pro-chivalric Arthurian romance whose hero is Lancelot. In the process, he reverses its message. Whereas the French *Queste* explains the difference between earthly and heavenly chivalry, Malory presents a vision of ideal knighthood that is compatible with holiness and salvation. In other words, Malory denies the contradiction between chivalry and holiness and turns quasi-hagiography into its opposite: hagiographic romance. Like its thirteenth-century predecessors, Malory's hagiographic romance is definitely romance and not hagiography. It promotes the chivalric code in direct contradiction of its anti-chivalric source. Thus, Malory not only disagrees with his source, but makes a conscious decision to correct it.

---

[711] See Knight 99-122; Moi 11-33.

Conclusion

Malory's *Sankgreal* and the fifteenth-century lives of St. Katherine sound surprisingly alike because both reflected and reacted to the same changes. In the opening chapter of *Autumn of the Middle Ages*, Huizinga describes the late Middle Ages this way: "When the world was half a thousand years younger all events had much sharper outlines than now. The distance between sadness and joy, between good and bad fortune, seemed to be much greater than for us; every experience had that degree of directness and absoluteness that joy and sadness still have in the mind of a child."[712] The story of these two great literary genres during this period is largely about the loss of ideals and the blurring of distinctions. In a sense, the world was growing up. England was growing up faster than most, regretting the loss of youthful innocence on the way, but not, of course, enough to stop, to cease breaking traditions. As both the Church and the feudal system lost power and prestige to the rising national state, those who derived their status from these institutions, namely knights and clerics, made compromises, accommodating the new situation. The chivalric and religious literature they left is the record both of their accommodation and their resistance to it. Naturally, both had a keener eye for the other's compromises than for their own. Yet, both seem to feel a new and pressing need to justify privileges that they sense they are about to lose. The authors attempt to breathe new life into old ideals while, paradoxically, rejecting their models in order to describe the world as they understand it.

Both genres reflect the declining influence of the Roman Church. As the most prominent institution of the central Middle Ages, the Church influenced nearly every facet of life. That it provided the *raison d'être* for the clergy is obvious, but its role in shaping lay society is nearly impossible to overstate. Among other things, the Church was instrumental in the creation of chivalry, as we now understand it. A ruling warrior class had existed in most of Europe, and it continued to exist in the chaos after the fall of Charlemagne's empire. However, until the Church initiated the Peace of God, the Truce of God, and eventually the crusades, warriors lacked the code of conduct whose decline Malory and other secular writers justifiably deplored. The Church also brought a measure of order and stability to Europe in the early Middle Ages, when both were lacking. Thus, even when other institutions became more powerful, life without a strong Church must have been unimaginable.

When the Church did weaken, due to internal strife and the growth of royal power, England felt the secularizing effects very quickly. By the fourteenth century, England was a cohesive political unit with sophisticated government institutions, and the lay public soon began to resent the intrusion of foreign powers in English affairs. Because of the weakness of the papacy and the increasing patriotism of the citizens, the English crown was able to win practical independence from Rome long before its actual break with the Roman Church. In the late Middle Ages, English patriotism often took the form of anti-papal demonstrations, and anti-clerical feeling only increased as the papacy became less assertive in its dealings with the crown. Thus, the English attitude toward the clergy and the papacy in the late Middle Ages well explains why Henry VIII was able to establish an independent Church of England without provoking revolution,

---

[712] Huizinga 1.

as such a move surely would have done anywhere else in Europe.

Both Malory and the hagiographers who were his contemporaries reflect in their work the decreasing importance of the organized Church in daily life. In the *Tale of the Sankgreal*, Malory consistently alters his source to make abstract concepts more concrete and spiritual ideals more practical. The goal of the quest, instead of spiritual perfection, is a much more attainable "worthiness," as defined by the High Order of Knighthood. Malory understood that holiness was a necessary part of knighthood, that none of the knight's finer qualities would exist without it. Therefore, his idea of proper knightly conduct includes a practical version of Christian morality. Malory was not, however, interested in spiritual understanding divorced from the world of action. Galahad achieves the Grail because he adheres perfectly to the knightly code, not because he is God's chosen servant or because he has a spiritual understanding that the others lack. He is a perfect knight, but not a saint, as he is in the French *Queste del Saint Graal*. However, Malory is much more interested in Lancelot, who represents the best of "earthly, sinful" knights. Reinterpreting the outcome of Lancelot's Grail Quest as nearly complete success, he offers his contemporaries a practical model of knightly conduct.

Malory utterly rejects the distinction between *chevalarie celestial* and *chevalerie terriene* that is so important to his source. For this reason, he has Meliant undertake the quest without confessing his sins. The failure to confess is an identifiable breach of true chivalry, which includes standard Christian practice. As the highest quest, the search for the Holy Grail demands perfect adherence to the chivalric code. Therefore, achievement of the Grail is difficult, but theoretically possible for all the knights who attempt it. In short, Malory's Grail Quest is not about the ineffable Grail, as its source is, but about the knights who search for it. Malory is interested in character, and each knight's success or failure reveals his character; his character does not reveal the Grail.

Likewise, the fifteenth-century lives of St. Katherine show an interest in earthly morality, at the expense of otherworldly perfection. Capgrave's Katherine is a saint, not only because of her spirituality, but also because of her behavior. She studies assiduously, remains chaste, and rules justly. She wins the debate with the scholars, not because she is inspired by the Holy Ghost, but because she studies hard and makes good arguments. In the 1420 *passio*, Porphiry does not become a Christian through an understanding of spiritual truths. He is converted only when, at Katherine's command, he throws his sword away. Thus, even some hagiographers of the fifteenth century were more concerned with overt behavior than their models were.

The reason, I believe, is the same for both. In the thirteenth century, when the Old French *Queste* and the *South-English Legendary* were written, both the Church and the feudal system were at their strongest and most hopeful. The Church was beginning ambitious reforms to improve the quality of pastoral care and make religion a larger part of the daily life of the laity than ever before. The friars, through skillful preaching and learned guidance, were leading masses of people in cities to fuller participation in religious practice than had previously been possible for laymen. Chivalry was also in flower, with the crusading movement at its height and the military religious orders at their most powerful. The art of war was growing in sophistication, and the quasi-religious rituals of knighthood had created an elite brotherhood of warriors. In such a world, writers of both chivalric and religious texts could formulate higher ideals. They could work, as visual artists did, to create the perfect knight or the perfect holy woman. While no real person could meet these ideals, real people could strive for them and become better people by doing so.

By the fifteenth century, these high hopes had fallen flat. The episcopate consisted mostly of secular aristocrats who made no attempt to stay out of politics. The best educated, most capable clergymen lived comfortably on their benefices and left the direct care of souls to an ill-educated, poorly paid underclass. Knights were either avoiding their military service and devoting themselves to business and banking or selling their skills to the highest bidder. The population in general was growing more worldly and anti-clerical every day. At such a time, few people were seeking a better understanding of spiritual perfection. Malory was already asking too much when he suggested that knights act like knights. On the other hand, while the chivalric ideal was impossible truly to live up to, its civilizing effects were real enough. The idea that those with power had a responsibility to use it in the service of justice and for the protection of the weak was a powerful concept in which Malory clearly believed, despite his own apparent failure to live up to it.

However, even Malory's portrayal of ideal knighthood is a product of chivalry in decline. True knighthood requires a functioning feudal system, which England, by Malory's time, did not have. Knights tried to redefine their obligations in terms of loyalty to a monarch, but a professional soldier in the king's service is not a knight. A knight has administrative and judicial authority. In his own province, the knight enforced the law and otherwise maintained the social order. His new position as professional man-at-arms did not entail using his sword for the righting of wrongs, but for whatever purpose his employer engaged him. Thus, as an ideal to strive for, Galahad was not only unrealistic, but also far from what an England, now short of knights and wracked by civil war, needed. His achievement of the Grail, though admirable, does nothing for Camelot. Clearly (to Malory), England needed more knights like Lancelot, who would do their best to be loyal and fulfill their obligations. What Malory did not perceive was that the failure of knights to be chivalrous was not, for once, a failure of human beings to do the right thing, but the failure of an outmoded institution to function correctly.

The decline of the feudal system led to the rise of patriotism and national politics. By the beginning of the Wars of the Roses, both the clergy and the laity were deeply involved in national issues. The clergy had become politicized either because they were political men already or because their patrons were involved in politics. Either way, their fortunes were dependent upon the outcome of a national struggle for power. Accordingly, Capgrave and Bokenham, both of whom had aristocratic patrons, offer a politicized version of St. Katherine as a just ruler who believes in monarchical government. In Bokenham's version, the politics are most obvious: wishing to make Katherine perfect, he makes her a Yorkist. His evil emperor makes typical Lancastrian arguments against the worthiness of women, and his Katherine makes the Yorkist rebuttal. She also makes the logical Yorkist argument that a king who is not "ruled by reason" has no right to rule a nation. By the time Bokenham wrote his life of the St. Katherine, Henry VI was far from being ruled by reason, though he was not permanently to lose his sanity until a serious illness six years later. Capgrave's politics are less obvious, but a close analysis of the parliamentary debate shows his Katherine to be more or less a Lancastrian. Her reverence for royalty and contempt for disloyal lords mirror Capgrave's own attitudes. For Capgrave, right conduct means loyalty to the ruler, whoever the current ruler may be. Therefore, any of Katherine's arguments against the need for her to marry could just as easily be arguments in support of Henry VI. Instead of arguing for the competence of women as rulers, she argues that a ruler who cannot personally lead troops into battle can still be an effective ruler and that no one, no matter how capable, can govern without the support of the nobles. The involvement of clerics in such secular political issues was a fairly recent phenomenon, which illustrates the growing importance of royal and aristocratic patronage in the English Church.

Malory, less approvingly, testifies to the role of knights in national politics. With affecting vividness, he shows the foolishness of Englishmen, who, already in Arthur's time, could not remain content even with the best king. In one of his few direct addresses to his audience, Malory reproaches Englishmen for their fickleness and disloyalty. (The criticism is especially poignant, considering that the writer was probably in prison at the time for following the Earl of Warwick against Edward IV.) Contrary to Guinevere's self-critical assessment, her affair with Lancelot does not ruin Camelot. The *Morte D'arthur* is not one long treatise against adultery. The affair becomes important only when the ambitious and discontented Mordred, along with the equally discontented Orkney faction, wants to ruin the Round Table. Realizing that the only way to accomplish his goal is to set Arthur against Lancelot, Mordred manipulates the three central characters into fighting one another for his own political gain. While he succeeds in destroying Camelot, he pays for it with his life. The message for Malory's countrymen is clear: no one wins. Malory knew this better than most.

Thus, both Malory's Grail Quest and the fifteenth-century lives of St. Katherine praise the pursuit of perfection in a world where perfection really is not possible. Certainly, they regret the decline of institutions that gave them power and respect. In the emerging social order, neither Malory nor Capgrave held the privileged positions that they would once have had. They now had to spend their time worrying about making a living, about pleasing patrons and employers. However, in judging them, we have to remember that the Church and the feudal system had been the only sources of values for centuries. Someone whose sense of the good is intimately connected with one or the other of those institutions will regret its waning influence, and not necessarily for selfish reasons. Writers of this time had no way of knowing that equally viable institutions were emerging and would provide the security and even inspiration for achievement that the weakened Church and feudal system could no longer provide.

For us, the greatest difficulty of writing about the Middle Ages is taking it on its own terms and not as a temporary interruption of progress while people waited for the Renaissance. Even the term Middle Ages implies a sense of transition that people who lived it could not possibly have felt. Furthermore, the lack of good information about how people saw themselves and their times invites us to fill the void with our own prejudices and expectations. In other words, we know too much about the Renaissance and too little about events that preceded it. We have difficulty imagining how people in the autumn of the Middle Ages perceived their world without becoming distracted by what they failed to perceive. In this effort, historians such as Huizinga and Bloch can be of great assistance to literary scholars. They allow us to gain a better understanding of literary texts by helping us to picture the situation of both writer and audience.

Ferguson refers to the fifteenth century as the Indian summer of English chivalry. In a sense, the Catholic Church in England was in its own Indian summer. Knights and clerics could see that the institutions that gave meaning to their lives were in disrepair, and they naturally fought to continue them. They no more imagined the end of knighthood than modernists, seeing the decline of religion, art, literature, etc., really expected these things to disappear. Like Malory and Capgrave, we still regret the loss of ideals, of the ability to believe in perfection, while most of the time accommodating ourselves to life as it is. Thus, we, too, respond to tales of chivalry and lives of the saints. They offer us, as they did their original audiences, heroic examples of loyalty, bravery, and faith in a world that despairs of perfection. They remind us that unattainable ideals still have the power to improve us.

Appendix

Sequence of Historical Events and Literary Compositions

1096-1099	First Crusade
1119 or 1120	Founding of the Knights Templar
1129	Templars receive formal recognition at the Council of Troyes
1145-1149	Second Crusade
1187-1192	Third Crusade
1198-1204	Fourth Crusade
1200-1240	Composition of Katherine Group, including Early-English *Seinte Katerine*
1205	King John clashes with Innocent III over vacant see of Canterbury
1216	King John dies; Henry III succeeds to the throne
1220	Anonymous Cicstercian monk composes *La Queste del Saint Graal*
1272	Henry III dies; Edward I succeeds to the throne
c.1285	*Legenda Aurea* *South-English Legendary*
1291	Acre falls to the Muslims
1303	Pope Boniface VIII kidnapped by Philip IV of France, dies of "shock"

1307	Philip IV orders the Templars' arrest
	Edward I of England dies; Edward II succeeds to the throne
1308	Edward II orders the Templars' arrest
1309	Pope Clement V moves residence to Avignon
1312	Clement V officially suppresses order of the Temple
1314	Jacques de Molay and Geoffroi de Charnay burned at the stake
1327	Edward II of England dies; Edward III succeeds to the throne
1346	Battle of Crecy
1349	Temporary truce between England and France, due to effects of plague
1351	Statute of Provisors
1352	Statute of Praemunire
1356	Battle of Poitiers
1377	Edward III dies; Richard II succeeds to the throne
1378	Pope returns to Rome—Schism
1381	"Peasant's Revolt"
1384	Death of Wycliffe
1388	Merciless Parliament
c.1390	Composition of *The Canterbury Tales* by Chaucer
1399	Henry Bolingbroke deposes Richard II; reigns as Henry IV
1400	Richard II dies in Tower of London
1413	Henry IV dies; Henry V succeeds to throne
1414	Sir John Oldcastle's revolt
1415	Battle of Agincourt
1417	End of "Babylonian Captivity" of papacy
1420	*S. Kateryne* (*passio* only)
	Prose Legend (*vita* and *passio*)
1421	Henry V dies, 31 August, succeeded by infant Henry VI
1422-1437	Minority of Henry VI

1438-1445	John Capgrave writes *Life of St. Katherine of Alexandria*
c.1445	Painting of St. Catherine by follower of Rogier Van der Weyden
1446	Henry VI pledges close connection with Lynn Priory
1447	Osbern Bokenham writes *Legendys of Hooly Wummen*
1453	Final expulsion of English from France (July)
	Henry VI goes insane (August)
1455	Beginning of Wars of the Roses
1460	Richard of York dies at Battle of Wakefield
1461	Crowning of Edward IV
1462-1463	Malory fights with Warwick for Edward IV
Mid-1460s	Malory fights with Warwick against Edward IV
Late 1460s	Malory imprisoned, writes most of his *Works*
1471	Edward, Prince of Wales, dies at Battle of Tewkesbury
	Henry VI dies in Tower of London
	Malory dies in Newgate prison
1483	Edward IV dies; Edward V succeeds to the throne
	Richard III deposes Edward V; Edward V murdered
1485	Henry Tudor defeats Richard III at Bosworth Field; reigns as Henry VII
	End of Wars of the Roses
	Caxton publishes Malory's works as *Le Morte D'Arthur*

Bibliography

Primary Sources:

The Ancrene Riwle. Ed. and trans. M.B. Salu. Intro. Gerard Sitwell. Notre Dame: Univ. of Notre Dame Press, 1955.

Andreas Capellanus. *On Love.* Ed. and Trans. P.G. Walsh. London: Duckworth, 1982.

Bokenham, Osbern. *Legendys of Hooly Wummen.* Ed. Mary S. Serjeantson. London: EETS 206, 1938.

Capgrave, John. *Abbreuiacion of Cronicles.* Ed. Peter J. Lucas. Oxford: Oxford University Press, 1983.

---. *Liber Illustribus Henricis.* Ed. and intro. Francis Charles Hingeston. Rolls Series. London: Her Majesty's Stationery Office, 1869. Rpt. Kraus-Thomson Organization Ltd., 1970.

---. *The Life of Saint Katherine.* Ed. Carl Horstmann. Intro. F.J. Furnivall. London: EETS O.S. 100, 1893.

---. *The Life of Saint Katherine.* Ed. Karen A. Winstead. Kalamazoo, MI: Medieval Institute Publications, 1999.

Chaucer, Geoffrey. *The Riverside Chaucer.* Ed. Larry Benson. 3rd ed. Oxford: Oxford University Press, 1987.

Chrétien de Troyes. *Arthurian Romances.* Trans. and intro. D.D.R. Owen. London: Orion, 1993.

The Dream of the Rood. A Guide to Old English. Ed. Bruce Mitchell and Fred Robinson. 5th ed. Blackwell: Oxford, 1992: 33-40.

Early South-English Legendary. Ed. and Intro. Carl Horstmann. London: EETS O.S. 87, 1887.

Froissart, Jean. *Chronicles.* Ed. and trans. Geoffrey Brereton. London: Penguin, 1968.

Guy of Warwick: The First or 14th-Century Version. Ed. Julius Zupitza. London: EETS E.S. 59, 1891.

Hali Meiðhad. Ed. F.J. Furnivall. Rev. Oswald Cockayne. EETS 18, 1866, 1922.

Kempe, Margery. *The Book of Margery Kempe.* Ed. Sanford Brown Meech. Oxford: Oxford University Press, 1940.

King Horn, A Middle English Romance. Ed. Joseph Hall. Oxford: Oxford University Press, 1901.

Þe Liflade ant te Passiun of Seinte Iuliene. Ed. S.R.T.O. d'Ardenne. London: EETS O.S. 248, 1961.

A Medieval French Reader. Ed. C.W. Aspland. Oxford: Clarendon Press, 1979.

Monstrelet, Enguerrand de. *Chronicles.* Trans. Thomas Johnes. London: Henry G. Bohn, 1853.

Petroff, Elizabeth Alvilda, ed. *Medieval Women's Visionary Literature.* Oxford: Oxford University Press, 1986.

La Queste del Saint Graal. Ed. Albert Pauphilet. Paris: Librairie Ancienne Honore Champion, 1921.

The Quest for the Holy Grail. Trans. E. Jane Burns. *Lancelot-Grail: The Old French Arthurian Vulgate and Post-Vulgate in Translation.* Ed. Norris J. Lacy. Vol IV. New York: Garland Publishing, 1995.

Registrum Simonis de Sudbiria. Ed. R.C. Fowler and C. Jenkins. Canterbury and York Society, 1938.

Registrum Simonis de Langham. Ed. A.C. Wood. Canterbury and York Society, 1947-8.

S. Kateryne. Altenglische Legenden, Neue Folge. Ed. Carl Horstmann. New York: Hildescheim & Olms, 1881.

Saint Katherine. Chaste Passions: Medieval English Virgin Martyr Legends. Ed. and trans. Karen Winstead. Ithaca: Cornell University Press, 2000.

Seinte Katerine. Ed. and intro. S.R.T.O. d'Ardenne and E.J. Dobson. London: EETS S.S. 7, 1981.

Seinte Katerine. Ed. and intro. Eugen Einenkel. London: EETS O.S. 80, 1884.

St. Katherine of Alexandria: The Late Middle English Prose Legend in Southwell Minster MS 7. Ed. and Intro. Nevanlinna, Saara and Irma Taavitsainen. Cambridge: D.S. Brewer, 1993.

Sir Gawain and the Green Knight. Ed. William Vantuono. New York: Garland, 1991.

Snappe's Formulary. Ed. H.E. Salter. Oxford Historical Society 80: 1923.

The Rule of the Templars. Intro. and trans. Upton-Ward, J.M. Woodbridge: Boydell Press, 1992.

Malory, Sir Thomas. *The Works of Sir Thomas Malory.* Ed. and intro. Eugene Vinvaer. Oxford: Oxford University Press, 1971.

Seinte Marherete. Ed. Francis Mack. London: EETS O.S. 193, 1934.

Secondary Sources:

Atkinson, Stephen. "Malory's Lancelot and the Quest of the Grail." *Studies in Malory.* Ed. James W. Spisak. Kalamazoo, MI: Medieval Institute Publications, 1985.

Barron, W.R.J. *English Medieval Romance.* Essex: Longman House, 1987.

Barber, Malcolm. *The Trial of the Templars.* Cambridge: Cambridge University Press, 1978.

Bell, Rudolph M. *Holy Anorexia.* Chicago: Univ. of Chicago Press, 1985.

Benson, Larry. *Malory's* Morte Darthur. Cambridge, MA: Harvard University Press, 1976.

Bloch, Marc. *Feudal Society.* Trans. L.A. Manyon. Chicago: University of Chicago Press, 1961.

Boase, Roger. *The Origin and Meaning of Courtly Love: A Critical Study of European Scholarship*. Manchester: Manchester University Press, 1977.

Borst, Arno. *Medieval Worlds: Barbarians, Heretics and Artists*. Trans. Eric Hansen. Chicago: University of Chicago Press, 1991.

Bradbury, Nancy M. *Writing Aloud: Storytelling in Late Medieval England*. Urbana and Chicago: University of Illinois Press, 1998.

Bray, Jennifer Relvyn. *The Legend of St. Katherine in Later Middle English Literature*. Ph.D. Thesis. Birkbeck College: University of London, 1984.

Brewer, Derek. "the hoole book." *Essays on Malory*. Ed. J.A.W. Bennett. Oxford, Clarendon Press, 1963. 41-63.

Brewer, Derek, ed. *Malory: The Morte Darthur*. Evanston, IL: Northwestern University Press, 1974.

Bynum, Caroline Walker. *Jesus as Mother: Studies in the Spirituality of the High Middle Ages*. Berkeley: Univ. of California Press, 1982.

Cartwright, Frederick F. *Disease and History*. New York: Signet, 1972.

Crane, Susan. *Insular Romance: Politics, Faith, and Culture in Anglo-Norman and Middle English Literature*. Berkeley: Univ. of California Press, 1986.

Delany, Sheila, intro. and trans. *A Legend of Holy Women*. By Osbern Bokenham. Notre Dame: University of Notre Dame Press, 1992. Trans. of *Legendys of Hooly Wummen*.

---. *Impolitic Bodies: Poetry, Saints, and Society in Fifteenth-Century England*. Oxford: Oxford University Press, 1998.

Dickinson, J.C. *An Ecclesiatical History of England: The Later Middle Ages From the Norman Conquest to the Eve of the Reformation*. London: A&C Black, 1979.

Dobson, E.J. *The Origins of* Ancrene Wisse. Oxford: Clarendon Press, 1976.

Dyer, Christopher. *Standards of Living in the Later Middle Ages: Social Change in England c. 1200-1520*. Cambridge: Cambridge University Press, 1989.

Ferguson, Arthur B. *The Indian Summer of English Chivalry: Studies in the Decline and Transformation of Chivalric Idealism*. Durham: Duke University Press, 1960.

Ffoulkes, C.J. *The Armourer and his Craft From the XIIth to the XVIth Century*. London: Longman, 1912.

Field , P.J.C. *The Life And Times Of Sir Thomas Malory*. Rochester, NY : D.S. Brewer, 1993.

Finlayson, John. "Definitions of Middle English Romance." *The Chaucer Review* 15 (1980): 44-62, 68-81.

Furnivall, F.J., intro. *Life of St. Katherine of Alexandria*. By John Capgrave. Ed. Carl Horstmann. London: EETS O.S. 100, 1893.

Gibson, Gail McMurray. *The Theater of Devotion: East Anglian Drama and Society in the Late Middle Ages*. Chicago: University of Chicago Press, 1989.

Green, Richard Firth. *Poets and Princepleasers: Literature and the English Court in the Late Middle Ages*. Toronto: Univ. of Toronto Press, 1980.

Housley, Norman. *The Later Crusades: From Lyons to Alcazar*. Oxford: Oxford University Press, 1992.

Huizinga, Johan. *The Autumn of the Middle Ages*. Trans. Rodney J. Payton and Ulrich Mammitzsch. Chicago: University of Chicago Press, 1996.

Ihle, Sandra Ness. "Invention of Character in Malory's Grail Book." *Medieval Studies in Honor of Douglas Kelly*. Ed. Keith Busby and Norris J. Lacy. Amsterdam: Rodopi, 1994.

---. *Malory's Grail Quest: Invention and Adaptation in Medieval Prose Romance*. Madison: University of Wisconsin Press, 1983.

Jacob, E. F. *The Fifteenth Century: 1399-1485*. The Oxford History of England. Ed. Sir George Clark. Oxford: Clarendon Press, 1961.

C. Johnson and H. Jenkinson. *English Courthand*. Oxford: Oxford University Press, 1915.

Keegan, John. *The Face of Battle*. New York: Viking Press, 1976.

Knight, Stephen. "The Social Function of Middle English Romances." *Medieval Literature: Criticism, Ideology and History*. Ed. David Aers. Brighton: Harvester, 1986.

Knowles, David. *The Religious Orders in England*. London: Cambridge University Press, 1960.

224

Kraemer, Alfred Robert. *Malory's Grail Seekers and jFifteenth-Century English Hagiography*. New York: Peter Lang, 1999.

Kurvinen, Auvo. "The Source of Capgrave's Life of St. Katherine of Alexandria." *Neuphilologische Mitteilungen* 61 (1960): 268-324.

Lawrence, C.H. *The Friars: The Impact of the Early Mendicant Movement on Western Society*. London: Longman Group, 1994.

Legman, G., Henry Charles Lea, Thomas Wright, George Witt, Sir James Tennent, and Sir William Dugdale. *The Guilt of the Templars*. New York: Basic Books, Inc., 1966.

Kittredge, George Lyman. *Sir Thomas Malory*. Barnstable: Priv. print, 1925.

Mahoney, Dhira. "The Truest and Holiest Tale: Malory's Transformation of *La Queste del Saint Graal*." *Studies in Malory*. Ed. James W. Spisak. Kalamazoo, MI: Medieval Institute Publications, 1985.

Matthew, Gervase. "Ideals of Knighthood in Late-Fourteenth-Century England." *Studies in Medieval History Presented to Frederick Maurice Powicke*. Ed. R.W. Hunt, et. al. Westport, CT: Greenwood Press, 1948.

Matthews, William. *The Ill-Framed Knight: A Skeptical Inquiry Into The Identity Of Sir Thomas Malory*. Berkeley: University of California Press, 1966.

McFarlane, K.B. *John Wycliffe and the Beginnings of English Nonconformity*. New York: Macmillan, 1953.

McNamara, JoAnn. *A New Song: Celibate Women in the First Three Christian Centuries*. Women and History 5: 1983.

McNamara, JoAnn and John E. Halborg with E. Gordon Whatley, trans. *Sainted Women of the Dark Ages*. Durham, NC : Duke University Press, 1992.

McNeill, William. *Plagues and Peoples*. Garden City, New York: Anchor Press, 1976.

Mehl, Dieter. *The Middle English Romances of the Thirteenth and Fourteenth Centuries*. New York: Barnes and Noble, 1969.

Mertes, Kate. "Aristocracy." *Fifteenth-Century Attitudes: Perceptions of Society in Late Medieval England*. Ed. Rosemary Horrox. Cambridge: Cambridge University Press, 1994.

Moi, Toril. "Desire in Language: Andreas Capellanus and the Controversy of Courtly Love." *Medieval Literature: Criticsm, Ideology & History.* Ed. David Aers. Brighton: Harvester, 1986.

Moore, John C. *Love in Twelfth-Century France.* Philadelphia: University of Pennsylvania Press, 1972.

Moorman, Charles. "'The Tale of the Sankgreall': Human Frailty." *Malory's Originality: A Critical Study of* Le Morte Darthur. Ed. R.M. Lumiansky. Baltimore: Johns Hopkins Press, 1964. 184-204.

Noble, Thomas and Thomas Head, ed. and intro. *Soldiers of Christ: Saints and Saints' Lives from Late Antiquity and the Early Middle Ages.* University Park: Pennsylvania State University Press, 1995.

Oman, Charles. *The Art of War in the Middle Ages A.D. 378-1515.* 2 vols. New York: Burt Franklin, 1924.

Pantin, W.A. *The English Church in the Fourteenth Century.* Toronto: University of Toronto Press, 1980.

Pearsall, Derek. "John Capgrave's *Life of St. Katherine* and Popular Romance Style." *Medievalia et Humanistica: Studies in Medieval & Renaissance Culture.* N.S. 6. *Medieval Hagiography and Romance.* Ed. Paul Maurice Clogan. Cambridge: Cambridge University Press, 1975.

Rigby, S.H. *English Society in the Later Middle Ages: Class, Status and Gender.* London: Macmillan, 1995.

Riley-Smith, Jonathan. *The Crusades: A Short History.* New Haven: Yale University Press, 1987.

Russell, Frederick. *The Just War in the Middle Ages.* Cambridge: Cambridge University Press, 1975.

Ryding, William. *Structure in Medieval Narrative.* The Hague: Mouton, 1971.

Salisbury, Joyce E. *Perpetua's Passion: The Death and Memory of a Young Roman Woman.* New York: Routledge, 1997.

Sigerist, Henry E. *Civilization and Disease.* Chicago: University of Chicago Press, 1943.

Strohm, Paul. "The Origin and Meaning of Middle English *Romance*." Genre 10 (1977) 1-28.

226

---. "Storie, Spelle, Geste, Romance, Tragedie: Generic Distinctions in the Middle English Troy Narratives." *Speculum* 46 (1971): 348-59.

Sumption, Jonathan. *The Hundred Years War I: Trial By Battle*. Philadelphia: University of Pennsylvania Press, 1990.

Thompson, A. Hamilton. *The English Clergy and Their Organization in the Later Middle Ages*. Oxford: Clarendon Press, 1947.

Thompson, James Westfall and Edgar Nathaniel Johnson. *An Introduction to Medieval Europe*. New York: Norton, 1937.

Thomson, John. *The Later Lollards: 1414-1520*. Oxford: Oxford University Press, 1965.

Thornton, Ginger and Krista May. "Malory as Feminist? The Role of Percival's Sister in the Grail Quest." *Sir Thomas Malory: Views and Re-Views*, ed. D. Thomas Hanks. New York: AMS, 1992.

Tolkien, J.R.R. "*Ancrene Wisse* and *Hali Meiðhad*." *Essays and Studies of the English Association* 14 (1929): 104-126.

Tucker, P.E. "Chivalry in the *Morte*." *Essays on Malory*. Ed. J.A.W. Bennett. Oxford: Clarendon Press, 1963. 64-103.

Vale, Malcolm. *War and Chivalry: Warfare and Aristocratic Culture in England, France and Burgundy at the End of the Middle Ages*. Athens: University of Georgia Press, 1981.

West, Constance Birt. *Courtoisie in Anglo-Norman Literature*. Oxford: Oxford University Press, 1938.

Weiss, Victoria. "Grail Knight or Boon Companion? The Inconsistent Sir Bors of Malory's *Morte Darthur*." *Studies in Philology* 94 (1997): 417-27.

Whatley, E. Gordon. "An Introduction to the Study of Old English Prose Hagiography: Sources and Resources." *Holy Men and Holy Women: Old English Prose Saints' Lives and Their Contexts*. Albany, NY: State University of New York Press, 1996.

Winstead, Karen. "John Capgrave and the Chaucer Tradition." *The Chaucer Review* 30 (1996): 389-402.

---. "Piety, Politics, and Social Commitment in Capgrave's *Life of St. Katherine*." *Medievalia et Humanistica* N.S. 17 (1991) 59-80.

---. Virgin Martyrs: Legends of Sainthood in Late Medieval England. Ithaca: Cornell University Press, 1997.

INDEX

MEDIAEVAL STUDIES

1. Edelgard E. DuBruck (ed.), **New Images of Medieval Women: Essays Toward a Cultural Anthropology**

2. M. Kilian Hufgard, **Saint Bernard of Clairvaux: A Theory of Art Formulated From His Writings and Illustrated in Twelfth-Century Works of Art**

3. Nancy van Deusen (ed.), **Paradigms in Medieval Thought Applications in Medieval Disciplines: A Symposium**

4. Nicole Crossley-Holland (ed.), **A Fifteenth-Century Franciscan French Office: Translation and Commentary of the** *Hours of the Passion*

5. Richard J. Utz (ed.), **Literary Nominalism and the Theory of Rereading Late Medieval Texts: A New Research Paradigm**

6. Ian Thomson and Louis Perraud, **Ten Latin Schooltexts of the Middle Ages: Translated Selections**

7. William L. Urban, **Dithmarschen, A Medieval Peasant Republic**

8. Elizabeth Mary McNamer, **The Education of Heloise: Methods, Content, and Purpose of Learning in the Twelfth-Century**

9. Ross Sutherland, **Cligès et le mystère de Terre Sainte du Templier: L'hérésie sacrée du sépulcre de la Christie**

10. Arnoldo Carlos Vento, **Tres Civilizaciones del Mundo Medieval: Crítica, Análisis y Crónicas de las Primeras Cruzadas**

11. **Six Medieval French Farces**, translated, with an Introduction and Commentary by Thierry Boucquey

12. Ronald E. Pepin, **An English Translation of** *Auctores Octo*, **A Medieval Reader**

13. M. Kilian Hufgard, **Bernard of Clairvaux's Broad Impact on Medieval Culture**

14. Thomas Renna, **Jerusalem in Medieval Thought, 400-1300**

15. Elizabeth Leigh Smith, **Middle English Hagiography and Romance in Fifteenth-Century England: From Competition to Critique**